Perceptions of the European Union in New Member States

The book explores the views of elites alongside those of the wider population in the European Union. The chapters place the new member states – and the potential candidate Serbia – on the map of Europe in this context for the first time. The volume's comparative method goes beyond the standard old member states versus new member states divide. It assesses regional differences within Central Europe and evaluates the problem of European and national identity formation, perception of external threats to the EU (including Russia), differences between economic and political elite views about the integration process and the connection between national performance and public opinion about Europe. Even though, in each country, positive views are dominant about the integration process, heterogeneous views prevail behind the image of a unifying Europe.

The book's major contribution is that it makes the new member states more visible and provides hard evidence while remaining theoretically driven. Furthermore, it covers the most important topics that emerge in studies concerning European integration. The book is intended for those interested in European integration in general but Central and Eastern European comparativists will find it particularly useful.

This book was published as a special issue of *Europe-Asia Studies*.

Gabriella Ilonszki is Professor of Political Science and Head of the Centre for Elite Studies at Corvinus University of Budapest, Hungary.

Perceptions of the European Union in New Member States

A Comparative Perspective

Edited by Gabriella Ilonszki

First published 2010 by Routledge
2 Park Square, Milton Park, Abingdon, Oxfordshire OX14 4RN

Simultaneously published in the USA and Canada
by Routledge
711 Third Avenue, New York, NY 10017

First issued in paperback 2014

Routledge is an imprint of the Taylor & Francis Group, an informa business

© 2010 University of Glasgow

This book is a reproduction of Europe-Asia Studies, volume 61, issue 6. The Publisher requests to those authors who may be citing this book to state, also, the bibliographical details of the special issue on which the book was based

Typeset in Times by Value Chain, India

All rights reserved. No part of this book may be reprinted or reproduced or utilised in any form or by any electronic, mechanical, or other means, now known or hereafter invented, including photocopying and recording, or in any information storage or retrieval system, without permission in writing from the publishers.

British Library Cataloguing in Publication Data
A catalogue record for this book is available from the British Library

ISBN 13: 978-1-138-87482-4 (pbk)
ISBN 13: 978-0-415-57490-7 (hbk)

CONTENTS

	Series page	vi
	List of Contributors	vii
	Gabriella Ilonszki Introduction: A Europe Integrated and United—But Still Diverse?	1
1	*Heinrich Best* History Matters: Dimensions and Determinants of National Identities among European Populations and Elites	8
2	*Miguel Jerez-Mir, José Real-Dato & Rafael Vázquez-García* Identity and Representation in the Perceptions of Political Elites and Public Opinion: A Comparison between Southern and Post-Communist Central-Eastern Europe	29
3	*Irmina Matonytė & Vaidas Morkevičius* Threat Perception and European Identity Building: The Case of Elites in Belgium, Germany, Lithuania and Poland	53
4	*Mladen Lazić & Vladimir Vuletić* The Nation State and the EU in the Perceptions of Political and Economic Elites: The Case of Serbia in Comparative Perspective	72
5	*Spyridoula Nezi, Dimitri A. Sotiropoulos & Panayiota Toka* Explaining the Attitudes of Parliamentarians towards European Integration in Bulgaria, Greece and Serbia: Party Affiliation, 'Left–Right' Self-placement or Country Origin?	87
6	*Zdenka Mansfeldová & Barbora Špicarová Stašková* Identity Formation of Elites in Old and New Member States (with a Special Focus on the Czech Elite)	105
7	*György Lengyel & Borbála Göncz* Elites' Pragmatic and Symbolic Views about European Integration	125
8	*Gabriella Ilonszki* National Discontent and EU Support in Central and Eastern Europe	144
	Index	161

Routledge Europe-Asia Studies Series

A series edited by Terry Cox
University of Glasgow

The Routledge Europe-Asia Studies Series focuses on the history and current political, social and economic affairs of the countries of the former 'communist bloc' of the Soviet Union, Eastern Europe and Asia. As well as providing contemporary analyses it explores the economic, political and social transformation of these countries and the changing character of their relationships with the rest of Europe and Asia.

Challenging Communism in Eastern Europe
1956 and its Legacy
Edited by Terry Cox

Globalisation, Freedom and the Media after Communism
The Past as Future
Edited by Birgit Beumers, Stephen Hutchings and Natalia Rulyova

Power and Policy in Putin's Russia
Edited by Richard Sakwa

1948 and 1968 – Dramatic Milestones in Czech and Slovak History
Edited by Laura Cashman

Perceptions of the European Union in New Member States
A Comparative Perspective
Edited by Gabriella Ilonszki

Symbolism and Power in Central Asia
Politics of the Spectacular
Edited by Sally N. Cummings

List of Contributors

HEINRICH BEST is currently Professor of Sociology at the University of Jena. He is also Co-Director of the multidisciplinary Collaborative Research Centre 'Social Development after Structural Change'. Professor Best's publication list includes 35 books or special issues of journals and 125 journal and book contributions as primary author and editor. His recent publications include *Elites and Social Change. The Socialist and Post-Socialist Experience* co-edited with R. Gebauer and A. Salheiser (Reinhold Krämer Verlag, 2008) and *Democratic Representation in Europe: Diversity, Change and Convergence*, co-edited with M. Cotta (ECPR, 2007). *Address*: Institute of Sociology, Friedrich Schiller University Jena, Carl-Zeiss-Strasse 2, 07743 Jena, Germany. Email: *Heinrich.Best@uni-jena.de*.

BORBÁLA GÖNCZ is a PhD candidate at Corvinus University of Budapest, Institute of Sociology and Social Policy. Her research topic concerns attitudes towards the European Union in Hungary, its different factors of influence, and European identity among elites and the general public. *Address*: Corvinus University of Budapest, 1093 Fővám tér 8, Budapest, Hungary. Email: *borbala.goncz@uni-corvinus.hu*.

GABRIELLA ILONSZKI works for the Institute of Political Science at Corvinus University of Budapest where she heads the Centre for Elite Studies. Her research interests include parliamentary government, gender studies and the selection and election of politicians in CEE. Her most recent publication is an edited volume, *Amatőr és hivatásos politikusok* [*Amateur and Professional Politicians*] (Új Mandátum, 2008). *Address*: Corvinus University of Budapest, 8 Fővám tér, Budapest, Hungary. Email: *gabriella.ilonszki@uni-corvinus.hu*.

MIGUEL JEREZ-MIR is Professor of Political Science and Head of the Department of Political Science and Public Administration at the University of Granada. A Fulbright Scholar at Yale University and former Prince of Asturias Chair at Georgetown University, he has published widely on political and economic elites in contemporary Spain and political science as a discipline. He is currently responsible of the Spanish elite survey for the Intune project. *Address*: Department of Political Science and Public Administration, Faculty of Political Sciences and Sociology, University of Granada, c/o Rector López Argüeta, 18001 Granada, Spain. Email: *mjerez@ugr.es*.

MLADEN LAZIĆ is Professor of Sociology in the Department of Sociology, Faculty of Philosophy, Belgrade. His main research interests include social stratification, economic and political elites, and social change. He has published and edited numerous books, including *Belgrade in Protest* (CEU Press, 1999); *Promene i otpori* [*Resistances to Social Change*] (Filip Višnjić, 2005). *Address*: Faculty of Philosophy, University of Belgrade, Čika Ljubina 18–20, 11000 Belgrade, Serbia. Email: *bigalazi@eunet.yu*.

GYÖRGY LENGYEL is Professor of Sociology at Corvinus University of Budapest. He heads the research seminar of the sociology PhD programme and gives lectures on economic and general sociology. He has studied economics, history and sociology, and he is Doctor of the Hungarian Academy of Sciences. His research topics are elites, entrepreneurs, social impacts of information technology and European integration. *Address*: Corvinus University of Budapest, 1093 Fővám tér 8, Budapest, Hungary. Email: *gyorgy.lengyel@uni-corvinus.hu*.

LIST OF CONTRIBUTORS

ZDENKA MANSFELDOVÁ is a senior researcher and head of the Department of the Sociology of Politics at the Institute of Sociology, Academy of Sciences of the Czech Republic. Her research focuses on political institutionalisation and representation of interests in both political terms (parties, parliament) and the non-political mesostructures of social interests. *Address*: Institute of Sociology, Academy of Sciences of the Czech Republic, Jilska 1, 110 00 Prague 1, Czech Republic. Email: *zdenka.mansfeldova@soc.cas.cz*.

IRMINA MATONYTĖ, PhD, is a senior researcher at the Institute for Social Research in Vilnius, Lithuania, where since 2004 she has coordinated the Framework 6 project Intune. She is professor in the MA programmes 'European Studies' and 'Democracy and Civil Society' at the European Humanities University in Vilnius. She has published (in Lithuanian, French and English) over 20 articles and contributed several chapters to collectively edited volumes on political leadership and elites, women in politics and civil society in post-communist Lithuania, Poland, Hungary, Estonia, Latvia and Moldova. *Address*: Saltoniškių g. 58, LT-08105, Vilnius, Lithuania. Email: *matonyte@ktl.mii.lt*.

VAIDAS MORKEVIČIUS is a research fellow at the Kaunas University of Technology, Lithuania. Since 2005 he has also worked as a junior researcher at the Institute for Social Research in Vilnius, Lithuania, for the Framework 6 project Intune. His main research interests are attitudes and behaviour of political elites and analysis of political discourse. *Address*: Saltoniškių g. 58, LT-08105, Vilnius, Lithuania. Email: *vaidas.morkevicius@ktu.lt*.

SPYRIDOULA NEZI is a PhD candidate in political science at the University of Athens, where she obtained her BA degree. She obtained her Masters in Political Behaviour from the University of Essex, UK. Her research interests are in the area of political parties, party competition and political methodology. Since November 2005 she has worked as a research assistant to Professors Ilias Nikolakopoulos and Dimitri A. Sotiropoulos on the Intune project. Since 2000 she has participated in various comparative European projects in the area of political behaviour. *Address*: National and Kapodistrian University of Athens, Faculty of Political Science and Public Administration, 6 Themistokleous Street, 106 78 Athens, Greece. Email: *roulanezi@gmail.com*.

JOSÉ REAL-DATO is lecturer in Political Science and Administration at the University of Almería, Spain. His research interests are the study of the careers of political elites, the theory of policy change, and Spanish and European research training policies. His most recent publications are 'Mechanisms of Policy Change: A Proposal for a Synthetic Explanatory Framework', *Journal of Comparative Policy Analysis*, 11, 1, March 2009, pp. 117–43; and (with Miguel Jerez-Mir) 'Cabinet Dynamics in Democratic Spain (1977–2008)', in K. Dowding & P. Dumont (eds) *The Selection of Ministers in Europe: Hiring and Firing* (Routledge, 2008). *Address*: Department of Public Law, Faculty of Law, University of Almería, Carretera de Sacramento, 04120 Almería, Spain. Email: *jreal@ual.es*.

DIMITRI A. SOTIROPOULOS is Associate Professor of Political Science at the University of Athens. He has studied at the University of Athens (LLB 1984), the London School of Economics (MSc 1986) and Yale University (MA 1987; MPhil 1988; PhD 1991). His publications include the volumes *Is Southern Europe Doomed to Instability?* co-edited with T. Veremis (Frank Cass, 2002); and *The State and Democracy in the New Southern Europe* co-edited with R. Gunther and P. Nikiforos Diamandouros (Oxford University Press, 2006). *Address*: National and Kapodistrian University of Athens, Faculty of Political Science and Public Administration, 6 Themistokleous Street, 106 78 Athens, Greece. Email: *dsotirop@hol.gr*.

BARBORA ŠPICAROVÁ STAŠKOVÁ is a researcher in the Department of the Sociology of Politics at the Institute of Sociology, Academy of Sciences of the Czech Republic. Her field of specialisation is civil society and citizen participation in the post-communistic regimes, community involvement in the public sphere and political communication and campaign.

Address: Institute of Sociology, Academy of Sciences of the Czech Republic, Jilska 1, 110 00 Prague 1, Czech Republic. Email: *barbora.staskova@soc.cas.cz*.

PANAYIOTA TOKA is a PhD candidate in political science at the University of Athens, where she obtained a BA and an MA degree. She has conducted research on political parties, political elites, and local administration. From 1998 to 2001 she was a member of the editorial board of the Greek journal *International Relations Tribune*. Since November 2005 she has been working as a research assistant for Professors Ilias Nikolakopoulos and Dimitri A. Sotiropoulos on the Intune project. *Address*: National and Kapodistrian University of Athens, Faculty of Political Science and Public Administration, 6 Themistokleous Street, 106 78 Athens, Greece. Email: *pantoka2@gmail.com*.

RAFAEL VÁZQUEZ-GARCÍA is currently assistant lecturer in the Department of Political Science and Public Administration at the University of Granada (Spain). He has been visiting researcher at several European universities. His special focus is on the study of civil society and political leadership and elites. Among his recent publications are 'Creating Social Capital and Civic Virtue: Historical Legacy and Individualistic Values. What Civil Society in Spain', in D. Purdue (ed.) *The Changing Structure of Civil Society* (Routledge/ECPR Political Science Series, 2008); *Nation-State vs. the EU in the Perceptions of Political and Economic Elites. A Comparison among Germany, Spain and Poland* (The BMW Center for German and European Studies. Working Paper Series, 16-08) (with M. Jerez). *Address*: Department of Political Science and Public Administration, Faculty of Political Sciences and Sociology, 7 University of Granada, c/o Rector López Argüeta, 18001 Granada, Spain. Email: *rvazquez@ugr.es*.

VLADIMIR VULETIĆ is Associate Professor of General Sociology in the Department of Sociology, Faculty of Philosophy, Belgrade. His main field of research is globalisation. His published works, among others, include: *Globalizacija—mit ili stvarnost* [*Globalization—Myth or Reality*] (Belgrade, 2003); *Između nacionalne prošlosti i evropske budućnosti* [*In Between National Past and European Future*] (Belgrade, 2008). *Address*: Faculty of Philosophy, University of Belgrade, Čika Ljubina 18–20, 11000 Belgrade, Serbia. Email: *vuleticv@sbb.co.rs*.

Introduction: A Europe Integrated and United—But Still Diverse?

GABRIELLA ILONSZKI

THE CHAPTERS IN THIS VOLUME GIVE AN OVERVIEW of some research findings of a European project, called Intune. The project (with the title 'Intune' or 'IntUne', standing for 'Integrated and United? A Quest for Citizenship in an Ever Closer Europe') has been financed by the European Union within the 6th Framework Programme, Priority 7, 'Citizens and Governance in a Knowledge Based Society'.[1] The project started in September 2005, spans for four years, covers 18 European countries, involves 29 European institutions and more than 100 scholars across Eastern and Western Europe. These sheer numbers themselves indicate the ambition of the main organisers: the project has been coordinated by the University of Siena and headed by Maurizio Cotta and Pierangelo Isernia and the participants have included sociologists, political scientists, policy analysts and linguists.

One major aim of the project has been to explore the views of elites and the wider population on the European Union with the help of questionnaire surveys in two waves: in the spring of 2007 and in the spring of 2009, respectively. The contributions to this volume all analyse the survey results of the 2007 wave. This can be regarded as one of the first systematic comparative surveys, which covers both old and new member states. Out of the new member states Estonia, Lithuania, Poland, the Czech Republic, Slovakia, Hungary, Bulgaria—and Serbia as a potential future candidate—are included.

The project's academic value is enhanced by the fact that the population and elite questionnaires were a joint effort of academics working in the two fields of elite and mass opinion; thus as a result the mass views and the elite views can be easily compared. The mass survey was built on a national sample of 1,000 in each country while a selected group of the national elites (120 respondents per country) were asked to answer structured questions on their perceptions of identity, representation and scope of governance mainly in relation to the European Union (EU) and to their

---

I would like to thank Terry Cox, Editor of *Europe-Asia Studies* for his encouragement to put this volume together and Sarah Lennon for her expertise and patience in dealing with various queries during this process.

[1]For the project's homepage see www.intune.it.

national polity. Some questions referred to the respondents' social and political background.

Each national elite sample consisted of 80 national MPs and 40 members of the economic elite. As for the 80 MPs, the sample was proportional according to seniority, gender, age, party and tenure. At least between 15 and 25 senior (frontbench) politicians—former or present ministers, junior ministers, presidents or vice presidents of the parliamentary groups or standing committees and EU commissioners—were included. In countries with smaller parliaments the quota of 80 political elite members was achieved by approaching MPs starting from the top (senior) politicians. Within the economic elites the top leaders of the largest enterprises and banks were interviewed according to a roll-down design: in case of refusal the deputy and then the next largest enterprise was approached, always one person per organisation. The sample was based on the 'Top 500 firms' lists of the respective countries. In addition to these economic top leaders between six and 12 leaders of the largest business associations—leaders of organisations of industrialists, employers, bankers, entrepreneurs and chambers—were interviewed. Table 1 below summarises the number of interviews in each country with the composition of political and economic respondents—as well as the countries where the mass survey was also conducted. As can be seen there is no total overlap between the two country groups. There was no mass survey conducted in the Czech Republic and Lithuania. (At the same time, a mass survey only was carried out in Slovenia, which has been used in one of the contributions to this volume.) The majority of essays in

TABLE 1
SAMPLE SIZE IN EACH COUNTRY

Country	Elite survey			Mass survey
	Political elite	Economic elite	N	N
Austria	81	35	116	1,000*
Belgium	80	44	124	1,000
Bulgaria	83	45	128	1,000
Czech Republic	80	42	122	none
Denmark	60	40	100	1,000
Estonia	72	40	112	1,000
France	81	43	124	1,000
Germany	80	43	123	1,000
Great Britain	50	21	71	1,000
Greece	90	36	126	1,000
Hungary	80	42	122	1,000
Italy	84	42	126	1,000
Lithuania	80	40	120	none
Poland	80	42	122	1,000
Portugal	80	40	120	1,000
Serbia	80	40	120	1,000
Slovakia	80	40	120	1,000
Spain	94	55	149	1,000
Total	**1,415**	**730**	**2,145**	**16,000**

Note: *The Austrian mass survey was conducted later thus its results are not covered in each article.

the volume analyse the results of the elite survey but in some cases the mass survey results are also included.

The contributors to this volume are all members of the so-called elite working group within the Intune Project, who were involved in the national elite surveys, in addition to other theoretical or empirical parts of the project.

One major goal of the contributions is 'to place' the new member states—and the potential candidate Serbia—on the 'map' of Europe with the help of surveys that had been thus far restricted to the old member states. To find their place we have found the comparative method to be the best possible approach but the rich material made it possible to exceed the more common opposition of old member states and new member states and seek for other explanatory factors. Some chapters follow a regional comparison (differentiation between Southern European countries and new member states in Central and Eastern Europe), others locate a country or a group of countries in a wider comparative framework or look inside the new member state group, still others follow an overall EU level comparison. In addition, some chapters make use of comparisons between mass and elite, and between political leaders and economic leaders, and make issue-related comparisons as well.

Although the essays are mainly based on the elite survey they reflect on and react to a general and obvious transformation of the European project in relation to its citizens. This concerns the end of the period of permissive consensus and the beginning of a period when the European Union seems to face the increasing challenge of whether it can continue and perform well (or better) without a more active participation of the population. People's involvement and their identification with the EU and the role of the elite in creating and responding to national and European identities are the central thoughts and concerns in the essays.

Public views on the European Union and the future of the integration process will largely depend on how European citizens identify with Europe, how national and European identities are intertwined, and how the elites think about these issues. The importance of this question is reflected most explicitly by four contributions (Best; Mansfeldová and Stašková; Jerez-Mir, Real-Dato and Vázquez-García; and Lengyel and Göncz), which represent different comparative routes. Best connects historical analysis with current survey results; Mansfeldová and Stašková place the Czech case in the European perspective; Jerez-Mir, Real-Dato and Vázquez-García choose to pursue a comparison between Southern Europe and Central and Eastern Europe in this field; while Lengyel and Göncz, with a general perspective, propose a new conceptual framework to understand identity formation.

Best examines identity formation on the mass and elite level with a focus on South Eastern Europe. Following Stein Rokkan's footsteps Best analyses the effects of state formation and nation formation on the perceptions of national identity. By examining population and elite responses to several 'identity questions', involving potential definitions of nationality (from language through religion to birthplace), he finds that construction of mass identities is first of all directed by 'historical givens and experiences'. Behind this general statement he is able to identify mass and elite differences and also some regional differences. For example, the 'nativistic' understanding of national identity (having parents who are nationals or being born within the boundaries of the nation state) is stronger among the population than among elite members and generally stronger in the new member states than in the old member states. The importance of historical legacy and long term explanations in the understanding of identification not only on the national, but also on the European level, is a conclusion that re-emerges in other writings as well, among others in the contributions of Jerez-Mir, Real-Dato and Vázquez-García. The rationale of their comparison between Southern Europe and Central and Eastern Europe is founded on an apparent difference between the two regions with respect to the European Union: the former group has an overall positive and the latter group an overall negative view on integration. Nevertheless, when representation and identity issues are analysed in concrete terms regional heterogeneity comes to light, rooted in historical and institutional explanations.

Mansfeldová and Stašková single out the Czech case to explore how national and European identities of political and economic elites are being formed. They find that the Czech elites—both the political and economic ones—are amongst the most Eurosceptic in the EU: they emphasise the role of the national state as opposed to the EU—although their general evaluation is largely positive, for example they claim that their country has benefited from the entry. More generally, Mansfeldová and Stašková distinguish between the 'origin', 'civic' and 'cultural' components both of national and of European identities—although these have different explanatory strength on the two levels. Lengyel and Göncz also deal with the problem of identity on the basis of the elite survey data. When writing about European identity academic literature generally differentiates between an essentialist or cultural dimension and a constructivist or civic dimension, the former emphasising common ethno-cultural traits while the latter the civic attitudes and behaviour of the people. On the basis of survey evidence they find that identity components can be grouped into a primordial and into a decisional category, the latter including both the cultural and the civic components that are somehow related to the decisions of the individual, and the former including traits that are established by birth. A further differentiation between the pragmatic and symbolic aspects of EU support proves that eventually four country groups can be identified based on identification and support, and while these do not follow a clear division between old member states and new member states, in some respects this regional division prevails. For example, old member states' elites tend to be more attached to Europe both in symbolic and pragmatic ways.

Identity is put to a kind of policy test by Matonytè and Morkevičius. The future of the European project partly depends on how European citizens will identify with it— and how the elites will think about it. As Matonytè and Morkevičius contend, cohesion of the EU is a *sine qua non* for 'European' political decisions. Since cohesion is built on positive and negative feelings at the same time they conceptualise cohesion with the help of threats: how do national elites think about threats in the EU context? What do they think about the entry of Turkey, about the USA's EU connections and about the role of Russia? Survey evidence proves that there are no unified perceptions with regard to external threats but these rather depend on the political–historical experiences of the given countries. For example, countries in the old Eastern bloc regard Russia as a threat, while the old member states perceive it differently. These views might also relate to (potential) EU policies. For example, the dominant majority of those who see better social security (as opposed to competitiveness) to be the major aim of the EU are more sceptical of close relations between the USA and some EU countries.

It is not surprising that Serbia has attracted much interest in more than one essay. It is an interesting case in itself while it also offers an analytical opportunity to see the effect of membership on EU views. Distinctions between old membership, new membership, more recent membership (Bulgaria being among the surveyed countries) and no membership in the European Union often appear to have an explanatory strength. While we can rely on experiences and well established views in the old member states, more ambivalences might prevail in the new member states and prospective members might cherish more illusions and expectations about the institution.

Lazić and Vuletić put the Serbian case in a comparative focus by seeking to determine the comparative strength of pro-EU and pro-national attitudes. This is a really challenging question because during an extended period of more than a decade of the 'blocked transformation' the Serbs blamed the West for the failures of their regime but they remained pro-EU at the same time. The authors' hypothesis is that in the EU countries, where secessionist or irredentist sentiments prevail—as they have done in Serbia—pro-nation-state attitudes will be stronger than pro-EU attitudes. This assumption is complemented—and indeed weakened—by another one, namely that the EU is regarded as a solution (mainly an economic safeguard) to economic problems. This assumption has been confirmed in another contribution (by Ilonszki), which claims that among the new member states we can observe an escape route scenario that explains EU support: the worse the economic perceptions in a country, the more 'EU-philia' can be observed. Moreover, in a pre-accession period only the positive expectations and not real world problems prevail in this respect. All in all, Lazić and Vuletić find that out of the countries under investigation the Serbian elite has been the most divided on this issue: pro-EU or pro-nation-state attitudes are equally evident as post-communist experience and national problems push Serbia towards more pro-national attitudes but positive (not yet tried) expectations concerning the EU pull it towards pro-Europeanism. The impact of legacy and the concrete political situation matter equally. Some other chapters, introduced above, also comment on the particularity of the Serbian case. Best witnesses the dilemma—indeed the dividedness—of the Serbian elite as opposed to the population in their approach to national identity, and Jerez-Mir, Real-Dato and Vázquez-García note that the Serbian political elite shows the lowest level of attachment to one's country in the survey data.

The dividedness of the Serbian elite is once more reinforced in the contribution of Nezi, Sotiropoulos and Toka who seek to answer the question of whether it is left–right placement or country of origin that best explains attitudes to the EU. At first glance the answer seems easy: the political elite from older member states (in this case Greece—as compared to Bulgaria and Serbia) and from parties located closer to the centre are more pro-European. The first finding confirms the importance of length (or prospect) of membership in the EU and the second warns that only concrete analysis can explain heterogeneity. The Greek Socialist party family tends to trust the EU less than either the Bulgarian or the Serbian respondents from the same party families. Although the Greek case is particular in this respect, this is just one piece of evidence among many that left and right appear differently in the EU context between the old and new member states, and left–right dividing lines are often blurred in the new member states. For example, a survey question asked whether enhancing competition or ensuring social security should be the goal of the European Union. The difference between the answers of the old member states and new member states is particularly high among politicians who place themselves on the left: more than one third of left wing politicians in the new member states as compared with only about one tenth in the old member states regard economic competitiveness as the main aim of the EU. The difficulty of understanding left and right might explain why party-based comparisons are relatively infrequent in the essays. Moreover, one can add that Central and East European countries are under several constraints at the same time: in addition to a general scepticism concerning the role of parties on the European level, now that their representative functions and connections have been challenged also on the national level, in some Central and East European countries party consolidation and party system consolidation have not yet been finalised.

The Intune project offers a rich source to extend our knowledge on the European Union and further publications are planned on the basis of its findings in the near future. Still, this collection will remain of particular interest because it makes the new member states more visible and puts an emphasis on region-based comparisons. Overall, the contributions offer insights into the 'EU-motivations' in some single countries, and they also prove that in addition to a division between old member states and new member states, other divisions and comparisons that are regional, sub-regional or topical are similarly fruitful. At the same time the authors warn that behind the image of a unifying Europe and the overall positive views about the integration process diversity and heterogeneity prevail: the complexity of long term historical legacies, institutional variance, political and economic interests do play a role. This multifaceted social, historical, religious (not to mention political) diversity has to be calculated when we want to understand elite and mass opinion on European integration.

At the end of such an extended undertaking it is appropriate to ask some general questions as well. What can the new member states add to the European project? This question is relevant because fairly often only the 'problem' side of their entry is emphasised, particularly in the context of identity formation and citizenship. Thomassen and Back (2008, p. 19) claim that '[s]ince the 2004 enlargement brought in a number of countries with a low sense of citizenship, this might have a lasting effect on the development of citizenship in the Union'. The 2004 European Parliament elections confirmed this statement with their low level turnout (on average turnout was lower in the new member states than in the old ones). The Intune Project data also confirm some of this approach. But admittedly, the EU is important for the new member states. This is confirmed by survey evidence: without exception in each country the majority of respondents have positive views about the integration process. Also, the European Union may have a positive impact in helping to overcome old, historically rooted conflicts between the new member states, and also in helping to strengthen democratic norms and institutions.

And what can the new member states add to the European Union? They can possibly add and strengthen new perspectives, including a perspective which emphasises the multifaceted character of the European Union. The enlargement of the EU itself due to increasing diversity will lead to a situation where the old governance model cannot perform well any longer. Ideally, '... the import of diversity will render the hierarchical mode of governance largely inadequate. The enlarged EU will have to embrace more flexible, decentralised and soft modes of governance ... (that is) a plurilateral mode of governance' (Zielonka 2007, p. 188). This development might be a value in itself.

Corvinus University of Budapest

References

Thomassen, J. & Back, H. (2008) *European Citizenship and Identity after Enlargement*, EUI Working Papers 2008/02, available at: http://cadmus.iue.it, accessed 15 May 2009.

Zielonka, J. (2007) 'Plurilateral Governance in the Enlarged European Union', *Journal of Common Market Studies*, 45, 1, pp. 187–209.

History Matters: Dimensions and Determinants of National Identities among European Populations and Elites

HEINRICH BEST

DISCUSSIONS OF MASS, GROUP, OR COLLECTIVE IDENTITY tend to be characterised by an abundance of theoretical and conceptual disputes and a relative lack of empirical foundation; in particular there is a lack of comparative studies based on systematic and reliable data (Bruter 2005, pp. 101–09). The dominant paradigm for both sociological and socio-psychological studies of mass identity is the constructivist approach. This emphasises, to varying degrees, the invented and constructed character of mass identity as opposed to essentialist understandings of the concept which assume a unique core or essence of identity (Scott & Marshall 2009, pp. 330–33). It is evident that any research following the constructivist approach requires clearly specified and carefully defined indicators targeting the determinants and dynamics of the underlying processes of identity formation for collectivities in various contexts. Because such data are difficult and costly to obtain, studies of the emergence of mass identities are usually based on insecure empirical grounds. It is therefore of specific relevance for the study of mass identity that the Intune project has provided a rich supply of data on the formation of mass identities in 18 European states, applying a multitude of indicators which specifically target the process of identity formation at elite level and in the general population.[1]

The present study scrutinises the hypothesis that the 'invention' or 'construction' of mass identities is not an arbitrary process of first composing and then imposing a narrative of 'sameness', 'belongingness' or 'common destiny' to some population, but that it is constrained and directed by specific historical givens and experiences shaping the collective memories and conditions of living of the same population. When it comes to national identities I assume that it is the processes of state formation and nation building that leave a specific and inextinguishable trace in the collective mind. Liah Greenfield (1992, p. 17) has pointed to the fact that 'the adjustment of the idea of the nation to the situational constraints of the relevant agents involves its conceptualisation in terms of indigenous traditions'. This conceptualisation further distinguishes every national identity and 'makes national identity a matter of historical

---

[1] For further details, see the editor's introduction to this collection.

contingency rather than necessity' (Greenfield 1992, p. 17). Contrary to Greenfield, however, I do not conceptualise national identity as an outcome of the mere 'availability of ideas' at the time of its formation, but rather as the result of a targeted response to a challenge posed to a collectivity of people at a critical juncture of a nation's historical development. History matters here insofar as it constrains the broad design or 'structural plan' of constructed identities. Because in Europe these historical challenges are located in deep layers of historical experience, the fundamental design of national identities should be relatively invariant with regard to more recent developments.

It is obvious that I am introducing here an essentialist element into a constructivist approach by assuming that there is an inertia present in mass identities which protects them from being transformed continuously by the forces of social and political change. Whether this is the case or not is a matter to be decided by empirical scrutiny through combining macro-historical patterns of state formation and nation building with individual manifestations of national identities in different European societies.

The following study first addresses state formation and nation building as central aspects of macro-structural modernisation processes in Europe (Rokkan 1999). In a second step it focuses on analysing the effects of historical conditions and the course of state formation and nation building on contemporary populations' perceptions of their national identity. In these analyses Stein Rokkan's macro-structural theory of state formation and nation building, which underlies his conceptual map of Europe,[2] will be combined with constructivist theories of national identity formation (Anderson 1991; Hobsbawm 1990). A major interest of the study lies in the question of to what extent constructs of national identities are shared within national populations. To establish the universality of national identities, data for the general population will be compared with data for political and economic elites.

Rokkan's macro-structural theory of (West-) European state formation and nation building attributes the development and contemporary manifestations of national and political diversity in Western and Central Europe to historical regional differences in political, economic and cultural conditions (Rokkan 1999, pp. 135–90; Flora 1999, pp. 70–91). The distance from Rome as the centre of the Catholic Church, with its claim of universalistic religious homogeneity, is taken here as the main cultural variable in the process of nation building. The process of European state formation, however, depends heavily on the distance from the City Belt, a zone of concentrated economic activity and infrastructural development that was formed at the beginning of the late Middle Ages and stretched from Flanders, via the Rhineland and eastern France, to northern and central Italy. The consolidation of modern states was favoured in those regions of Europe that were positioned midway between the City

---

[2] Rokkan's conceptual map of Europe 'has been designed as a "schematic system of co-ordinates generated through the combination of one territorial", one economic, and one cultural variable in the model' (Rokkan 1999, p. 141). Its original design was included in several articles and book chapters published in the 1970s and early 1980s. Its final and 'canonised' version can be found in a posthumous edition of Rokkan's collected works which has been compiled by Peter Flora with Stein Kuhnle and Derek Urwin (Rokkan 1999). Peter Flora's introduction to this edition gives a comprehensive presentation of Rokkan's conceptual designs and theoretical work (Flora 1999).

Belt and the less developed hinterland. Such a location meant that the emerging states had access to the economic resources of the City Belt as well as room to expand their territories. With regard to nation building, Rokkan assumes a south–north gradient of Rome's influence: at the northern periphery of Europe, where national Protestant churches were formed early and became firmly established over time, the processes of nation building were easier to accomplish than in areas closer to the central institutions of the universalistic Catholic Church. According to these geographical specifications, Rokkan's conceptual map includes only those parts of Western and Central Europe that were at some stage under the control of the Catholic Church. For example, South Eastern Europe is only covered up to the eastern borders of the western part of the Roman Empire in the Balkans and up to the southern border of the Habsburg Empire. The rest of Eastern and South Eastern Europe is *terra incognita* on Rokkan's conceptual map, either forming part of a 'Mediterranean Periphery' or with unspecified conditions regarding state and nation building.

If one wants to extend Rokkan's conceptual map to include Eastern and South Eastern Europe, it is necessary to find the generic factors of state and nation-building equivalent to the City Belt and the distance from Rome. Here I suggest using the distance from Byzantium and the range of the Slavic mission of the Orthodox Church, which has been—with its early Slavic translation of the Bible and the introduction of the Cyrillic alphabet—a defining as well as an embedding factor of culture formation (Herrin 2007). Through its inheritance of Muslim and Turkish minorities, the territorial and temporal scope of the Ottoman Empire was, on the other hand, an important factor of ethnic–cultural differentiation in South Eastern Europe. Being a multi-ethnic empire it prevented the formation of national states within its borders up to the middle of the nineteenth century. The territorial range of the Ottoman Empire can also be used to define an economic axis related to state building, because the territories under its control were part of an integrated trading area in the eastern Mediterranean (Imber 2002; McCarthy 2001).

In my adaptation of Rokkan's conceptual map, the axes for state and nation building in South Eastern Europe are rotated by 45 degrees. While the axis of state formation stretches from west to east, the axis of nation formation is drawn in a north–south direction. Here the east–west axis rather marks the direction of cultural differentiation and nation building along the division line formed by the schism of 1054 between the Orthodox and the Catholic Churches. The north–south axis defines the requirements for state formation by the southern limits of the Habsburg *reconquista* on the one hand, and by the duration or the rigour of the rule of the Ottoman Empire on the other hand.

The second part of my theoretical and conceptual considerations addresses the impact of territorial conditions and historical processes underpinning nation building and state formation in South East Europe on the appropriation and shaping of current populations' national identities in this region of Europe. In other research contexts, constructive theories of national identity formation have shown the connection between macro and micro processes in the shaping of ideas and self-definitions. In his classic work, Benedict Anderson (1991) conceptualised nations as imagined communities with collective identities based on cognitive constructs and their normative correlates. During the formation of such communities, the constructors of imagined communities are not free in the selection of their constituting elements, but remodel and reassemble cultural traditions and institutional relicts of the past (Smith 2008). Anderson attributes a crucial role to elites as both producers and propagators when it comes to the formation of imagined communities and collective identities. The gap between elites and masses is an issue of particular significance when it comes to nation-building in 'latecomer nations' of Eastern Europe. Studies of Eastern European nationalism have shown that different patterns of inclusion and exclusion in defining the nation emerge according to which segment of the elite acquires a dominant role in the process of state formation and nation building (Kohn 1945). In Eastern Europe it was particularly 'aristocratic' and 'bureaucratic nationalism', as opposed to the 'bourgeois nationalism' dominating in the West, which put its imprint on the development of national states (Sugar 1969).

In the following, the components and subjects of the study are discussed. I also address whether—and if so in which way—the specific conditions of state and nation building in South Eastern Europe have shaped the process of forming national identities within elites and general populations. The specific profiles of South Eastern European national identities should be revealed in comparing them with findings from other European countries. The empirical basis of the study is formed by the series of pan-European surveys that were conducted in 2007 under the auspices of the Intune project. Apart from a number of topics that are specific to Europe, the subjects of the surveys were national identity constructions and the self-images of economic and political elites as well as of the general population.

We have here the first simultaneous multi-country survey of political and economic elites, as well as of masses and elites, and the first pan-European elite survey including post-communist societies of East, Central and South East Europe. In this study, the geographical core of South East Europe is covered by Serbia, Bulgaria and Greece. Its northern periphery is represented by Hungary. Slovenia is only included as far as the general population is concerned, as no elite surveys were executed there.

In the following discussion the focus will be on a set of items concerning national identity. These items were worded almost identically in both the elite and the population surveys. The interviewees were asked to specify the characteristics that qualify someone to be a member of their nation. For this purpose, they were offered a set of eight items referring to widespread definitions of nationality currently used in public debate and found in the theoretical literature (see Table 1). Here we find references to the cultural identity of a nation (mastering languages), to the status of a person in the polity (being a citizen), to the emotive bases of national identities (to feel, for example, Bulgarian), to *ius soli* (to be born in the country), or *ius sanguinis* (to have parents who hold citizenship). When these items are submitted for factor analysis, two main factors can be detected in all three populations: one includes ascribed characteristics, such as being born in the country or stemming from a family with citizen status, the other encompasses acquired or acquirable characteristics, such as respecting the laws of the country or holding citizenship. It is remarkable that, in these analyses, cultural definitions of nationality are attributed differently by the different populations. Sometimes cultural definitions are classed as essentialistic with regard to ascribed characteristics, whereas at other times they are listed as constructivistic as acquired characteristics. This is also valid for the

TABLE 1
NATIONAL IDENTITY

Question: People differ in what they think it means to be [national]. In your view, how important is each of the following to be [national]?
How important is it ...

A.	... **to be a Christian**[a]
B.	... to share [country] cultural traditions
C.	... **to be born in [country]**[a]
D.	... **to have [national] parents**[a]
E.	... to respect [national] laws and institutions
F.	... to feel [national]
G.	... **to master the language(s) of the [country]**[a]
H.	... **to be a country citizen**[a]

Note: [a] Bold items are represented in Figures 1–5.
Possible answers:
1. Very important
2. Somewhat important
3. Not very important
4. Not important at all

characteristic of being Christian as a defining criterion for nationality. In the general population cultural definitions of nationality tend to be included in the essentialistic cluster of criteria of nationality, whilst among political elites they tend to be part of the constructivist factor, and the position of economic elites is somewhere in-between both patterns. These factor analysis findings are a first hint concerning the ambivalent status of culture as either an essentially exclusive or a potentially inclusive criterion of nationality.

The following presentation of results is limited to five out of the eight definitions of nationality surveyed. The criterion for selection was the strength of factor loadings. The interpretation only refers to differences between elites and non-elites at the level of national aggregates.

I will begin with mastery of the national language as a criterion for national identity. Here, on the notion that this is a necessary qualification, we have consistently the highest agreement between elite and population and the smallest differential between countries. Serbia is an exceptional case because it includes in its (former) national territory—particularly, if one considers Kosovo—large native minorities with their own languages. The claim to these populations and their settlement areas is at the cost of a heterogeneous national communication space. Serbian elites are obviously more prepared than the general Serbian population to pay this price. On the other hand Croatians and Bosnians, who speak languages very similar to Serbian and who are part of the same space of social communication, cannot be distinguished nationally from Serbians by their languages. Figure 1 shows that, apart from a few exceptions like Serbia, the concept of nation as a homogeneous space of communication is shared between elites and masses alike and is highly consensual between European countries in East and West (Deutsch 1966). This applies even to a multilingual country like Belgium where each cultural community can consider its language as a 'national' language.

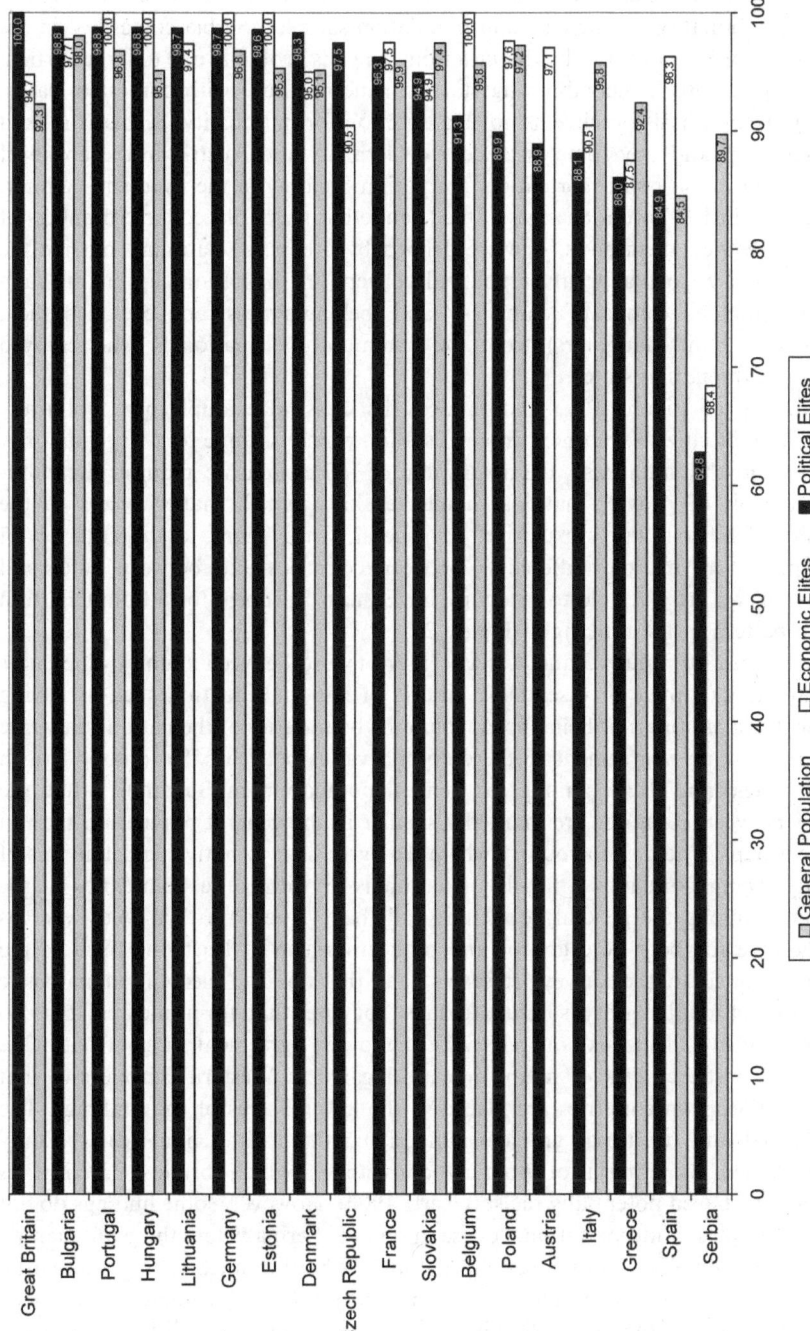

FIGURE 1. To be a [National] it is Important to Master the [National] Language (percent agreement)

The special status of Serbia becomes evident when the importance of citizenship is a criterion of nationality. In the elite and population samples, Serbia comes last in the ranking of European countries by this criterion, which is probably due to large Serbian minority populations in neighbouring states, including those with contested status. Regarding the emphasis on citizenship as a criterion for nationality, Serbia is ranked next to Hungary and—by some distance—to Germany and Austria in the group of losers in the process of state formation and nation building in the twentieth century. In all these countries, border changes of the twentieth century placed large numbers of people who defined themselves, or were defined by others, as nationals outside the realm of citizenry, so that legal or political conceptions of nationality cut through historically founded claims of 'sameness' and 'belongingness' and excluded these 'prodigal sons' (and daughters) from the community of nationals who enjoyed citizenship of the nation state.

Ranking top of Figure 2 we find France, the classical example of a politically defined nation of citizens, but next comes Estonia, which is home to a large minority of Russians. In the latter case, the acquisition of full citizenship requires the cultural qualification of proving national language skills, which makes access to the community of citizens fairly exclusive. In general, with regard to the criterion of citizenship, we see marked differences between countries and between elites and non-elites but we are not able to recognise an Eastern European or a South Eastern European pattern in the ranking of Figure 2.

As can be seen in Figures 3 and 4, between-group and between-country differences with regard to ascriptive or essentialist criteria of national identity, such as having parents who are nationals or being born within the boundaries of the nation states, are particularly striking. Agreement to these criteria varies between 5% (among British economic elites) and 91% (among the general population in Bulgaria), while the variations between countries are markedly smaller in the general population than in both elite groups. There is no country where the agreement to nativistic definitions of nationality (being born into a family of nationals or within the boundaries of the nation state) among the general population falls below the 50% threshold, whereas this is the case for both elite groups and both criteria in at least one third of the countries included in the survey. It seems that the atavistic element in nativistic definitions of national identity is harder to digest for elites than for non-elites. It is also significant that five of the six countries with the lowest agreement rates of both elite groups to nativistic criteria of nationality are located in Western Europe and that all Western European countries are placed in the lower halves of the rankings. The obvious social and territorial gradients underlying these differentials can be only partly explained by criteria of political correctness, which brands nativism as ethnocentric and even potentially racist (Geertz 1966). However, some findings do not fit into this simplistic interpretation. A case in point is Serbia where there are marked differences between elites and masses and the masses have a much stronger nativistic orientation than the political elites. However, I attribute these differences between elites and non-elites in the case of Serbia not to a shortcoming of political correctness among the masses, but to an after effect of the Yugoslavian supra-national concept of the state: Serbian elites combine this concept with visions of the dominance of Greater Serbia. Regarding Bulgaria, the differences between elites and non-elites are

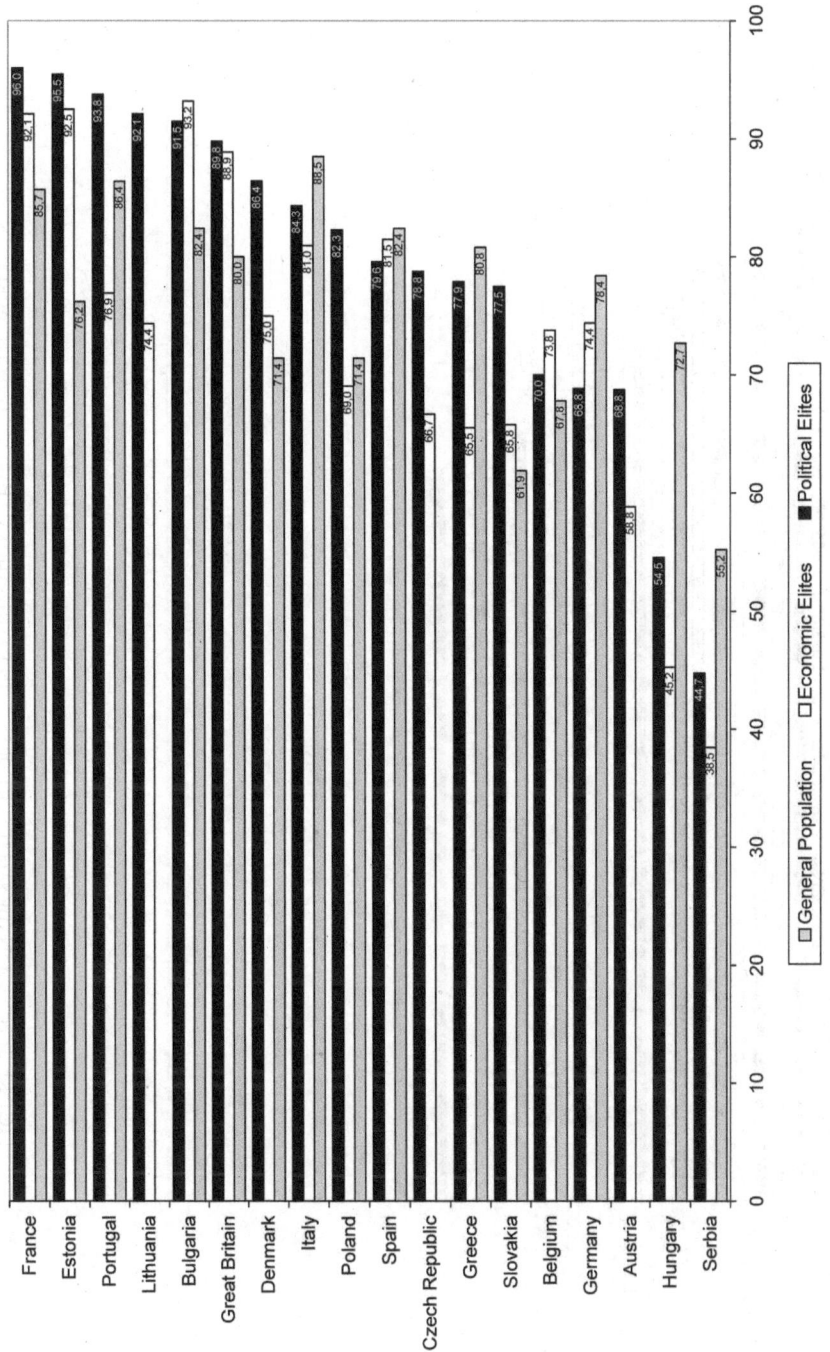

FIGURE 2. TO BE A [NATIONAL] IT IS IMPORTANT TO BE A [COUNTRY] CITIZEN (PERCENT AGREEMENT)

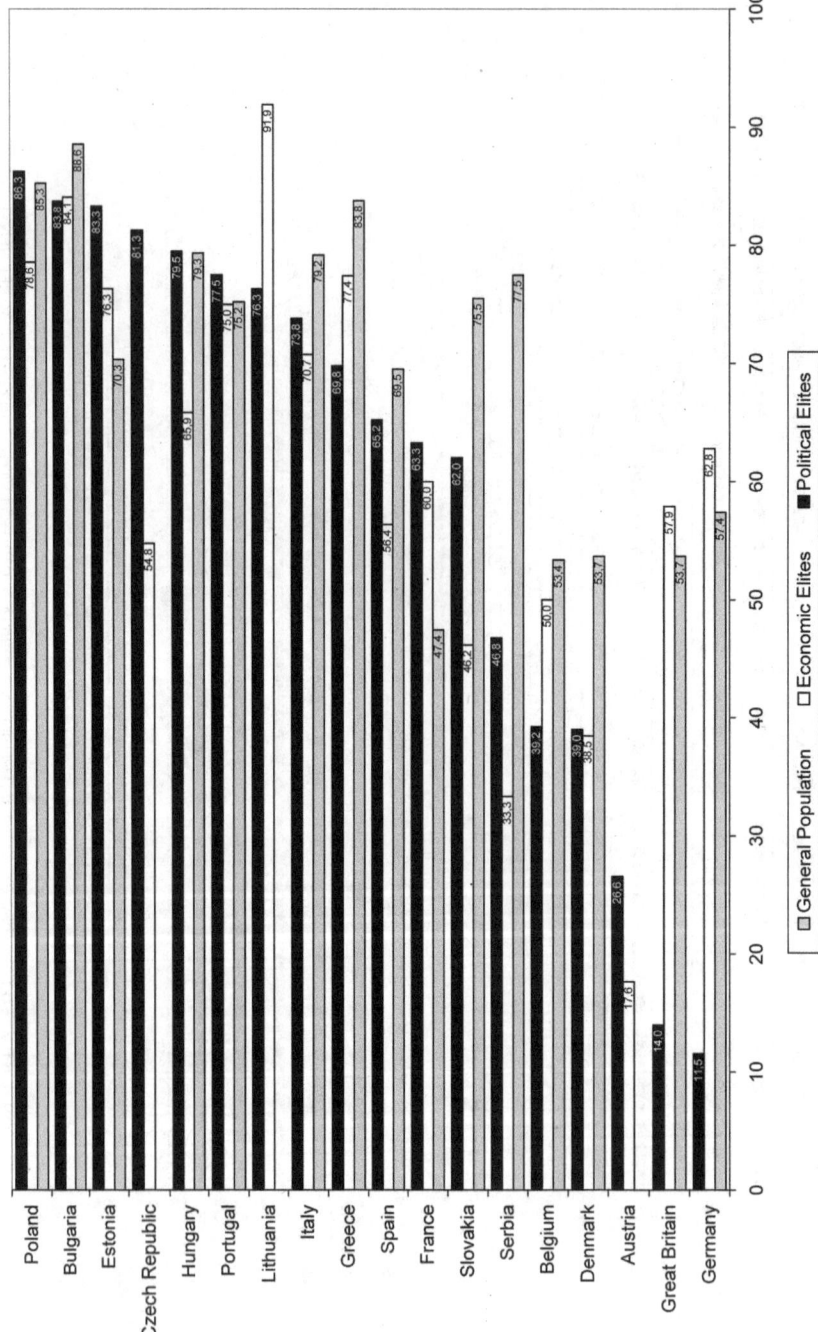

FIGURE 3. TO BE A [NATIONAL] IT IS IMPORTANT TO HAVE [NATIONAL] PARENTS (PERCENT AGREEMENT)

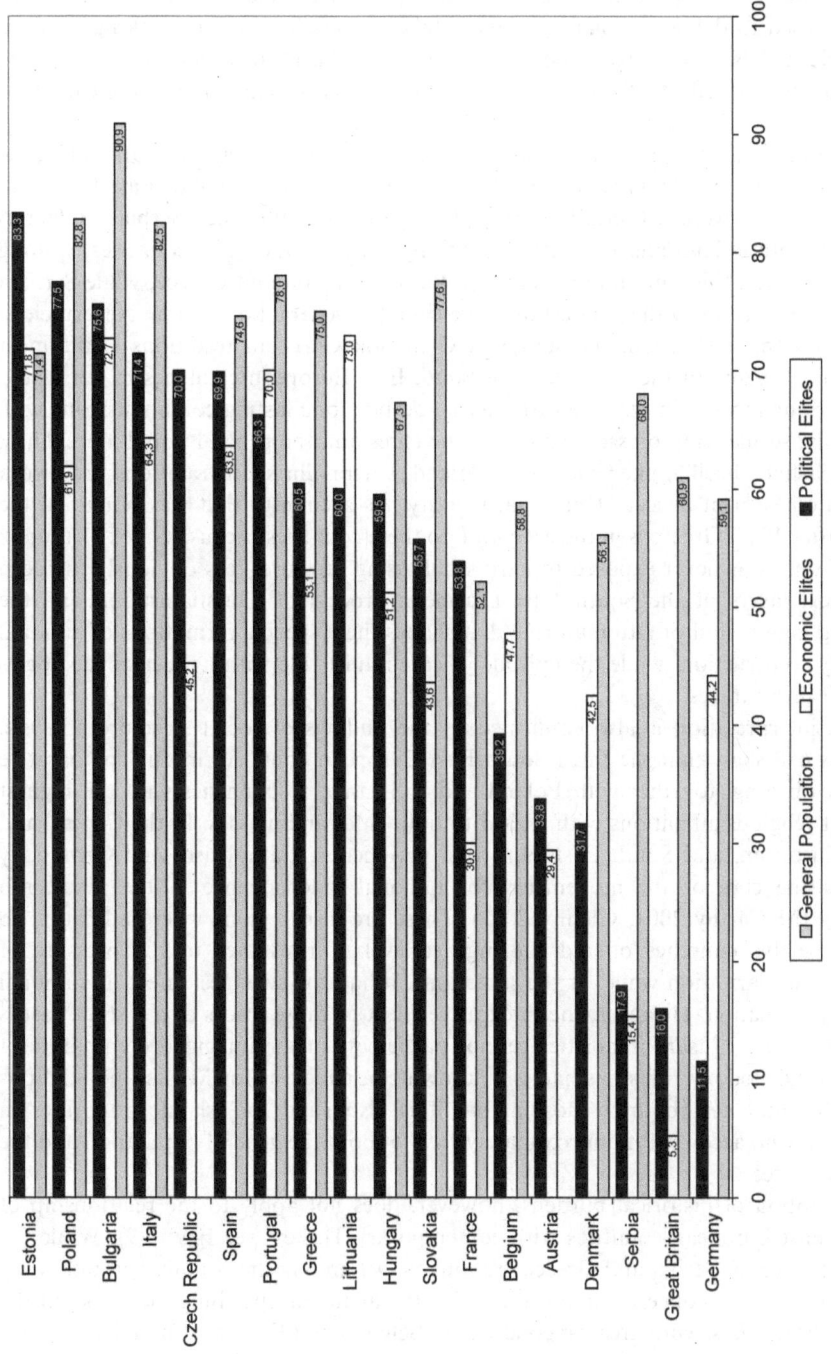

FIGURE 4. TO BE A [NATIONAL] IT IS IMPORTANT TO BE BORN IN [COUNTRY] (PERCENT AGREEMENT)

clearly smaller and we can recognise a stronger concordance between the different criteria used to define nationality. Greece takes a middle position, ranking between Bulgaria and Serbia. Thus, a homogeneous South East European cluster resulting from a unifying effect of common historical experiences cannot be found in these rankings.

However, when we pass on to Christianity as a defining criterion for nationality, the picture changes in a significant way. Figure 5 shows the three South East European countries that were culturally shaped by Orthodoxy (Greece, Serbia, Bulgaria) together with Poland and Italy clearly ranking ahead of the other countries. Among elites, however, this top ranking is only valid for Bulgaria and Greece, while Serbian elites once more show the greatest distance from the general population. Nevertheless, even with this restriction, the stamp of Orthodox Christian traditions is the most distinctive feature of the core group of South East European countries in our study. This is equally valid in the case of Bulgaria, despite long lasting communist rule with its strong secularising pressures on both the elites and the general population. Thus, Bulgaria finds itself ranked alongside Poland, where Christian traditions are also a central constituent aspect of national identity. As a country that was bound to the West after 1945, Greece is in the exception to these countries because Greek Orthodox Christianity was never exposed to hard secularising pressure. It is obviously the deep historical layers of the South East European process of Christianisation and the ensuing long period of Ottoman rule that shapes these specific formations of national identity construction, while the episode of communist rule with its secular ideologies has left fewer traces.

This interpretation is also confirmed by the findings of social structure analysis. Figures 6–8 show that the three South East European countries in our comparative analyses belong, together with Poland and Lithuania, to countries with the highest level of religious affiliations with regard to both elites and masses. In the Central and East European, and South East European peripheries, Catholicism and Orthodoxy formed the core of the movements for national independence in the nineteenth century (McCarthy 2001; Glenny 2001). These are also regions where affiliation to the respective churches offered the highest level of resistance to the pressure of modern secularisation while, at the same time, it had the strongest effect on national identity formation. However, the integrative effect of those traces of a distant past is limited in that Muslim minorities cannot participate in the imagined community of national Orthodoxy. This has had well known consequences for Muslim populations in Serbia and neighbouring Bosnia, but it is also valid for Islamic minorities in Bulgaria, who account for approximately 10% of both the general population and the political elites.

The notion of historical burdens, however, does not apply to the relationship of South East European countries with contemporary Turkey (see Figure 9). While the political elites of Serbia and Greece are ranked last among the countries in our study when it comes to concerns about a Turkish threat to Europe, Bulgaria ranks in the middle field. Those with greatest concern are Belgium and France, although a Turkish threat scenario had no (or only a very remote) historical impact on them. This result supports a theoretical approach that connects the construction of national identities to the substance of historical experiences and narratives, rather than to contemporary

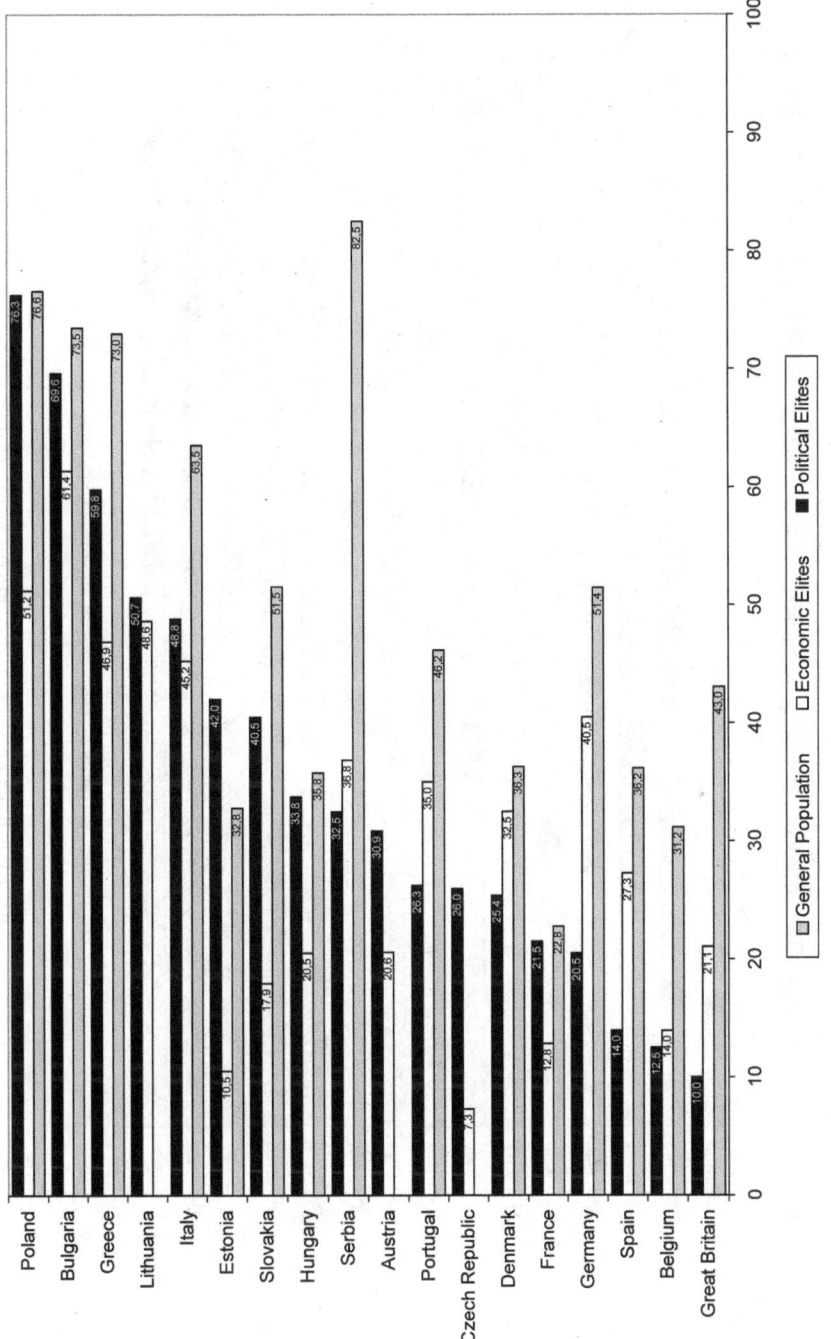

FIGURE 5. TO BE A [NATIONAL] IT IS IMPORTANT TO BE A CHRISTIAN (PERCENT AGREEMENT)

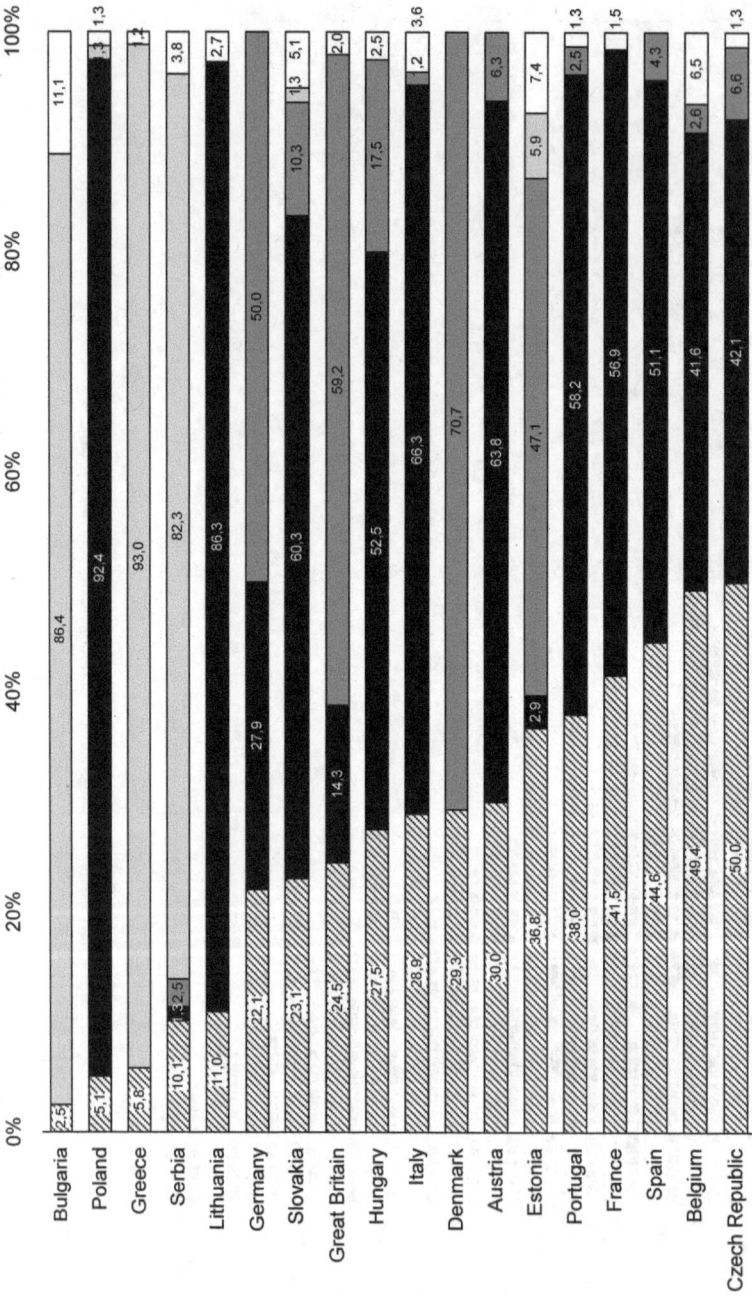

FIGURE 6. RELIGIOUS CONFESSION: POLITICAL ELITES (PERCENT)

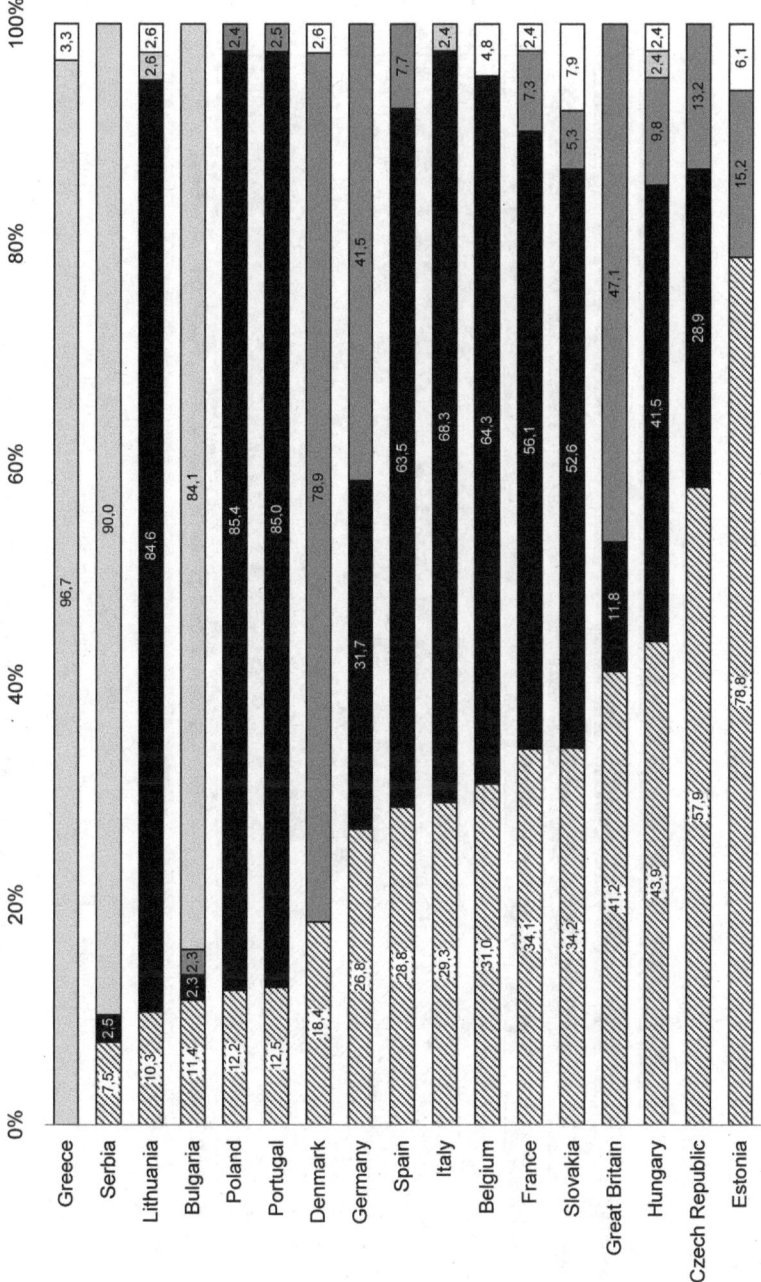

FIGURE 7. RELIGIOUS CONFESSION: ECONOMIC ELITES (PERCENT)

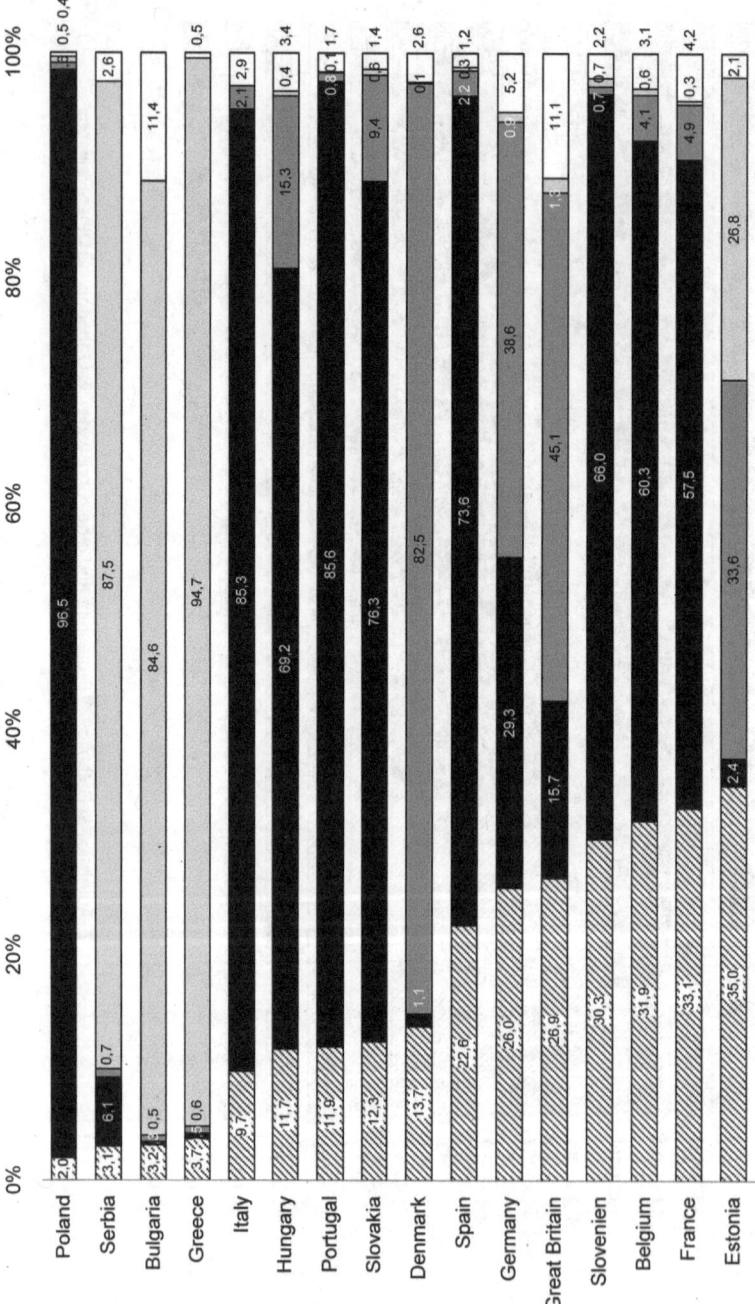

FIGURE 8. RELIGIOUS CONFESSION: GENERAL POPULATION (PERCENT)

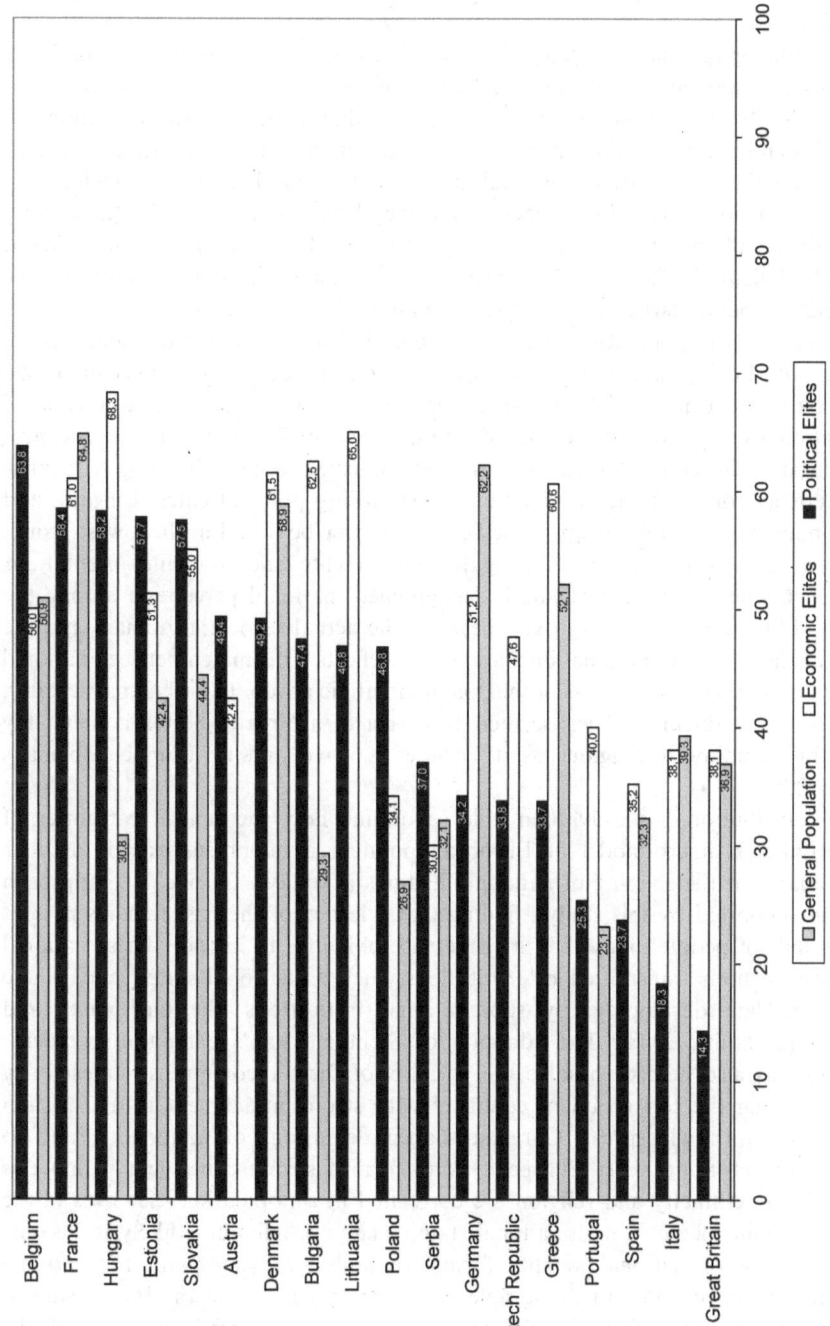

FIGURE 9. THE ENLARGEMENT OF THE EU TO INCLUDE TURKEY IS A BIG THREAT FOR THE COHESION OF THE EU (PERCENT AGREEMENT)

disputes about foreign policy or the problems resulting from modern migration processes.

In the following—the last step of the comparison—I will discuss the cumulative percentages of agreement with all five aspects of nationality used in this study (see Figures 10–12). The question posed here is to what extent do the definitions of national identity used in this study form a clear-cut pattern of in-group relations. To establish the exclusivity of national identity definitions I used the percentage of interviewees who named simultaneously all five characteristics of national identity as criteria of affiliation. This indicates a high level of exclusiveness that makes it extremely difficult for immigrants or members of ethnic or religious minorities to be considered as being part of the national community.

For the general population, we once more find Bulgaria, Greece and Serbia, together with Poland and Italy, in the top-ranking group defined by an accumulation of criteria of exclusion and inclusion (Figure 12). Although this cannot be equated with nationalism, it does, however, indicate a widespread readiness to exclude people who do not comply with the complete opening code of national identity characteristics for the national community. Regarding political elites, Bulgaria and Greece remain in this top group, while Serbia can now be found in the lowest group. However, in my opinion, the clear gap between elite and non-elite orientations in Serbia is due less to a particularly 'enlightened' national perception among the Serbian political elites than to a gap between the actual territorial domain and the historical claim of a Serbian nation state, which reflects a mismatch between national borders and the settlement areas of the dominant ethnic group. In Serbia, particularly, the elites face a dilemma, because their construct of a Greater Serbia is inevitably multi-ethnic and multi-religious as it includes Kosovo and its Islamic Albanians (Glenny 2001).

This contribution has only been able to outline how the central categories of Stein Rokkan's macro-model of European political development can be used as an *explanans* for the shaping of national identities in today's Europe. The approach has been supported by this study's finding that a legacy of the past remains present in the minds of people today that are otherwise oblivious to history. These national legacies have been transmitted by institutions, such as national states, and, where those were late developing, by supranational institutions like Orthodoxy and Catholicism (Smith 2008). The adaption of Stein Rokkan's comparative macro-sociology has also helped to solve the paradox of former communist states today ranking among the top group of countries with strong attachment to a Christian Church and with widespread Christian-shaped definitions of nationality, and to explain why the South East European states form a strong contingent within this group. Where ethnicity and religion are correlated in a population that lives in the sphere of dominance of a multinational state or empire, religion is likely to become a core element of national identity formation and a rallying point for national independence movements. In the sample of countries included in the Intune survey, this was the case for Catholic Poland and Lithuania, which were part of the Orthodox Russian Empire, and for Orthodox Bulgaria, Serbia and Greece, which were part of the Islamic Ottoman Empire. To the present day, Christianity forms an important element of national identities in these countries. The participation of

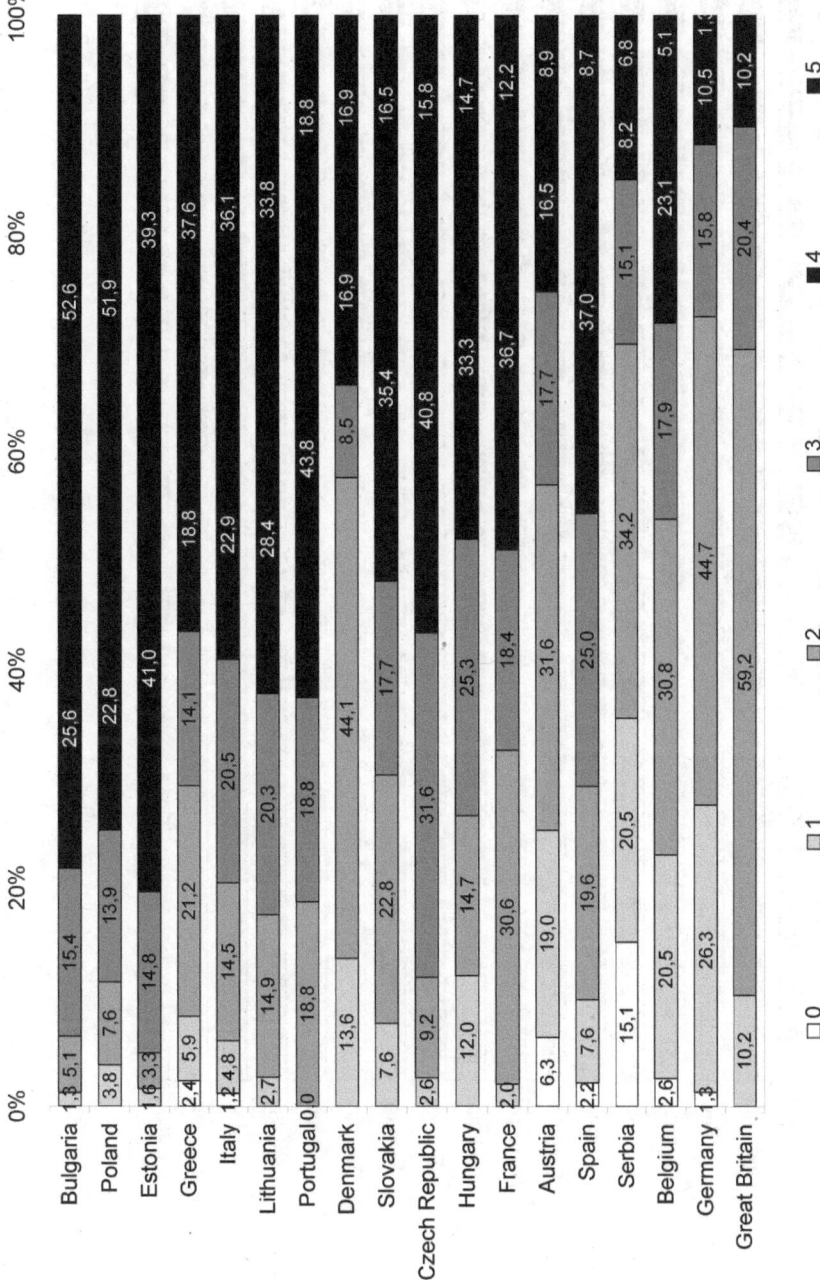

FIGURE 10. FREQUENCY OF AGREEMENT TO CRITERIA OF NATIONALITY (SEE TABLE 1): POLITICAL ELITES (PERCENT)

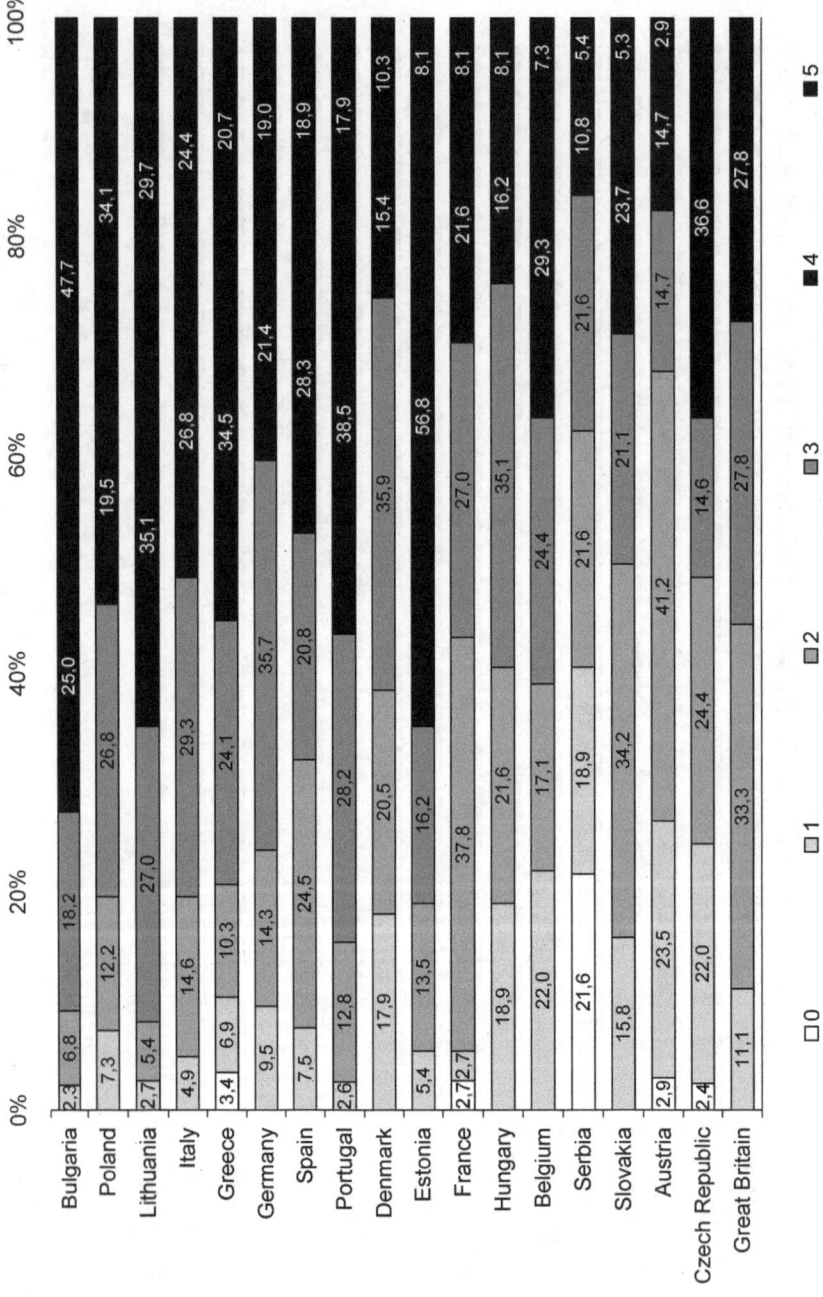

FIGURE 11. FREQUENCY OF AGREEMENT TO CRITERIA OF NATIONALITY (SEE TABLE 1): ECONOMIC ELITES (PERCENT)

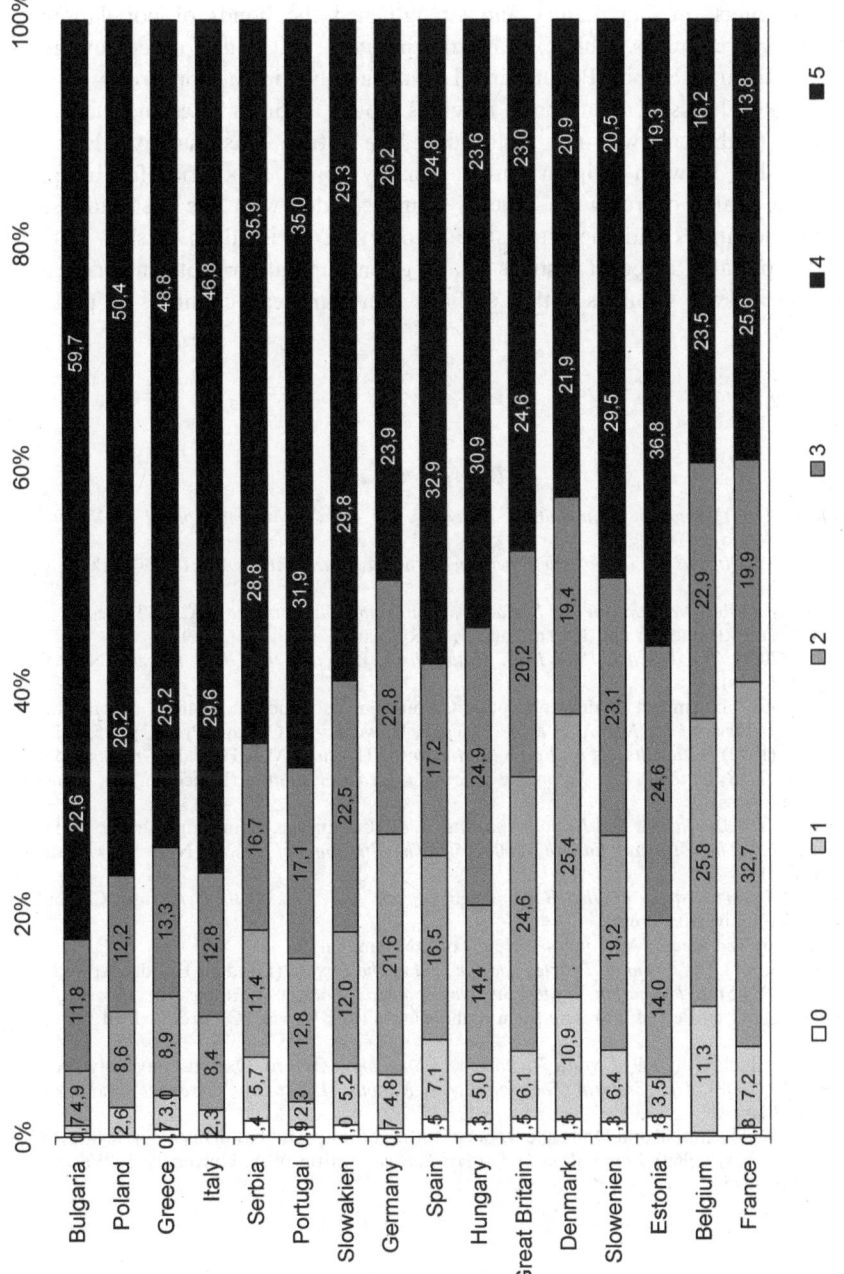

FIGURE 12. FREQUENCY OF AGREEMENT TO CRITERIA OF NATIONALITY (SEE TABLE 1): GENERAL POPULATION (PERCENT)

the Orthodox or Catholic Church in all their national liberation movements had a vitalising effect on Christianity and strengthened the bonds of populations to their respective churches. This explains the paradox that four former communist countries (Bulgaria, Serbia, Poland and Lithuania) rank in the top group of those with the highest levels of affiliation to religious groups amongst elites and the general population. (Lithuania was not included in the Intune mass survey.) However, the relationship between religion and nationality comes at a price for both: the universalistic claim of religious belief systems collides with the restricted scope of national identities and the integrative ideology of nationalism clashes with the reality of a plurality of belief systems in any given population. Both inconsistencies have led to massive conflicts within and between European countries in past and recent times.

University of Jena

References

Anderson, B. (1991) *Imaged Communities: Reflections on the Origins and Spread of Nationalism* (London, Verso).
Bruter, M. (2005) *Citizens of Europe? The Emergence of a Mass European Identity* (New York, Palgrave Macmillan).
Deutsch, K. W. (1966) *Nationalism and Social Communication* (Cambridge, MA, MIT Press).
Flora, P. (1999) 'Introduction and Interpretation', in Rokkan, S. (1999), pp. 1–91.
Glenny, M. (2001) *The Balkans 1804–1999. Nationalism, War and the Great Powers* (New York, Penguin Books).
Geerz, C. (1966) 'The Impact of the Concept of Culture on the Concept of Men', in Platt, J. (ed.) (1966) *New Views of the Nature of Man* (Chicago, University of Chicago Press), pp. 53–118.
Greenfield, L. (1992) *Nationalism. Five Roads to Modernity* (Harvard, MA, Harvard University Press).
Herrin, J. (2007) *Byzantium: The Surprising Life of a Medieval Empire* (Princeton, NJ, Princeton University Press).
Hobsbawm, E. (1990) *Nations and Nationalism since 1780* (Cambridge, Cambridge University Press).
Imber, C. (2002) *The Ottoman Empire 1300–1650. The Structure of Power* (New York, Palgrave Macmillan).
Jelavich, B. (1983) *History of the Balkans: Eighteenth and Nineteenth Centuries* (Cambridge, Cambridge University Press).
Kohn, H. (1945) *The Idea of Nationalism* (New York, Macmillan).
McCarthy, J. (2001) *The Ottoman Peoples and the End of the Empire* (London, Hodder Arnold).
Rokkan, S. (1999) *State Formation, Nation-Building, and Mass Politics in Europe. The Theory of Stein Rokkan* [edited by Peter Flora with Stein Kuhnle and Derek Urwin] (Oxford, Oxford University Press).
Scott, J. & Marshall, G. (2009) *Oxford Dictionary of Sociology* (Oxford, Oxford University Press).
Smith, A. D. (2008) *The Cultural Foundations of Nations. Hierarchy, Covenant, and Republic* (Oxford, Blackwell).
Sugar, P. F. (1969) 'External and Domestic Roots of Eastern European Nationalism', in Sugar, P. F. & Lederer, I. (eds) (1969) *Nationalism in Eastern Europe* (Seattle, WA, University of Washington Press), pp. 46–54.

Identity and Representation in the Perceptions of Political Elites and Public Opinion: A Comparison between Southern and Post-Communist Central-Eastern Europe

MIGUEL JEREZ-MIR, JOSÉ REAL-DATO & RAFAEL VÁZQUEZ-GARCÍA

EUROPEAN UNION INTEGRATION AND THE INHERENT processes of political development and institution building are shaped by interactions between elites and masses. In their initial steps, scholars noted the predominantly intergovernmental, elite-driven flavour of these processes (Inglehart 1970; Lindberg & Scheingold 1970).[1] It has been during the last few years—as the process of European integration has deepened and the number of 'Europeanised' policy areas has expanded—that national arenas have also been increasingly concerned with European Union (EU) affairs, reinforcing the role of national elites and mass public opinion on European integration (Dalton & Eichenberg 1998). National elites' perception of Europe is a significant factor in understanding the current European integration process as well as the future perspectives for the continent (Slater 1994; Wessels 1999; Holmberg 1999; Jenny *et al.* 2006; Haller 2008). Further, the study of political elite's attitudes and values could be very useful for understanding the nature of change processes within the EU since, as Putnam has argued, 'elite composition is more easily observable than are the underlying patterns of social power, it can serve as a kind of seismometer for detecting shifts in the foundation of polities and politics' (Putnam 1976, p. 166).

A great deal of empirical evidence is available regarding mass attitudes and orientations towards processes of European integration and identity-building (Gabel 1998; McLaren 2002; Díez 2003). Conversely, systematic comparative research on national European elites is much less abundant (Best *et al.* 2005), although during the last decade the number of comparative studies has increased, mainly oriented towards party elites (Aspinwall 2002; De Winter & Gómez-Reino 2002; Evans 1998; Hug & König 2002; Hooghe 2003; Johansson 2002; Jolly 2007; Ladrech 2002; Marks *et al.* 2002; Netjes & Binnema 2007; Ray 1999, 2003a). In conjunction with some other

---

The authors would like to acknowledge the assistance of Francisco J. Alarcón-Gonźlez in the management of data used in this essay.

[1]For a review, see Haller (2008, p. 35).

factors, elite behaviour and how it interacts with still unsettled public preferences may be decisive in steering towards a new system of legitimation (Pridham 2007, p. 565). Concerning this interaction, support for a bottom-up process is outlined mainly by Carrubba (2001), while other authors find evidence for a top-down process (Wessels 1995; Ray 2003b; Gabel & Scheve 2007a, 2007b). Moreover, with few exceptions—most notably Wessels (1995) and Steenbergen et al. (2007)—there have been no outstanding efforts to estimate the impact of both processes simultaneously. A major problem in this field has been the evident lack of systematic comparative projects on the relation between elites and mass opinion towards Europe.[2] In order to gain comprehensive knowledge from a systematic retrieval of these studies we now have the Intune project,[3] which maps the main conceptions of identity and their multiple interconnections among sets of actors crucial to the construction of European identity: elites, citizens and the mass media.

As an output of Intune, like the other essays in this collection, this work aims to make a contribution to the comparative literature on political elites and mass public opinion regarding attitudes towards EU integration along several European countries. More specifically, we concentrate on the comparison of political elites and public attitudes along two basic dimensions of the European integration process: identity and representation. Our comparison is focused on two geographic areas within the EU: Central and Eastern European post-communist countries (CEEPC) and Southern Europe.

Why compare these geographical areas?

Table 1 measures support for European integration in the countries included in the samples of the Intune project, all of which are members of the EU except Serbia. One of the things that is immediately noticeable is that, in general terms, with the exceptions of Bulgaria and Poland for political elites and mass public opinion, respectively, the average level of support among elites and the public in CEEPC countries is below the European mean. In contrast, those countries traditionally grouped under the category of Southern Europe (Greece, Italy, Portugal and Spain) (Malefakis 1995; Bruneau et al. 2001) all display levels of support above the cited average. Besides this, regional patterns are consistent for different types of interviewees, and elite and public opinion views do not differ substantially within countries (with the exception of Spain, Hungary and Bulgaria). These results are corroborated by those offered by other sources and scholars. Thus, higher levels of Euroscepticism have been found in CEEPC countries (Hughes et al. 2002; Rohschneider & Whitefield 2006, 2008), while Southern Europe has traditionally been more supportive of the EU (Brinegar et al. 2004; Llamazares & Gramacho 2007).

Inter-regional differences and intra-regional similarities make these geographical areas suitable for comparison. Such features are directly related to the conditions

---

[2]However, some exceptions are Slater (1994), Spence (1997), CIRCAP (2006) and Haller (2008).

[3]'Integrated and United? A Quest for Citizenship in an Ever Closer Europe', project, approved under the 6th Framework Programme of the European Commission. For details, see the official website, available at: www.intune.it, last accessed 15 April 2009.

TABLE 1
Opinions on Whether 'The European Union should be Strengthened'

	Political elite				Public		
Country	Mean	N	Standard deviation	Country	Mean	N	Standard deviation
Spain	8.13	94	1.60	Portugal	6.75	844	2.95
Italy	7.72	82	2.45	Italy	6.70	974	3.04
Greece	7.57	90	2.37	Greece	6.62	963	3.11
Germany	7.41	70	1.72	Poland	6.46	880	2.45
Belgium	7.27	79	2.61	Spain	6.46	980	2.64
Denmark	6.78	58	2.93	Slovenia	5.74	954	3.01
Portugal	6.74	77	2.42	Denmark	5.73	958	2.70
Bulgaria	6.67	79	2.42	Germany	5.70	983	2.68
France	6.48	44	2.24	Serbia	5.64	776	2.78
Hungary	6.43	79	2.32	Slovakia	5.51	981	2.22
Austria	6.38	79	2.69	Belgium	5.41	985	2.89
Lithuania	6.34	80	1.85	Bulgaria	5.36	683	2.52
Serbia	6.33	72	2.71	Hungary	5.22	764	2.32
Slovakia	6.21	78	2.16	France	5.20	989	2.95
Poland	6.03	78	2.32	Estonia	4.79	815	2.62
Czech Republic	5.53	80	2.75	Great Britain	4.51	963	2.72
Estonia	4.87	71	2.19	Austria	–	–	–
Great Britain	4.65	48	2.85	Czech Republic	–	–	–
Slovenia	–	–	–	Lithuania	–	–	–
Europe	6.6	1,338	2.52	Europe	5.75	14,492	2.82

Question: Some say European unification should be strengthened. Others say it already has gone too far. What is your opinion? Please indicate your views using a 10-point scale. On this scale, '0' means unification 'has already gone too far' and '10' means it 'should be strengthened'. What number on this scale best describes your position?
Responses: 0–10.
Source: Intune Project. Author's own elaboration using the Intune project database.

experienced during the process of accession by both groups of countries. Despite the fact that both CEEPC and Southern European countries joined—respectively—the EU and the European Economic Community (EEC) shortly after experiencing transitional processes from non-democratic regimes,[4] there were different conditions surrounding the processes.

Regarding CEEPC countries, their societies have characteristics that differentiate them from those countries involved in previous stages of European integration (Bozoki 2003). They shared the same fate during a great part of the twentieth century, while they were kept under the close and vigilant observation of the Soviet Union. After the demise of communist regimes, the common Leninist legacy was shaped by the immediate context of elite interests, norms, institutions and international pressures (Crawford & Lijphardt 1995; Geddes 1995; Hanson 1995), resulting in a divide within the CEEPC countries—where liberal democratic rules of the game took root alongside authoritarian features that characterised the Soviet empire (Way & Levitsky 2007; Eckiert et al. 2007).

---

[4]This particular condition does not apply to Italy, a founding member of the EEC.

Along with the transition to democratic regimes, the process of accession to the EU also constituted an element that reinforced the existence of a common ground affecting these countries and that 'marked the beginning of a new era for Europe' (Rohrschneider & Whitefield 2006, p. 142). Conditionality imposed on these countries during this process influenced the acceptance, among their citizens and elites, of newborn political and economic institutions (Cameron 2007; Schimmelfennig 2007; Schimmelfennig & Scholtz 2008), yet this happened perhaps, in diverse and contradictory ways (Tucker *et al.* 2002). Despite the fact that national elites (usually the prospective 'winners' of the process) in candidate CEEPC countries were strongly committed to the 'return to Europe' (Grabbe & Hughes 1998; Higley *et al.* 1998), the process of accession also fuelled uncertainty, a lack of enthusiasm, and growing scepticism in public opinion (and sometimes among political elites as well) about the consequences of EU membership, thus creating a gap between the behaviour and attitudes of the 'pro-Europe' national elites and rising levels of Eurosceptic public opinion in some applicant countries (Hughes *et al.* 2002, p. 328; Taggart & Szczerbiak 2001). The power structures of the former communist state influenced the values, behaviour and democratic potential of the post-communist MPs or, at least, made the post-communist parliamentarians different from their counterparts in the older democratic regimes (Crowther & Matonyte 2007, p. 284). In any case, both publics and elites strongly supported the idea of integration with the West and the EU in general, although they were sceptical about specific integration instruments (Rohrschneider & Whitefield 2006, p. 142).

In the case of Southern European countries, democratic transition and consolidation were facilitated by the moderation shown by both the general public and elites (Malefakis 1995, p. 75), which included a clearly pro-European stance, resulting in political systems with little resemblance to their pre-democratic predecessors (Bruneau *et al.* 2001, p. 81). Besides, democratisation processes in these countries (with the exception of Italy) were favoured by the support they received from other European countries and European international organisations. In this respect, for Greece, Portugal and Spain the advantages of joining the EEC clearly outnumbered the effects of conditionality.

Identity and representation as basic dimensions of attitudes toward EU integration

One question that arises from these data is whether such alignments between public and elite opinion along clear geographical borders are maintained when considering more specific dimensions of the European integration process, such as identity and representation. Identity can be understood both as a feature (or a set of features) attributed to a group of individuals on the basis of which they can be observed and perceived from the outside as having significant elements of commonality, and as a feeling—or an array of feelings—shared by individuals, which define their belonging to a group of similar people. Identities are multiple in nature. Hence, one may have a single identity, but it will be made up of many levels of loyalty and identification. It often implies an implicit or explicit comparative dimension: one's group identity emerges more strongly when compared to another group's identity. Identity normally has a positive connotation for those who share it, but it may also have a negative image when attributed to individuals from other groups (Müller-Härlin 2003, pp. 269–71).

Particularly, patriotism is an attitude that is often associated with citizenship—and also identity—and indicates a pride or predisposition to expressing enthusiasm towards symbols of the polity. It presupposes an intense identification with the community. It is difficult to conceive patriotism without strong feelings of identity. However, there may be feelings of identity without patriotism. The discussion in the Constitutional Convention about the religious and cultural identity of Europe shows that, even if this topic has become increasingly relevant, it is not easy to find a strong consensus on the elements of a European identity. Meanwhile, it is important to note that, according to surveys, feelings of a common European identity—which coexist with feelings of national identity—already exist and have a greater or lesser intensity among the populations of the old continent (Eder 2001; Delanty 2005). It is clear that increasing numbers of Europeans do identify in one way or another with Europe, and claim to have some kind of European identity, often alongside a national identity. Moreover, many other scholars have emphasised how multiple identities—local, regional, national and European—reinforce, rather than exclude, each other (Bruter 2005). The question of a European identity and demos must therefore be seen in relation to entrenched national identities (Fossum 2001). In this sense, studying European identity requires a simultaneous consideration of other types of territorial identification.

Regarding representation, it can be said that this concept is still the dominant instrument through which citizens exercise their prerogatives of self-government and by which political elites of a community are legitimised in their governing role and kept accountable (Pitkin 1967; Manin 1997; Schmitt & Thomassen 1999). In the modern democratic state, the experience of representation is limited to citizens. Only citizens as members of the polity are represented. Viewed from the other side of the relationship, representation has a crucial role in the construction of citizenship. While performing such representative roles, elites contribute to the 'production' and 'reproduction' of citizenship (both as members of the community and as a system of entitlements) and of identity. Hence, European elites and institutions play a central role in the construction of the representative link with European citizenship. In this sense, alignments and aggregations among MEPs within the European Parliament along ideological rather than purely territorial lines show that, to some extent, European representation exists (Hix et al. 2007). In this respect, here we use the degree to which interviewees trust EU institutions as a proxy for the existence of such a European representation link.

Results[5]

As we have noted above, the aim of this essay is to check whether general patterns detected in both geographical regions regarding general EU support are maintained

---

[5]As is the case for the rest of the works in this special issue, we have used the database of the Intune Project Survey on European Elites and Masses. The questionnaire was administered between February and May 2007, in 18 European countries (all of them members of the European Union, except Serbia). The number of cases included in the elite and public opinion samples differ. Thus, the post-communist countries considered in the political elite survey are Bulgaria, the Czech Republic, Estonia, Hungary, Lithuania, Poland, Serbia and Slovakia. For the public opinion survey, while the Czech Republic and

when considering more specific identity and representational dimensions of European citizenship. In this section, we limit ourselves to present detailed and systematic descriptive evidence, leaving more analytical treatment (looking for causal patterns) for a future occasion.

Dimension 1: identity

As stated in the previous section, studying European identity also requires paying attention to other types of territorial identification (see Table 2).

First of all, we explore how interviewees feel attached to national and sub-national territorial levels. There is a near unanimity among political elites about being attached to their own cities, with a percentage above 90 points in all cases. The results for Estonia, Lithuania and Serbia are situated below the European average of 95.9%, and Hungary and Poland show a total agreement on this issue. The degree of attachment of Southern European elites is only slightly lower, with Spain and Portugal showing extreme values (96.8% and 91.1 respectively). Serbia has the lowest score with 91%. In contrast, public opinion shows a lower level of attachment to the local community than political elites, although the minimum (84.9% in Estonia) is also quite high. Once more, the highest levels are found in post-communist countries, where publics show a tighter bond to their town than in Southern Europe. The only post-communist country where the public shows a lower level of attachment to the local community, compared with Southern European ones, is the abovementioned Estonia. As to differences between the two categories of interviewees within countries, in all cases the political elites have higher scores than public opinion, and they are above 10% in Slovakia, Spain, Greece and Estonia.

There is no pattern regarding regional attachment along geographic areas. Concerning political elites, along the heterogeneity among post-communist countries is outstanding: attachment to this level ranges from 100% in Poland to 76.3% in Hungary, or less than 70% in Serbia. This wide range clearly suggests the different perceptions of the regional realities existing in each country, independently of the geographic area we consider. If looking for regularities, political elites in Southern Europe usually show more homogeneous positions, all above the European average of 88.2%. The Polish, Czech, Spanish, Greek and Bulgarian political elites' attachment to their regions is above 95%, while that of the Serbian, Hungarian and Lithuanian elites does not reach 80%. Public opinion is more heterogeneous both among and within countries. Thus, the attachment of Hungarian and Serbian publics to their regions is much higher than that of their political elites (respectively, 13.3% and 12.2% higher).

Regarding the degree of attachment to one's country, once more we observe heterogeneity within geographical areas and between types of interviewees. For political elites, the level of attachment ranges from a minimum in Serbia of 89.9% to 100% in Bulgaria, the Czech Republic, Estonia and Poland. This is the level of government which political elites manifest the highest degree of attachment, with the

Lithuania were not in the sample, Slovenia—absent from the elite survey—was included. Although the respective totals are considered, comparisons take into account only the countries included in both samples.

TABLE 2
ATTACHMENT TO DIFFERENT LEVELS OF POLITICAL COMMUNITIES (VALID PERCENTAGES)

	Attachment to your town		Attachment to your region		Attachment to your country		Attachment to Europe	
	Political elite	Public	Political elite	Public	Political elites	Public	Political elites	Public
Bulgaria	98.8 (80)	93.8 (1,005)	95.1 (81)	92.0 (1,005)	100.0 (81)	95.7 (1,005)	80.5 (81)	48.2 (1,005)
Czech Republic	97.5 (80)		96.3 (80)		100.0 (80)		75.0 (80)	
Estonia	95.8 (71)	84.9 (1,000)	85.7 (70)	78.6 (1,000)	100.0 (71)	92.0 (1,000)	84.1 (69)	52.1 (1,000)
Greece	96.6 (87)	85.7 (1,000)	95.5 (88)	86.5 (1,000)	98.9 (89)	93.4 (1,000)	80.7 (88)	49.8 (1,000)
Hungary	100.0 (79)	90.1 (1,002)	76.3 (80)	89.6 (1,002)	98.8 (80)	96.5 (1,002)	92.5 (80)	83.1 (1,002)
Italy	93.9 (82)	85.2 (1,012)	89.2 (83)	83.6 (1,012)	94.0 (84)	92.5 (1,012)	92.7 (80)	78.9 (1,012)
Lithuania	94.7 (76)		79.7 (69)		97.4 (77)		84.3 (70)	
Poland	100.0 (80)	91.5 (999)	100.0 (80)	92.0 (999)	100.0 (80)	95.7 (999)	93.8 (80)	74.7 (999)
Portugal	91.1 (79)	85.1 (1,000)	93.8 (80)	87.9 (1,000)	98.8 (80)	93.0 (1,000)	96.3 (80)	71.3 (1,000)
Serbia	91.0 (78)	86.0 (1,005)	69.4 (72)	81.6 (1,005)	89.9 (79)	87.1 (1,005)	69.7 (76)	56.2 (1,005)
Slovakia	97.5 (80)	86.0 (1,082)	93.8 (80)	79.6 (1,082)	97.5 (80)	88.5 (1,082)	91.3 (80)	58.3 (1,082)
Slovenia		87.5 (1,018)		84.5 (1,018)		94.3 (1,018)		71.1 (1,018)
Spain	96.8 (94)	85.7 (1,002)	95.7 (94)	78.0 (1,002)	93.5 (93)	80.3 (1,002)	91.5 (94)	59.2 (1,002)
Southern Europe	94.7 (342)	85.4 (4,014)	93.6 (345)	84.0 (4,014)	96.2 (346)	89.8 (4,014)	90.1 (344)	64.8 (4,014)
Post-communist (6)	97.2 (462)	88.7 (6,093)	87.0 (463)	85.5 (6,093)	97.7 (473)	92.5 (6,093)	85.4 (467)	62.0 (6,093)
Europe	95.9 (1,394)	86.1 (13,136)	88.2 (1,385)	82.7 (16,136)	95.2 (1,405)	90.3 (16,136)	85.6 (1,388)	63.4 (16,136)

Question: People feel different degrees of attachment to their town or village, to their region, to their country and to Europe. What about you? Are you very attached, somewhat attached, not very attached or not at all attached to the following: (a) your town/village; (b) your 'region' [use the appropriate term for each country]; (c) country (e.g. 'Italy'); (d) Europe?

Responses: very attached, somewhat attached, not very attached, not at all attached. Percentages represent the sum of 'very attached' and 'somewhat attached'.

Source: Intune Project, Elite and Mass Surveys, 2007.

exception of Hungary, Serbia and Spain; in these three cases, local attachment predominates. In contrast, public opinion shows in general a lower degree of attachment to their countries, with differences ranging from Italy's 1.5% to 8% in Estonia, 9% in Slovakia and 13% in Spain. The national level is also the preferred level of political community for all the countries' publics, except Spain.

Compared with the territorial levels discussed above, the degree of attachment of political elites to Europe offers a wider range of variation along countries, both for political elites and for the general public. For the general public attachment to Europe is consistently below attachment to national and sub-national levels. The same occurs for the political elites, with the exceptions of Hungary, Italy, Lithuania and Serbia (where MPs feel more attached to Europe than to their region) and Portugal (where the political elite prefers the European level to both the regional and local levels, with the degree of identification always being above 90%). Unsurprisingly, political elites in Hungary, Italy, Lithuania and Serbia show the lowest levels of attachment to their region. Regarding the presence of patterns according to geographical areas, there seems to be a certain degree of geographical coherence for political elites in Southern European countries, as more than 90% of the Portuguese, Italian and Spanish political elites feel identified with Europe. However, the presence of such a hypothetical geographical pattern is complicated by the case of Greece, where the percentage only reaches 80.7%. In contrast, identification with Europe among political elites in post-communist countries is much more heterogeneous. Thus, in three post-communist nations (Poland, Hungary and Slovakia) more than 90% of MPs feel identified with Europe, while the figures for Bulgaria and the Czech Republic are 80.5% and 75%, respectively. Serbia occupies (once more) an extreme position, with only 68.7% of the interviewees showing attachment to Europe, which reflects a higher degree of Euroscepticism in this country.

Regarding public opinion's attachment to Europe, as with local and national identification, it is below that of political elites in all countries. The highest levels of public identification with Europe are found in Hungary, Italy and Poland (respectively, 83.1%, 78.9% and 74.1%). Portugal and Slovenia are also above the 70% mark. In contrast, the lowest levels of public attachment to Europe are found in Greece (49.8%) and Bulgaria (48.2%). The rest of the countries are all below the European mean (63.4%). Differences are more pronounced than in the previous types of attachment. Thus, in Estonia, Greece, Slovakia and Spain such differences reach more than 30%, while in Portugal the gap is of 25%. In sum, we can assert that European identity is still considered secondary both by national publics and political elites as compared with national and—with the abovementioned exceptions among political elites—sub-national levels. In addition, we can hypothesize that the degree of identification with Europe mostly depends on country-specific factors such as history and institutions.

European identity should also be analysed regarding its qualitative dimension, that is, what elements interviewees think are important in order to be considered truly European citizens. Here, it is interesting to compare such elements with those considered by interviewees as important in defining national identification.

Regarding national citizenship (Table 3), being Christian is by far the least significant element. We encounter great variations among countries, ranging from the

PERCEPTIONS OF THE EUROPEAN UNION IN NEW MEMBER STATES 37

TABLE 3
ELEMENTS OF BEING A NATIONAL CITIZEN

	To be Christian		To share cultural traditions		To be born in (country)		To have national parents		To respect national laws and institutions		To feel national		To master the country's language		To be a (country) citizen	
	Political elite	Public	Political elite	Public	Political elite	Public	Political elite	Public	Political elite	Public	Political elite	Public	Political elite	Public	Political elite	Public
Bulgaria	69.6 (79)	70.8 (1,005)	98.8 (91)	93.1 (1,005)	75.6 (82)	90.0 (1,005)	83.8 (80)	87.5 (1,005)	98.8 (80)	94.3 (1,005)	98.8 (82)	95.8 (1,005)	98.8 (82)	96.6 (1,005)	91.5 (82)	79.5 (1,005)
Czech Republic	25 (80)		96.3 (80)		70 (80)		81.3 (80)		93.8 (80)		97.5 (80)		96.3 (80)		78.8 (80)	
Estonia	40.3 (72)	28.6 (1,000)	97.2 (72)	92.5 (1,000)	83.3 (72)	69.4 (1,000)	83.3 (72)	71.3 (1,000)	98.6 (72)	94.5 (1,000)	97.2 (72)	83.2 (1,000)	95.8 (72)	94.9 (1,000)	87.5 (72)	72.7 (1,000)
Greece	57.8 (90)	74.2 (1,000)	84.4 (90)	94.2 (1,000)	57.8 (90)	76.1 (1,000)	66.7 (90)	84.6 (1,000)	93.3 (90)	93.4 (1,000)	95.6 (90)	95.5 (1,000)	82.2 (90)	92.7 (1,000)	74.4 (90)	80.9 (1,000)
Hungary	33.8 (80)	39.0 (1,002)	100 (79)	90.5 (1,002)	59.5 (79)	72.0 (1,002)	79.5 (78)	81.5 (1,002)	90.7 (75)	97.1 (1,002)	100 (79)	97.4 (1,002)	98.8 (80)	95.6 (1,002)	54.5 (77)	71.0 (1,002)
Italy	48.8 (84)	63.4 (1,012)	86.9 (84)	91.7	71.4 (84)	81.8 (1,012)	73.8 (84)	78.6 (1,012)	98.8 (84)	98.0 (1,012)	92.9 (84)	91.9 (1,012)	88.1 (84)	95.8 (1,012)	83.3 (84)	86.4 (1,012)
Lithuania	47.5 (80)		88.8 (80)		56.2 (80)		72.5 (80)		95 (80)		97.5 (80)		95 (80)		87.5 (80)	
Poland	76.3 (80)	74.3 (999)	98.8 (80)	93.5 (999)	77.5 (80)	82.2 (999)	86.3 (80)	83.6 (999)	93.8 (80)	93.2 (999)	100 (80)	97.0 (999)	88.8 (80)	97.3 (999)	81.3 (80)	69.3 (999)
Portugal	26.3 (80)	48.2 (1,000)	93.8 (80)	91.4 (1,000)	66.3 (80)	78.4 (1,000)	77.5 (80)	76.5 (1,000)	97.5 (80)	94.5 (1,000)	97.5 (80)	91.4 (1,000)	98.8 (80)	94.9 (1,000)	93.8 (80)	81.8 (1,000)
Serbia	32.5 (77)	80.7 (1,005)	86.1 (79)	88.6 (1,005)	18 (78)	66.3 (1,005)	46.8 (77)	75.7 (1,005)	89.5 (76)	84.2 (1,005)	82.1 (78)	89.2 (1,005)	62.9 (78)	87.3 (1,005)	44.7 (76)	54.1 (1,005)
Slovakia	40 (80)	53.3 (1,082)	97.5 (80)	82.3 (1,082)	55 (80)	77.5 (1,082)	61.3 (80)	75.7 (1,082)	92.5 (80)	93.1 (1,082)	93.8 (80)	91.0 (1,082)	93.8 (80)	96.8 (1,082)	77.5 (80)	60.9 (1,082)
Slovenia		32.0 (1,018)		93.5 (1,018)		67.2 (1,018)		66.9 (1,018)		93.9 (1,018)		92.4 (1,018)		97.4 (1,018)		69.7 (1,018)
Spain	14.0 (93)	34.3 (1,002)	72.8 (92)	82.0 (1,002)	69.9 (93)	75.0 (1,002)	64.5 (93)	69.5 (1,002)	93.5 (93)	93.2 (1,002)	82.6 (92)	84.4 (1,002)	84.9 (93)	83.9 (1,002)	79.6 (93)	81.8 (1,002)

(continued)

TABLE 3
(Continued)

	To be Christian		To share cultural traditions		To be born in (country)		To have national parents		To respect national laws and institutions		To feel national		To master the country's language		To be a (country) citizen	
	Political elite	Public	Political elite	Public	Political elite	Public	Political elite	Public	Political elite	Public	Political elite	Public	Political elite	Public	Political elite	Public
Southern Europe	36.9 (344)	55.1 (4,014)	85.3 (341)	89.8 (4,014)	62.4 (343)	77.8 (4,014)	71.3 (342)	77.3 (4,014)	96.5 (344)	94.8 (4,014)	93.5 (340)	90.8 (4,014)	89.2 (343)	91.8 (4,014)	83.6 (342)	82.7 (4,014)
Post-communist (6)	49.4 (469)	57.8 (6,093)	96.6 (470)	90.0 (6,093)	61.5 (470)	76.3 (6,093)	73.6 (466)	79.2 (6,093)	94.4 (463)	92.7 (6,093)	95.6 (468)	92.3 (6,093)	90.6 (468)	94.8 (6,093)	74.1 (460)	67.8 (6,093)
Europe	36.2 (1,387)	48.8 (16,136)	88.5 (1,393)	87.8 (16,136)	54.3 (1,393)	69.7 (16,136)	61.5 (1,325)	69.5 (16,136)	95.6 (1,392)	94.4 (16,136)	83.6 (1,389)	88.6 (16,136)	92.5 (1,395)	94.3 (16,136)	78.9 (1,353)	74.3 (16,136)

Question: People differ in what they think it means to be (national). In your view, how important is each of the following to be (national): (a) to be a Christian; (b) to share (country) cultural traditions; (c) to be born in (country); (d) to have (national) parents (e.g. 'Italian parents'); (e) to respect (national) laws and institutions; (f) to feel (national); (g) to master (language(s) of the country)/[in relevant cases] one of the official languages of the country; (h) to be a country citizen [never put as first]?

Reponses: Very important, somewhat important, not very important, not important at all. Percentages represent the sum of 'very important' and 'somewhat important'.

Source: Intune Project, Elite and Mass Surveys, 2007.

maximum level of agreement in Poland (76.3%) and Bulgaria (69.6%) to the minimum in Spain (14%). Once more, attitudes seem to be independent of geographical groups. Thus, Greek political elites occupy the third position in the ranking of those who consider being Christian an important component of nationality (57.8%), followed by Italy (48.8%). Other nations above the European average are two of the Baltic countries, Lithuania and Estonia, and Slovakia (with 47.5%, 40.3% and 40%, respectively). Regarding post-communist countries, there is also a sharp contrast between the maximum in Poland and the Czech Republic, where only 25% of MPs consider being Christian important. Compared with the public, political elites have a much more secular view of nationality, although in almost all countries both groups follow the same trend. Thus, common citizens consider being Christian an element of nationality to a greater extent in all countries except Poland (where, in fact, there is no difference between the two categories of interviewees) and Estonia. The contrast between political elites and the public is particularly sharp in Serbia (where the percentages agreeing are, respectively, 32.5% and 80.7%), followed by Portugal where 48.2% of the public considers being Christian important (22 percentage points above political elites) and Spain where such difference reaches 20.4%.

Sharing cultural traditions is widely accepted by political elites in almost all the countries as an important element of nationality. It also generates a high level of consensus; in all cases this element is above 84%, with the exception of Spain, where just 72.8% of political elites agree on this element. In this case, there seems to be a clearer geographical pattern regarding political elites. Thus, the percentages for Italy, Greece and Spain are below the European average (88.5%). The Spanish case (72.8%) is particularly remarkable. Portugal is the Southern European country with the highest proportion of support for this element (93.8%) among political elites, it is above all the post-communist countries except Lithuania (88.8%) and Serbia. Public opinion also shows considerable agreement with the idea of shared cultural traditions (in all countries above 82%). However, the geographic pattern disappears, Greece being the country whose citizens manifest the highest percentage of agreement (94.2%) while Spain shows the lowest level (82%).

Contrasts between political elites and public opinion vary in terms of their strength and direction. Thus, the sharpest difference concerns Slovakia, where the score for the political elite is 15.2% above that for public opinion. In Hungary, the political elite also scores considerably higher than public opinion in considering cultural traditions as an important element of nationality. On the other hand, there are the cases of Spain (where the figures for the political elite and the public are, respectively, 72.8% and 82%) and, particularly, Greece, whose citizens are the most supportive of the importance of cultural traditions but whose political elite has the second lowest score, after the Spanish elite.

As an element of nationality, being born in the country is considered of less importance and draws less consensus than sharing cultural traditions, with the Estonian political elite at the top with 83.3%, while Serbia shows an outlying 18%. Again, no geographical pattern is found. Political elites in Poland, Bulgaria, Italy, the Czech Republic and Spain show between 70% and 80%, while Hungary, Greece, Lithuania and Slovenia are between 55% and 60%. Thus, it cannot be concluded that there is a regular pattern according to geographical area.

As to the importance of being born in a particular country, political elites accord quite moderate importance to the fact of the nationality of parents as an element of national identity, with scattered percentages of support by country, ranging from a maximum of 86.3% in Poland to 61.3% in Slovakia and (once more) the outlying case of Serbia (46.8%). Regarding geographic areas, post-communist countries are located mainly in the upper half of the range, occupying the first five positions: Poland, Bulgaria, Estonia, the Czech Republic (all of them above 80%) and Hungary (79.5%). Nevertheless, the two countries at the bottom (the abovementioned Slovakia and Serbia) pull down the average to 73.6%, very similar to that of Southern Europe (71.3%). Here, the percentages range from Portugal's 77.5% to the 64.5% of Spain. In any case, all the considered countries (with the exceptions of Slovakia and Serbia) are above the European mean. Compared with political elites, geographical patterns in public opinion are less clear, with Bulgaria and Greece occupying the two first positions (87.5% and 84.6%, respectively), while Estonia, Spain and Slovenia appear at the bottom (with 71.3%, 69.5% and 66.9%), the last two being below the European mean of 69.5%.

For three further items, to respect national laws and institutions, to feel national, and to master the national language, there is a wide consensus on their great importance for having a national identity. Thus, along with sharing national cultural traditions, these items can be considered as important prerequisites of nationality. Regarding political elites, the percentages of those who agreed to the importance of these factors in all countries and categories of interviewees are above 80% (with the exception of the Serbian political elite concerning mastery of the country's language, where only 62.9% of the interviewees agree). Moreover, figures above 90% are extremely frequent in the case of respecting national laws and institutions. In all countries except Serbia (with a score of 89.5%) more than 90% of the political elite consider this item important for being a national. The trend is quite similar for the general public. In all countries the proportion of interviewees who think that respecting national laws and institutions is important for being a national is greater than 92% (with only the exception of Serbia which had a score of 84.2%).

A similar situation can be described about feeling national. More than 90% of the political elites agree with this requirement as an element of nationality, with the only exceptions being Spain (82.6%) and Serbia (82.1%), both countries having experienced quite complex processes of nation and state building, respectively. The same pattern appears with respect to the general public, where the positions of these two countries are inverted (89.2% in Serbia and 84.4% in Spain). Estonians express the lowest degree of support (83.2%), which implies a considerable gap (14 percentage points) between the public and the political elite, as compared with the rest of the countries.

There is also extensive agreement concerning the importance of mastering the country's language as a condition for being national, according to political elites. However, the degree of agreement in some countries is slightly lower for this item compared with the feeling national item. As usual, Serbian political elites show the lowest percentage of support (62.9%). With the exception of Poland, in the rest of the post-communist countries, more than 90% of the interviewees consider this condition important for being national. The figures for the Italian, Spanish and Greek political elites indicate that agreement there is below that percentage (88.1, 84.9 and 82.2% respectively), while, in contrast, Portugal shares first place with Bulgaria and Hungary (98.8%).

Finally, concerning the requirement of legal citizenship, the positions of the political elites range from the highest support in Portugal and Bulgaria (93.8% and 91.5% respectively) to the lowest in Hungary and Serbia (54.5% and 44.7% respectively), although most countries are between 74% and 88%. Thus, this item does not reflect a level of consensus as high as the three we have just examined. There is no clear pattern by geographical area. Finally, in many countries political elite opinions are in sharp contrast with those of the general public. In Bulgaria, Estonia, Poland, Portugal and Slovakia the position of elites is more than 10% above that of masses, while in Hungary and Serbia the public is markedly more in favour than their politicians of considering legal citizenship as an important element of nationality, the differences being 16.4% and 9.4%, respectively.

Regarding the components of European identity, we observe very similar patterns compared with national identity (Table 4). Therefore, in general terms, there is not much consensus among political elites on being Christian as an important component of European identity (the European average is 30.8%). Of course, geographical area patterns are not found here. Again, the Polish political elite leads the defence of Christianity in Europe with somewhat more than 64% (nevertheless, this is more than 12% below the percentage in this country that considered this feature to be important to be a national). Those with scores of above 40% are the same national elites that considered being Christian important for national identity: Bulgaria, Estonia, Italy and Lithuania. For the rest of the countries, this feature is also a less important element of European identity than for national identity in the abovementioned case of Greece, where 32.9% of the political elite consider Christianity an important feature, in contrast to the 57.8% that thought the same about national identity. Following the same pattern, in Serbia we find a score of 13.2% for European and 32.5% for national identity. In Portugal we find 16.3% for European and 26.3% for national identity. In contrast, being Christian is considered more important for being European than being national in the Czech Republic (33.3% as opposed to 25%), while in Hungary and Spain the positions are quite similar: 36.3% as opposed to 33.8% and 15.4% compared with 14%, respectively.

Comparing political elite opinion with that of the general public, there are considerable differences within countries. Thus, Greek public opinion leads the ranking, with 62.4% agreeing on the importance of Christianity for European identity. Unsurprisingly, the other three highest percentages correspond to Poland (61%), Italy and Bulgaria (both above 50%). Public opinion is also more prone than elites to consider being Christian an important feature of European identity in Portugal and Spain (41.5% and 32%, respectively), while the sharpest contrast appears in Serbia, where 46.1% of interviewees values Christianity, against 13.2% of the political elite. On the other hand, Estonian public opinion seems to have a less confessional view than their representatives, with a difference of 20.6% between both categories of interviewees.

With respect to the sharing of European cultural traditions as an element of European identity, the answers of the political elites resemble those given to the same question referring to national identity. Here, opinions are more consensual, and a

TABLE 4
ELEMENTS OF BEING A EUROPEAN CITIZEN

	To be Christian		To share European cultural traditions		To be born in Europe		To have European parents		To respect the European Union's laws and institutions		To feel European		To master a European language	
	Political elite	Public	Political elite	Public	Political elite	Public	Political elite	Public	Political elite	Public	Political elite	Public	Political elite	Public
Bulgaria	48.1 (81)	50.9 (1,005)	91.3 (80)	79.8 (1,005)	43.8 (80)	73.2 (1,005)	44.3 (79)	68.2 (1,005)	97.5 (81)	90.0 (1,005)	93.8 (80)	85.9 (1,005)	84.8 (79)	82.1 (1,005)
Czech Republic	33.3 (78)		85.9 (78)		46.8 (79)		51.9 (79)		87.3 (79)		92.4 (79)		94.9 (78)	
Estonia	47.2 (72)	26.6 (1,000)	95.8 (71)	77.8 (1,000)	78.3 (69)	54.0 (1,000)	76.4 (72)	50.1 (1,000)	97.2 (72)	82.9 (1,000)	95.8 (72)	72.8 (1,000)	100 (72)	85.7 (1,000)
Greece	32.9 (85)	62.4 (1,000)	77.4 (84)	64.5 (1,000)	53.5 (86)	53.9 (1,000)	50.6 (85)	48.1 (1,000)	96.5 (85)	85.7 (1,000)	98.9 (87)	67.3 (1,000)	90.7 (86)	85.2 (1,000)
Hungary	36.3 (80)	35.6 (1,002)	98.8 (80)	81.2 (1,002)	48.8 (80)	69.1 (1,002)	57.5 (80)	69.3 (1,002)	91.1 (79)	94.6 (1,002)	98.7 (78)	89.1 (1,002)	96.3 (80)	87.5 (1,002)
Italy	44 (75)	54.4 (1,012)	86.7 (76)	82.6 (1,012)	67.5 (83)	79.8 (1,012)	56.6 (83)	73.4 (1,012)	97.6 (82)	95.1 (1,012)	93.8 (81)	88.7 (1,012)	92.9 (84)	93.3 (1,012)
Lithuania	40 (75)		82.9 (76)		45.9 (74)		60 (75)		96.1 (76)		97.5 (79)		90.7 (75)	
Poland	64.6 (79)	61.0 (999)	92.5 (80)	81.1 (999)	64.6 (79)	74.6 (999)	72.2 (79)	67.8 (999)	85.9 (78)	86.9 (999)	98.7 (79)	84.9 (999)	88.5 (85)	86.5 (999)
Portugal	16.3 (80)	41.5 (1,000)	87.3 (79)	79.9 (1,000)	63.8 (80)	69.7 (1,000)	53.8 (80)	63.1 (1,000)	86.1 (79)	87.4 (1,000)	97.5 (79)	80.3 (1,000)	97.5 (80)	86.1 (1,000)
Serbia	13.2 (76)	46.1 (1,005)	94.8 (77)	77.4 (1,005)	25.3 (75)	62.4 (1,005)	20 (75)	62.2 (1,005)	89.6 (77)	82.8 (1,005)	91.8 (73)	81.9 (1,005)	85.5 (76)	82.8 (1,005)
Slovakia	43 (79)	44.0 (1,082)	91.3 (80)	72.0 (1,082)	59.5 (79)	69.5 (1,082)	64.6 (79)	65.6 (1,082)	97.4 (78)	87.9 (1,082)	97.5 (79)	82.9 (1,082)	93.7 (73)	88.8 (1,082)
Slovenia		30.2 (1,018)		77.9 (1,018)		58.4 (1,018)		51.9 (1,018)		88.5 (1,018)		77.6 (1,018)		89.9 (1,018)
Spain	15.4 (91)	32.0 (1,002)	75.5 (94)	65.8 (1,002)	54.8 (93)	72.2 (1,002)	48.9 (92)	63.4 (1,002)	97.9 (94)	89.8 (1,002)	95.7 (94)	79.6 (1,002)	87.2 (94)	87.1 (1,002)

(continued)

TABLE 4
(Continued)

	To be Christian		To share European cultural traditions		To be born in Europe		To have European parents		To respect the European Union's laws and institutions		To feel European		To master a European language	
	Political elite	Public	Political elite	Public	Political elite	Public	Political elite	Public	Political elite	Public	Political elite	Public	Political elite	Public
Southern Europe	27.1 (340)	47.6 (4,014)	81.5 (340)	73.2 (4,014)	59.6 (342)	68.9 (4,014)	52.4 (340)	62.0 (4,014)	94.7 (340)	89.5 (4,014)	96.5 (314)	79.0 (4,014)	91.9 (344)	87.9 (4,014)
Post-communist (6)	42.2 (467)	44.0 (6,093)	94.0 (468)	78.1 (6,093)	53.0 (462)	67.2 (6,093)	55.8 (464)	63.9 (6,093)	93.1 (465)	87.5 (6,093)	96.1 (461)	82.9 (6,093)	91.4 (464)	85.6 (6,093)
Europe	30.8 (1,382)	40.2 (16,136)	84.9 (1,376)	74.3 (16,136)	47.9 (1,379)	62.5 (16,136)	47.7 (1,378)	57.6 (16,136)	93.0 (1,383)	88.0 (16,136)	93.7 (1,382)	77.9 (16,136)	92.1 (1,385)	87.5 (16,136)

Question: People differ in what they think it means to be a European. In your view, how important is each of the following to be a European: (a) to be a Christian; (b) to share European cultural traditions; (c) to be born in Europe; (d) to have European parents; (e) to respect the European Union's laws and institutions; (f) to feel European; (g) to master a European language?

Responses: very important, somewhat important, not very important, not important at all. Percentages are the sum of 'very important' and 'somewhat important'.

Source: Intune Project, Elite and Mass Surveys, 2007.

certain geographical pattern is also identifiable, with post-communist MPs more interested in regarding European cultural traditions as a requisite for being European; Hungary leads the group with 98.8%, while only the Czech Republic and Lithuania are below 90%. In contrast, all Southern European countries are below that percentage, with Greece and Spain showing the lowest levels of support (77.4% and 75.5% respectively). Regarding public opinion, it is in general less committed than the political elites, and no country has a score of above 85%. Also, the geographical pattern disappears, the Italian people showing the highest level of agreement (82.6%), while the percentage of Portuguese citizens is 79.9%. Spain and Greece occupy the last two positions. Within countries, contrasts are also noticeable in Slovakia, Estonia and Hungary where the support of political elites is more than 15% above that of the general public regarding this element of European identity.

Being born in Europe and having European parents are considered, in general, much less important elements of European identity by political elites but, as with the issues in relation to national identity, there are some significant differences between countries. Regarding being born in Europe, geographical area patterns are difficult to sustain, for there is great heterogeneity in opinions, particularly among the elites of post-communist countries. Thus, the outlying case of Estonia is at the top, with 78.3% of the interviewees supporting the importance of being born in Europe. Three more post-communist countries (Poland, Slovakia and Hungary) are also above the European average (47.9%), although quite far below the Estonian political elite. In contrast, the lowest levels of support are found in other Eastern European countries, with Serbia as a bottom outlying case. (Only 25.3% of the Serbian interviewees viewed this item as important, following the trend with regards to national identity.)

A geographical area pattern seems to be more consistent for Southern European countries, all of them above the European average, ranging from 67.5% in Italy to 53.5% in Greece. Contrasts between elites and the public are also noticeable in all countries, with the exception of Greece. Apart from this country, the average difference between the importance given by political elites and public opinion to this element of European identity is 13.1% in favour of public opinion. The most extreme cases are Serbia (where the public's support is 37.1% above that of the political elite), Bulgaria and Hungary (where the percentages of elites and public are, respectively, 43.8% as opposed to 73.2%, and 48.8% as opposed to 69.1%). Four other countries show differences ranging from 10% to 18%: Poland, Slovakia (10% each), Italy and Spain. The only country where support is significantly higher among political elites is Estonia (with 78.3% as opposed to 54%).

Having European parents offers a similar picture. Percentages of support among national political elites range from the highest in Estonia of 76.4% to the outlying lowest in Serbia of 20%. Geographical regional patterns are a little more consistent than in the case of being born in Europe, mostly for Southern European countries. Thus, some differences of opinion about the importance of having European parents can be observed in post-communist countries, where Estonia, Poland, Slovakia, Lithuania and Hungary show the highest levels of opinion in favour of the importance of having European parents, all of them above 57%, while Bulgaria and Serbia have the lowest figures. In contrast, Southern European elites maintain more homogeneous positions, from a 56.6% score in Italy to 48.9% in Spain. When comparing the question of having European parents on the national and European levels, we observe that in some countries the difference between both percentages is significant, as in Bulgaria (39.4% of difference), the Czech Republic (29.4%), and Serbia (26.8%). On the other hand, comparing political elites with public opinion, the general trend is that public opinion is more likely to consider having European parents an element of European identity, with significant contrasts in the cases of Serbia (42.2% of difference) and Bulgaria (23.9%). Exceptions to this trend are Estonia, where the political elite's support is clearly above that of the general public (76.4% as opposed to 50.1%), and Greece and Poland, where public support is slightly lower (less than 5% difference).

As is the case with country nationality, the questions of respecting European laws and feeling European generate a greater consensus among political elites. Percentages of agreement on respecting European laws and institutions range from 97.9% of the Spanish political elite to 85.9% in Poland. Within this general consensus, it is difficult to ascertain geographical area patterns, although three Southern European countries (Spain, Italy and Greece) have scores of above 95%. Only four countries (Serbia, the Czech Republic, Portugal and Poland) are below 90%. Compared with public opinion, political elites generally put more emphasis in the importance of respect for European laws. The only cases where this trend reverses (Hungary, Portugal and Poland) are not significant; differences within these countries are below 3.5%. Besides, this item reflects higher levels of consensus among the public (percentages of support range from 95.1% in Italy to 82.2% in Serbia) and differences within countries are below 10%, with the exceptions of Estonia and Greece (14.3% and 10.8% of difference, respectively).

Consensus among national political elites on the importance of feeling European as an element of European identity is even higher, ranging from 98.9% in Greece to 91.4% in Serbia. In contrast, public opinion on this subject ranges from the highest score of 89.1% in Hungary to 67.3% in Greece. In this sense, differences within countries between categories of interviewees are also considerable, with several countries showing a difference of more than 10%, with Greece and Estonia above 20% (31.6% and 23% respectively).

Finally, mastering a European language also offers a high level of consensus among national political elites, similar to that of respecting European laws and institutions. Thus, it ranges from the 100% agreement in Estonia to 84.8% in Bulgaria, and only Poland, Spain, Bulgaria and Serbia are below 90%. Moreover, the Serbian elite's degree of agreement is much higher than that manifested for country nationality (85.5% for being European as opposed to 62.9% for being national). Differences between elite views and their respective public opinions are also quite small on this subject. On average the scores of the political elites are 5.2% higher than for public opinion, with only Estonia and Portugal having differences of above 10% (14.3% and 11.4% respectively).

In sum, the features that national publics and political elites consider most important for defining European identity are similar to those found for national identity: sharing (national or European) cultural traditions, respecting laws and institutions, feeling national or European, and mastering the country's (or a European) language (the latter is considered more important as a requisite for being European than for being national). All these conditions coincide with non-ascribed characteristics. That is, they depend more on the individual's behaviour than on his or her community, which would be the major feature of the two less supported features, country of birth and having a national (or European) parent. And again, geographical area patterns are difficult to ascertain, and when they appear, there are always elements of heterogeneity that hinder considering them as explanatory factors of different attitudes toward national and European identity. Thus, bearing all this in mind, it can be concluded that the main factors for defining national or European identity are to be found in national history and institutions.

Dimension 2: representation

As we noted above, trust in EU institutions constitutes an indicator of the existence of a representation relationship at the European level. It measures the extent to which confidence is placed in institutions as the most relevant actors to represent national or European interests of political elites and public opinion (see Table 5).

Compared with the identity dimension, the geographical patterns observed regarding general EU support are less clear here. In general terms, the European Parliament registers the highest level of confidence among political elites, most noticeably among the Greek elite (an average of 7.11 points on a scale of 10), while the lowest level of trust corresponds to the Serbian elite (4.73). Thus, along with Greece, the more supportive political elites are those of Lithuania and Hungary (6.38 and 6.37 respectively), while Spain, Italy and Portugal occupy the subsequent positions. Apart from the above-mentioned, the average confidence in the European Parliament is below the European average (6.05) in the remainder of the post-communist countries. Another interesting feature is that, with the exception of Greece and Serbia, there is significant public trust in the European Parliament, to a greater extent than is found in the national political elites. In this sense, differences are significant in Bulgaria (where the public's average confidence is 7.61, 1.84 points above that of the political elite), Estonia (7.54, 1.63 points above the elite), and Poland (6.64, 1.47 points above the elite).

Average levels of trust in the EU Commission range from the highest in Lithuania (6.29) to the least in Serbia (4.66). Here, it is even more difficult to identify any pattern according to geographical area. Besides, the differences between public and national political elites with respect to attitudes toward the EU Commission are more pronounced than for attitudes toward the European Parliament, usually with stronger support among the publics. (The only case where political elites' confidence is greater than that of the public is Hungary.) Thus, in Estonia the public's average trust (8.55) is 2.3 points above that of the political elite's, while such difference reaches 2.24 points in Bulgaria (8.02 as opposed to 5.78), 1.83 in Italy (7.37 as opposed to 5.54) and 1.7 in Poland (6.78 as opposed to 5.08). It would also be useful to know what the public thought of the European Commission and the European Council of Ministers but unfortunately only data on elite opinions are available on these institutions.

Finally, an interesting feature is that in all countries, public opinion trusts European institutions more than their respective national institutions.[6] Differences

---

[6]This comparison was only available for the public opinion survey. Data for national parliament not shown.

TABLE 5
Trust in European Union Institutions

	European Parliament		European Commission		European Council of Ministers
	Political elite	*Public*	*Political elite*	*Public*	*Political elite*
Bulgaria					
Mean	5.77	7.61	5.78	8.02	5.86
N	77	1,005	79	1,005	78
Standard deviation	2.33	4.05	2.26	4.13	2.34
Czech Republic					
Mean	5.26		4.89		5.31
N	80		80		80
Standard deviation	1.99		2.09		1.80
Estonia					
Mean	5.92	7.54	6.25	8.55	6.04
N	72	1,000	72	1,000	72
Standard deviation	1.36	3.26	1.40	3.54	1.37
Greece					
Mean	7.11	6.48	6.03	6.75	6.30
N	90	1,000	90	1,000	90
Standard deviation	1.65	3.06	2.02	3.14	1.85
Hungary					
Mean	6.37	6.48	6.13	5.44	6.16
N	79	1,002	80	1,002	79
Standard deviation	1.83	3.10	1.89	3.23	1.81
Italy					
Mean	6.17	6.78	5.54	7.37	5.53
N	83	1,012	83	1,012	83
Standard deviation	1.84	2.78	2.04	2.91	1.74
Lithuania					
Mean	6.38		6.29		6.38
N	80		80		80
Standard deviation	1.95		1.92		1.80
Poland					
Mean	5.18	6.64	5.08	6.78	5.10
N	80	999	80	999	80
Standard deviation	2.30	3.28	2.29	3.29	2.12
Portugal					
Mean	5.93	6.91	5.90	6.82	6.24
N	80	1,000	80	1,000	80
Standard deviation	2.10	3.42	2.16	3.20	2.07
Serbia					
Mean	4.73	4.52	4.66	4.76	4.71
N	79	1,005	78	1,005	80
Standard deviation	3.06	3.61	3.04	4.00	3.02
Slovakia					
Mean	5.68	6.24	5.58	6.52	6.41
N	80	1,082	80	1,082	80
Standard deviation	2.00	2.76	1.76	2.96	1.62
Slovenia					
Mean		7.19		7.33	
N		1,018		1,018	
Standard deviation		2.69		2.90	

(continued)

TABLE 5
(Continued)

	European Parliament		European Commission		European Council of Ministers
	Political elite	Public	Political elite	Public	Political elite
Spain					
Mean	6.29	6.37	6.16	6.57	6.05
N	94	1,002	94	1,002	93
Standard deviation	1.81	2.58	1.51	2.51	1.59
Southern Europe					
Mean	6.38	6.64	5.91	6.88	6.03
N	347	4,014	347	4,014	346
Standard deviation	1.89	2.98	1.94	2.97	1.83
Post-communist (6)					
Mean	5.59	6.50	5.57	6.67	5.71
N	467	6,093	469	6,093	469
Standard deviation	2.27	3.51	2.23	3.78	2.20
Europe					
Mean	6.05	6.44	5.54	6.64	5.75
N	1,397	16,136	1,399	16,136	1,394
Standard deviation	2.16	3.07	2.14	3.26	2.06

Question: Please tell me on a score of 0–10 how much you personally trust each of the following EU institutions to usually take the right decisions. 0 means that you do not trust an institution at all, and 10 means you have complete trust. The European Parliament?; The European Commission?; The European Council of Ministers [this question was not available in the public opinion survey]?
Reponses: no trust at all=0, 1, 2, 3, 4, 5, 6, 7, 8, 9, 10=complete trust.
Source: Intune Project, Elite and Mass Surveys, 2007.

are particularly great in Bulgaria, where on a scale of 0–10 the average public trust in the European parliament is 4.17 points above that of public trust in the national parliament, while the difference between trust in the EU Commission and trust in the national government rises to 4.29 points. In Poland, the figures are 2.92 and 3.07, respectively. In the case of Hungary, the difference is only significant for the parliamentary institutions, where we observe 2.02 points in favour of the EU Parliament.

Conclusions

In this essay, our aim was to contribute to the comparative literature on political elites and mass public opinion regarding attitudes towards EU integration, focusing on the comparison of two geographical areas within the EU, the CEEPC countries and Southern Europe. The rationale for this comparison was the existence of clear differences in general patterns of support for the EU between these geographical regions, where Southern European countries are clearly more pro-European than CEEPC ones. In this sense, along with comparing the views of political elites and public opinion on more specific dimensions of European citizenship (identity and representation), we also wanted to discover whether such geographical patterns were repeated along such dimensions.

The results of our analysis show that, in general, the answer is negative. Heterogeneity within regions on both dimensions points to the need to focus on country-specific factors (historical and institutional) in order to account for the attitudes of political elites and public opinion. Regarding the specific comparative results on European identity, such dependence on country-specific factors is clearly revealed by the heterogeneity on the level of attachment to Europe and the wide range between the lowest and the highest percentages. Besides, European identity is still considered secondary on the whole—with the certain exceptions discussed above among political elites in some countries—as both types of interviewees feel a weaker degree of attachment to Europe, compared to the other national and sub-national levels. However, it is also interesting that the elements considered important for European identity by both public and political elites are the same as those considered important for national identity: sharing cultural traditions, respecting European laws and institutions, feeling European and mastering a European language. Such similarity underscores the prevailing non-ascribed, liberal conception of identity both among national political elites and in public opinion.

Regarding the existence of a representation relationship at the European level, it is interesting that public opinion in all countries shows more trust in EU institutions than in their respective national parliaments or governments. In some cases (Bulgaria, Poland and Hungary), we see outstanding differences. This could be either a sign of the positive assimilation of the European representational bond by national citizenship or, more likely in our view, just a manifestation of the lower visibility of EU institutions. Finally, it is also significant that, in general terms, national public opinion trusts European institutions to a greater extent than their political elites do, which could be interpreted in terms of political elites' perception of a rivalry with European institutions. Nevertheless, in order to correctly interpret these and other regularities we have uncovered, further research is needed.

University of Granada
University of Almería

References

Anderson, C. J. (1996) 'The Dynamics of Public Opinion toward European Integration, 1973–93', *European Journal of International Relations*, 2, 2, pp. 175–99.
Aspinwall, M. (2002) 'Preferring Europe Ideology and National Preferences on European Integration', *European Union Politics*, 3, 1, pp. 81–111.
Best, H., Cotta, M. & Verzichelli, L. (2005) *Elites Position Paper for Kick-off Meeting*, Intune Papers No. EL-05-01M, Siena, 29 September–2 October, available at: http://www.intune.it, accessed 15 April 2009.
Blazyca, G. & Kolkiewicz. M. (1999) 'Poland and the EU: Internal Disputes, Domestic Politics and Accession', *Journal of Communist Studies and Transition Politics*, 15, 4, pp. 131–43.
Bohle, D. & Greskovits, B. (2007) 'The State, Internationalization, and Capitalist Diversity in Eastern Europe', *Competition and Change*, 11, 2, pp. 89–115.
Bozoki, A. (2003) *Central European Ways to Democracy*, Studies in Public Policy, Centre for the Study of Public Policy, University of Strathclyde, Glasgow, 2003/383.
Brinegar, A., Jolly, S. & Kitschelt, H. (2004) 'Varieties of Capitalism and Political Divides over European Integration', in Marks, G. & Steenbergen, M. (eds) (2004) *European Integration and Political Conflict* (Cambridge, Cambridge University Press).

Bruneau, T. C., Diamandouros, N., Gunther, R., Lijphart, A., Morlino, L. & Brooks, R. A. (2001) 'Democracy, Southern European Style', in Diamandouros, P. N. & Gunther, R. (eds) (2001) *Parties, Politics, and Democracy in the New Southern Europe* (Baltimore, MD, The Johns Hopkins University Press).

Bruter, M. (2005) *Citizens of Europe? The Emergence of a Mass European Identity* (London, Palgrave Macmillan).

Cameron, D. R. (2007) 'Post-Communist Democracy: The Impact of the European Union', *Post-Soviet Affairs*, 23, 3, pp. 185–217.

Carrubba, C. (2001) 'The Electorate Connection in European Union Politics', *Journal of Politics*, 63, 1, pp. 141–58.

CIRCAP (2006) *European Elites Survey 2006* (Siena, Centre for the Study of Political Change), available at: http://www.gips.unisi.it/circap, accessed 8 September 2008.

Conti, N. (2007) 'Domestic Parties and European Integration: The Problem of Party Attitudes to the EU, and the Europeanisation of Parties', *European Political Science*, 6, 2, June, pp. 192–207.

Cotta, M. & Isernia, P. (2007) *Integrated and United: A Quest for Citizenship in an 'Ever Closer' Europe*, Intune Papers No. TS-07-01 (Siena, Intune Project).

Crawford, B. & Lijphardt, A. (1995) 'Explaining Political and Economic Change in Post-Communist Eastern Europe: Old Legacies, New Institutions, Hegemonic Norms, and International Pressures', *Comparative Political Studies*, 28, 2, pp. 171–99.

Crowther, W. E. & Matonyte, I. (2007) 'Parliamentary Elites as a Democratic Thermometer: Estonia, Lithuania and Moldova Compared', *Communist and Post-Communist Studies*, 40, 3, pp. 281–99.

Dalton, R. J. & Eichenberg, R. C. (1998) 'Citizen Support for Policy Integration', in Sandholtz, W. & Sweet, A. S. (eds) (1998) *European Integration and Supranational Governance* (Oxford, Oxford University Press).

Delanty, G. (2005) 'The Quest for European Identity', in Eriksen, E. O. (ed.) (2005) *Making the European Polity. Reflexive Integration in the EU* (London, Routledge).

De Winter, L. & Gómez-Reino, M. (2002) 'European Integration and Ethnoregionalist Parties', *Party Politics*, 8, 4, pp. 483–503.

Díez-Medrano, J. (2003) *Framing Europe: Attitudes to European Integration in Germany, Spain, and the United Kingdom* (Princeton, NJ, Princeton University Press).

Eder, K. (2001) 'Integration through Culture? The Paradox of the Search for a European Identity', in Eder, K. & Giesen, B. (eds) (2001) *European Citizenship Between National Legacies and Post-National Projects* (Oxford, Oxford University Press).

Ekiert, G., Kubik, J. & Vachudova, M. A. (2007) 'Democracy in the Post-Communist World: An Unending Quest?', *East European Politics and Societies*, 21, 1, pp. 7–30.

Evans, G. (1998) 'Euroscepticism and Conservative Electoral Support: How an Asset Became a Liability', *British Journal of Political Science*, 28, 4, pp. 573–90.

Fossum, J. E. (2001) *Identity Politics in the European Union*, Working Papers, 01/17 (Oslo, ARENA).

Gabel, M. (1998) 'Public Support for European Integration: An Empirical Test of Five Theories', *Journal of Politics*, 60, 2, pp. 333–54.

Gabel, M. & Scheve, K. (2007a) 'Estimating the Effect of Elite Communications on Public Opinion Using Instrumental Variables', *American Journal of Political Science*, 51, 4, pp. 1013–28.

Gabel, M. & Scheve, K. (2007b) 'Mixed Messages, Party Dissent, and Mass Opinion on European Integration', *European Union Politics*, 8, 1, pp. 37–59.

Geddes, B. (1995) 'A Comparative Perspective on the Leninist Legacy in Eastern Europe', *Comparative Political Studies*, 28, 2, pp. 239–74.

Grabbe, H. & Hughes, K. (1998) *Enlarging the EU Eastwards* (London, RIIA).

Haller, M. (2008) *European Integration as an Elite Process. The Failure of a Dream?* (New York, Routledge).

Hanson, S. E. (1995) 'The Leninist Legacy and Institutional Change', *Comparative Political Studies*, 28, 2, pp. 306–14.

Henderson, K. (ed.) (1999) *Back to Europe: Central and Eastern Europe and the EU* (London, UCL Press).

Henjak, A. (2007) *Evolution of Support for European Integration 1990–2005*, Intune Papers, No. MA-07-01 (Siena, Intune Project).

Higley, J., Pakulski, J. & Weselowski, W. (eds) (1998) *Post-communist Elites and Democracy in Eastern Europe* (London, Macmillan).

Hix, S., Noury, A. & Roland, G. (2007) *Democratic Politics in the European Parliament* (Cambridge, Cambridge University Press).

Holmberg, S. (1999) 'Wishful Thinking among European Parliamentarians', in Schmitt, H. & Thomassen, J. (eds) (1999).
Hooghe, L. (2003) 'Europe Divided? Elites vs. Public Opinion on European Integration', *European Union Politics*, 4, 3, pp. 281–304.
Hug, S. & König, Th. (2002) 'In View of Ratification: Governmental Preferences and Domestic Constraints at the Amsterdam Intergovernmental Conference', *International Organization*, 56, 2, pp. 447–76.
Hughes, J., Sasse, G. & Gordon, C. (2002) 'Saying "Maybe" to the Return to Europe: Elites and the Political Space for Euroscepticism in Central and Eastern Europe', *European Union Politics*, 3, 3, pp. 327–55.
Inglehart, R. (1970) 'Public Opinion and Regional Integration', *International Organization*, 24, 4, pp. 764–95.
Jenny, M., Pollak, J. & Slominski, P. (2006) 'Political Elites and the Future of Europe: The Views of MPs and MEPs', in Puntscher, S. & Wessel, W. (eds) (2006) *The Making of a European Constitution. Dynamics and Limits of the Convention Experience* (Wiesbaden, VS Verlag für Sozialwissenschaften).
Johansson, K. M. (2002) 'Party Elites in Multilevel Europe. The Christian Democrats and the Single European Act', *Party Politics*, 8, 4, pp. 423–39.
Jolly, S. K. (2007) 'The Europhile Fringe? Regionalist Party Support for European Integration', *European Union Politics*, 8, 1, pp. 109–30.
Ladrech, R. (2002) 'Europeanization and Political Parties. Towards a Framework for Analysis', *Party Politics*, 8, 4, pp. 389–403.
Lindberg, L. & Scheingold, S. (1970) *Europe's Would-be Polity* (Englewood Cliffs, NJ, Prentice-Hall).
Llamazares, I. & Gramacho, W. (2007) 'Eurosceptics among Euroenthisiasts: An Analysis of Southern European Public Opinions', *Acta Politica*, 42, 2–3, pp. 211–32.
Malefakis, E. (1995) 'The Political and Socioeconomic Contours of Southern European History', in Gunther, R., Diamandouros, N. & Puhle, H. J. (eds) (1995) *The Politics of Democratic Consolidation. Southern Europe in Comparative Perspective* (Baltimore, MD, The Johns Hopkins University Press).
Manin, B. (1997) *The Principles of Representative Government* (Cambridge, Cambridge University Press).
Marks, G., Wilson, C. J. & Ray, L. (2002) 'National Political Parties and European Integration', *American Journal of Political Science*, 46, 3, pp. 585–94.
McLaren, L. (2002) 'Public Support for the European Union: Cost/Benefit Analysis of Perceived Cultural Threat?', *Journal of Politics*, 64, 2, pp. 551–65.
Müller-Härlin, M. (2003) 'The Political Reconstruction of National and European Identity in France and Germany after the Second World War', *Dialectical Anthropology*, 27, 3–4, pp. 269–78.
Netjes, C. E. & Binnema, H. A. (2007) 'The Salience of the European Integration Issue: Three Data Sources Compared', *Electoral Studies*, 26, 1, pp. 39–49.
Pennings, P. (2006) 'An Empirical Analysis of the Europeanization of National Party Manifestos, 1960–2003', *European Union Politics*, 7, 2, pp. 257–70.
Pitkin, H. (1967) *The Concept of Representation* (Los Angeles, CA, University of California Press).
Poguntke, T., Aylott, N., Ladrech, R. & Luther, K. R. (2007) 'The Europeanisation of National Party Organisations: A Conceptual Analysis', *European Journal of Political Research*, 46, 6, pp. 747–71.
Pridham, G. (2007) 'Legitimating European Union Accession? Political Elites and Public Opinion in Latvia, 2003–2004', *Party Politics*, 13, 5, pp. 563–86.
Putnam, R. (1976) *The Comparative Study of Political Elites* (Englewood Cliffs, NJ, Prentice Hall).
Ray, L. (1999) 'Measuring Party Orientations towards European Integration: Results from an Expert Survey', *European Journal of Political Research*, 36, 2, pp. 283–306.
Ray, L. (2003a) 'When Parties Matter: The Conditional Influence of Party Positions on Voter Opinion about European Integration', *Journal of Politics*, 65, 4, pp. 978–94.
Ray, L. (2003b) 'Reconsidering the Link between Incumbent Support and Pro-EU Opinion', *European Union Politics*, 4, 3, pp. 259–79.
Rohschneider, R. & Whitefield, S. (2006) 'Political Parties, Public Opinion, and European Integration in Post-Communist Countries: The State of the Art', *European Union Politics*, 7, 1, pp. 141–60.
Rohschneider, R. & Whitefield, S. (2008) 'Representation in New Democracies: Party Stances on European Integration in Post-Communist Eastern Europe', *The Journal of Politics*, 69, 4, pp. 1133–46.
Schimmelfennig, F. (2007) 'European Regional Organizations, Political Conditionality, and Democratic Transformation in Eastern Europe', *East European Politics and Societies*, 21, 1, pp. 126–41.

Schimmelfennig, F. & Scholtz, H. (2008) 'Political Conditionality, Economic Development and Transnational Exchange', *European Union Politics*, 9, 2, pp. 187–215.

Schmitt, H. & Thomassen, J. (eds) (1999) *Political Representation and Legitimacy in the European Union* (Oxford, Oxford University Press).

Slater, M. (1994) 'Political Elites, Popular Indifference, and Community-Building', in Nelsen, B. & Stubb, A. (eds) (1994) *The European Union: Readings on the Theory and Practice of European Integration* (Boulder, CO, Lynne Rienner).

Spence, J. (1997) *The European Union: A View from the Top* (Waver, Belgium, EOS Gallup Europe).

Steenbergen, M., Edwards, E. & de Vries, C. (2007) 'Who's Cuing Whom? Mass Elite Linkages and the Future of European Integration', *European Union Politics*, 8, 1, pp. 13–35.

Taggart, P. & Szczerbiak, A. (2001) 'Parties, Positions, and Europe: Euroscepticism in the EU Candidate States of Central and Eastern Europe', paper presented at the *Annual Meeting of the Political Studies Association*, Manchester, 10–12 April.

Tucker, J. A., Pacek, A. C. & Berinsky, A. J. (2002) 'Transitional Winners and Losers: Attitudes toward EU Membership in Post-Communist Countries', *American Journal of Political Science*, 46, 3, pp. 557–71.

Way, L. A. & Levitsky, S. (2007) 'Linkage, Leverage, and the Post-Communist Divide', *East European Politics and Societies*, 21, 1, pp. 48–66.

Wessels, B. (1995) 'Evaluations of the EC: Elite or Mass Driven', in Neidermayer, O. & Sinott, R. (eds) *Public Opinion and Internationalized Governance* (Oxford, Oxford University Press).

Wessels, B. (1999) 'Whom to Represent? Role Orientations of Legislators in Europe', in Schmitt, H. & Thomassen, J. (eds) (1999).

Threat Perception and European Identity Building: The Case of Elites in Belgium, Germany, Lithuania and Poland

IRMINA MATONYTĖ & VAIDAS MORKEVIČIUS

ONE OF THE IMPORTANT CONSTITUENTS OF COMMON IDENTITY is that the people concerned share a perception of the same external 'others' as threats. Therefore, it may be argued that European identity should be grounded in similar perceptions of threats and that truly European elites should share similar perceptions. In this study, elites' perception of three potential external threats to the cohesion of the European Union (EU) have been investigated: enlargement of the EU to include Turkey; the close relationships between some EU countries and the United States; and the interference of Russia in European affairs. On the basis of Belgian, German, Polish and Lithuanian elite survey data we explore whether there is evidence of a common European identity across the selected European states, or whether distinct European identities are emerging along the new–old dividing line between EU member states. We also examine whether individual-level factors such as elite left–right self-identification, different visions of the role and future of the EU, as well as the type of preferred national identity (achieved or ascribed), significantly shape perceptions of external threats and therefore constitute grounds for the formation of distinct European identities.

Social constructivism in European studies

The design of the European Union began with the Treaty of Rome (1957), which established the European Economic Community (EEC) and the European Atomic Energy Community (Euratom). The two entities played explicit instrumental roles to counteract actual threats and tensions arising mostly from the adversely competitive economic development of the biggest European states, and the new geopolitical and security environment created by the Cold War. The ensuing development of the EEC led to the creation of the European Community and then

---

This research was funded by a grant from the Intune project (Integrated and United: A Quest for Citizenship in an Ever Closer Europe) financed by the Sixth Framework Programme of the European Union, Priority 7, Citizens and Governance in a Knowledge Based Society.

the EU, and this was fully sanctioned by the Treaty on the Functioning of the EU. Member states have to respect, and candidate countries have to adapt to, the *acquis communautaire* which refers to the total body of EU law accumulated thus far. During the most recent process of enlargement of the EU, the *acquis* was divided into 31 chapters for the purpose of negotiation between the EU and the candidate states for the fifth enlargement. However, none of these developments established a 'contractual obligation' to develop a common European identity or to have the same national or supra-national perceptions of its political roles, responsibilities and expectations.

In the realist school of international relations literature, a threat is defined as a situation in which one agent or a group of agents has either the capability or intention to inflict a negative consequence on another agent or group (Davis 2000, p. 10). Similarly, the conflict school in social sciences sees all social processes as threat-driven, since there is always some power asymmetry between interacting groups (Sherif 1966). Historically the EU was created in the light of such a rational realist assessment of contemporaneous conflicts, and evolved as a structural-functionalist strategy, aimed at integrating national economic systems in order to avoid (or diminish) the internal and external threats that Europe faced in the second half of the twentieth century.

Yet, over time the EU evolved not as a mere political instrument to solve the pressing problems, but rather as a political project with all the attributes of a political, economic and socio-cultural agent. Important EU-level developments have challenged and impacted on collective nation-state identities and are constitutive of a European identity. These include the emergence of the European public space through the establishment of supra-national institutions and the formation of transnational European discourses, as well as the establishment of a European polity through the transfer of competences from the nation-state to the European level and the ensuing importance of inter-subjective meanings that people attach to the Europeanisation process as a whole (Risse 2001, p. 200). Such developments have led students of European integration to adopt a social constructivist approach where emphasis is placed on perceptions and representations of social situations and political choices, and where social processes are studied as constitutive of collective preferences and identities. Constructivists emphasise interactions between agents and structures in the context of the ongoing mutual constitution. Such an approach opens up 'the black box' of interest and identity formation, where agent interests emerge from and are endogenous to interaction with institutional structures (Jupille *et al.* 2003, p. 14). Constructivists often explore the role of social factors, including norms and culture, in constructing collective interests and identities. Such constructions come about through dynamic processes of persuasion or social learning (Jupille *et al.* 2003, p. 15). In the circumstances of profound social and political change, elites' dispositions become critical, since they largely define the field of socially thinkable and politically realisable options.

In mainstream political science, elites (especially party leaders) are understood as crafty promoters of ideas (including identity constructions), driven by their willingness to gain power (remain in government) and promote values and perceptions that suit their perceived instrumental interests. Diachronic analysis of threat framing by elites implies certain intentionality and leads to better understanding of the institutionalisation of certain political decisions and discourses. An issue can be framed as a threat to certain values and will therefore receive political attention; for instance, Russia in the early years of post-communism was perceived as an enemy to Estonian independence (Noreen & Sjostedt 2004). Salient threats, in turn, serve as mobilising referents for collective action; for instance, the European fear of competition from the United States in the defence sector led to the elaboration of the EU Research and Technology Development policy (Mörth 2003).

However, the assumption of national and European elites' capabilities and interest to follow such strategic thinking and purposeful political action rests on a certain exaggeration of their rationality and determination. Historians of the EU describe various failed scenarios and political elites' misunderstandings or missed opportunities in the course of European construction. In this essay we concentrate on the 'European elites in the making' and perform what may be called a synchronic analysis of them (as they exist at a point in time and not sequentially).

European identity building and threat framing

Social identity theory claims that prejudicial attitudes are typical for group-identity construction since individuals automatically sort themselves into categories and create groups of 'us' and 'them', while adopting norms, beliefs, values, attitudes and behaviour associated with the in-group. This prejudice is usually associated with a fear that the out-group has the capability, intention and potential to create nuisance for the in-group (Rousseau & Garcia-Retameo 2007, p. 747). This 'identitarian' approach rests on structural-functional presumptions and is criticised by social philosophers who claim that the distancing of 'us' (as a subject) from 'them' (as an object) by detachment may only be counteracted by experiential dynamics, known in social philosophy as politics of experience (mostly applied in the study of global nomadic cultures, feminism and the post-modern political 'action').

On the individual level of analysis, psychologists deal with the perception of threats against individuals and relate them to self-perception, self-esteem, confidence and trust. Some psychologists, epitomised by Freud, hold that the absence of imaginary threats and enemies is virtually impossible. Social psychologists argue that group-perceived threats are constitutive of collective identities. Collective views about potential threats might work in both directions: they might integrate and disintegrate a group, since social representation of threats depends on how the perceived power discrepancy between subgroups is being interpreted. The social constructivist approach focuses not so much on identified threats, but rather on their perception, since threats are not certain but only probabilistic (they may or may not be carried out) and a concrete threat framing may have spin off effects on further understanding of the situation and further social actions. Therefore, threat images, constructed and advanced by the (national) elites can be explained by collective identity formations, which in turn are linked to the process of elite socialisation. In this essay we focus on the views of national elites as Europeanisation takes place all over the European Union at the beginning of twenty-first century; after the collapse of communism and in the context of globalisation.

As a background definition of Europeanisation we use the one proposed by Radaelli (2000, p. 4):

> Europeanization refers to processes of construction, diffusion and institutionalization of formal and informal rules, procedures, policy paradigms, styles, 'ways of doing things' and shared beliefs and norms which are first defined and consolidated in the making of EU decisions and then incorporated in the logic of domestic discourse, identities, political structures and public policies.

Authors within the burgeoning Europeanisation literature on the whole agree that dominant beliefs and values are first specified and strengthened in the making of EU decisions and they are then reassessed and disseminated in domestic discourses and identities.

According to Risse (2001, p. 202), ideas about European order, as well as transnationally rooted European and national identity constructions, interact with given collective nation-state identities. The more such European political visions and identity-building resonate with ideas about the national political order embedded in collective nation-state identities, the more likely they are to merge with and be incorporated into these national collective views. It follows that the very content of the 'European' collective nation-state identity might also vary, depending on how various ideas about Europe resonate with visions of national identities.

Social constructivists dismiss the 'Europessimist' claim that European integration is impossible because a collective identity cannot be achieved. Rather, they claim that the impact of Europeanisation on collective identities and shifting loyalties evolves simultaneously along several dimensions, among which the national elites' political ideologies and orientations are the most prominent, and works in conjunction with the given nation-state identities.[1]

Empirical studies widely confirm that political ideology is a major factor that influences elites' attitudes towards different issues (Aberbach *et al.* 1981, pp. 115–69). It is extensively conceptualised that people with the orientation towards the political left usually emphasise issues of political and social equality, social security, solidarity as well as international peace and cooperation whereas people on the right put emphasis on issues of economic freedom and growth, competition, national and traditional moral values as well as state authority and military power (Budge *et al.* 2001).

The cohesion of the EU stands as a condition *sine qua non* for any meaningful 'European' political decision. Perceptions of external threats to the cohesion of the EU thus convey the national elites' feelings of belonging and concern for the EU. As to the conceptualisation of threats to EU cohesion perceived by the national elites, two types of threats might be distinguished: first, external threats (from other countries and problematic relations with them); and second, internal threats (such as increasing numbers of immigrants, nationalism, socio-economic differences, deficiencies of the welfare state and the effects of globalisation). In this study we concentrate on the first type of threats. The perceived threats to the cohesion of the EU are to be interpreted in

---

[1] For an outstanding analysis of how political debates and dominant national political discourses have related to the British, German and French Europeanisation since 1950s, see Risse (2001).

the context of the emergence of an EU identity and of Europeanisation taking place in the EU member states.

In the survey under consideration three countries external to the EU have been specified (Turkey, the USA and Russia), but in none of the cases was a particular country presented as an open enemy to the EU. Therefore, in the survey questionnaire the three external threats were framed as important referential 'others', vital for European self-identification and boundary setting, rather than as probable aggressors, threatening the very European project. In the questions specified, countries were put into the European context and the respondents were asked to place the countries on a scale according to how much they did or did not pose a threat to the cohesion of the EU. (This is synonymous to more abstract notions of otherness or sameness to 'Europeanism'.) Russia is presented in the clearest adversarial terms through its interference in EU affairs. The United States is not conceived as an external threat by itself; instead particularistic close relations between some EU countries and the United States are presented as threatening EU cohesion. Turkey (an EU candidate country since 2005) is a particular challenge, since it is sometimes seen as destabilising convenient European ways of thinking 'from within' and calling for a revision of European boundaries and values.

For this study we selected two countries representing those new EU member states that formerly belonged to the Warsaw Pact—Lithuania and Poland—and two countries representing founding EU member states—Belgium and Germany. These particular countries were selected since they differ in size, economic wealth and democratic experiences as well as having different degrees of influence on the workings of the EU. Therefore, our sample is rather diverse. Otherwise, the four selected EU member states are neighbouring countries, sharing recent common political relations and broad social interactions with other countries. (We do not go any deeper into history than to talk of deep-rooted Western values and lingering collective memories among the populations in these states.)

Hypotheses

Our hypotheses draw on the reasoning on 'variability' presented above; we claim that there is no unified perception of the external threats to EU cohesion among the elites in Belgium, Germany, Poland and Lithuania. We also hypothesise that the major factors that shape elites' perception of external threats to EU cohesion are their political ideologies as well as the socio-political experiences of their countries.

First, in a rational realist manner, we propose that an important factor which might be relevant in comparing elite attitudes across different countries is the historical and political relations of a given country with other countries. (After all, the European project itself started as an attempt to overcome some historical conflicts with the neighbouring states.) Therefore, we expect that elites in the new EU member states (formerly belonging to the Warsaw pact) should be rather sceptical about Russia's role in the region, and would be more likely to consider Russia's interference in European affairs as a threat to the cohesion of the EU. On the other hand, we expect elites in the old EU member states would not exhibit such fears but would be rather more likely to consider external threats as coming from the enlargement of the EU to include Turkey or close relationships between some EU countries and the United States. We examine these propositions by cross-tabulating three variables representing different potential external threats to the cohesion of the EU (measured from 1—not a threat at all, to 4—a big threat) and the country status variable (coded as 1—new EU member state, and 2—old EU member state). We also include the country status variable in further analyses as a control variable.

Similarly, we expect that elites whose values derive from the left of the political spectrum would be more likely to consider close relationships between some EU countries and the United States as a threat to the cohesion of the EU than those from the political right. We ground this assumption on the fact that the ideology of the political left stresses social justice and advances the welfare state while the United States does not cherish these values, but rather stresses individual liberties, responsibilities and market competitiveness. We test our hypothesis by regressing a variable related to the perception of the threat caused by close relationships between some EU countries and the United States with variables on ideological self-identification on the 11 point left–right scale (coded from 0—extreme left to 10—extreme right) and opinions on the main aim of the EU ('making the European economy more competitive in world markets' measured as 1, and 'providing better social security for all its citizens' measured as 2). We also include country status (new as opposed to old EU member state) as a control variable in the regression in order to check whether elites in the founding EU member states consider close relationships between some EU countries and the United States as a bigger threat to the cohesion of the EU than elites in the new EU member states.

We also expect that elites with values on the right of the political spectrum should more frequently consider enlargement of the EU to include Turkey as a threat to the cohesion of the EU than elites with left values. This assertion is grounded in the fact that right-wing ideology is conservative and stresses national traditional values, whereas left-wing ideology attaches importance to civil and human rights and allies itself with advocates of racial and gender equality and cultural tolerance (multi-culturalism). Turkey's integration into the EU means the inclusion of a very culturally distinct country—an issue that could be unsettling for the rightist elites. We test our hypothesis by regressing a variable related to the perception of the potential threat caused by Turkey's accession to the EU on two variables: ideological self-identification measured on the 11-point left–right scale, and a variable representing an opinion on whether being a true national (Belgian, German, Lithuanian or Polish) requires having ethnic (Belgian, German, Lithuanian and Polish) parents (measured from 1—not important at all, to 4—very important). We again include country status (new as opposed to old EU member state) as a control variable in order to check whether elites in the founding EU member states consider Turkey's integration into the EU as a bigger threat to the cohesion of the EU than elites in the new EU member states.

Finally, we expect that the elites with right-wing values should be more likely than those from the left to consider interference of Russia in European affairs as a threat to the cohesion of the EU. We ground this assertion on the fact that right-wing ideology values a strong sovereign state and its military prowess. Since Russia's interference in European affairs would undermine the sovereignty and power of the EU and their member states, this should be considered a threat, especially by adherents of right-wing values. We test our hypothesis by regressing a variable representing perceptions of the potential threat caused by Russian interference in European affairs on two variables—ideological self-identification on the 11-point left–right scale and opinion on whether over the next 10 years the EU should develop a single foreign policy toward outside countries (measured from 1—strongly against, to 4—strongly in favour). We also include the country status (old or new EU member state) as a control variable in order to check whether elites in the new EU member states consider the interference of Russia in European affairs as a bigger threat to the cohesion of the EU than elites in the founding EU member states.

Findings

The main finding from analysis of the survey data is the absence of a unified perception of external threats to EU cohesion among political and economic elites in Belgium, Germany, Poland and Lithuania (see Figure 1). The least divisive (but not the least important) of the elites' perceptions is related to the threat posed by the eventual enlargement of the EU to include Turkey: scepticism about Turkish membership of the EU oscillates between 40% and 60% among the respondents from

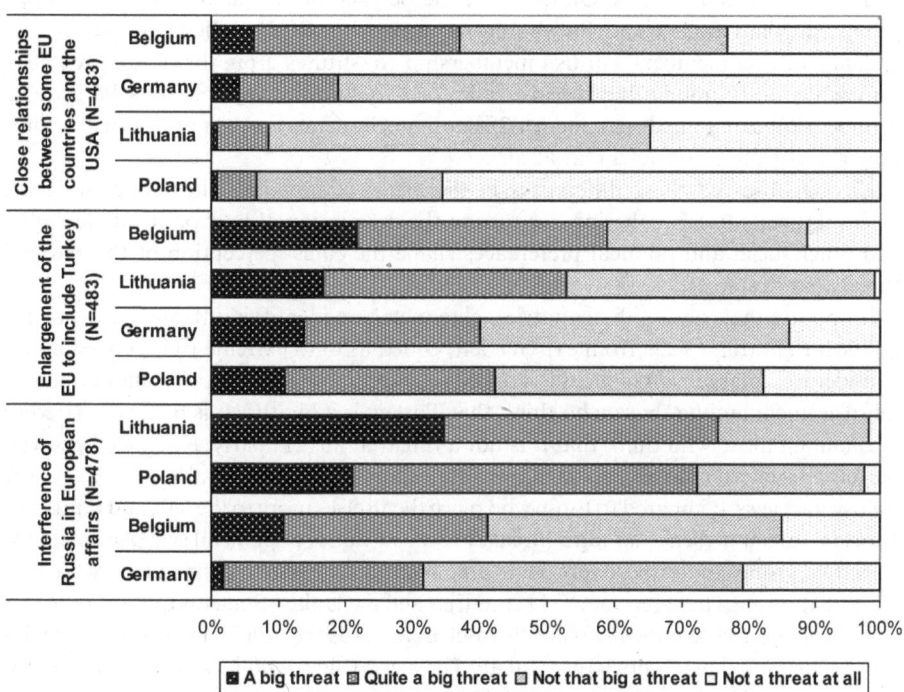

FIGURE 1. ELITES' PERCEPTION OF EXTERNAL THREATS TO EU COHESION (BELGIAN, GERMAN, POLISH AND LITHUANIAN ELITES, 2007)

the selected national elites. The close relationships between some EU countries and the United States are not generally framed as a big threat to EU cohesion by the national elites in any of the EU member states studied here. Perception of the interference of Russia in European affairs generates differences of opinion within and among the national elites in the EU.

For the German and, to a lesser degree, for the Belgian elites, Russian interference in European affairs is not a threat at all or not a big threat for EU cohesion, whereas for the Lithuanian and Polish elites it is a big or quite a big threat: only a small fraction (between 2% and 3%) of Lithuanian and Polish elite members think that it is not a threat at all, while 40% of Lithuanian and 25% of Polish elite members hold that it is a big threat. Meanwhile between 10% and 20% of the German and Belgian elites believe that Russia is not a threat at all and only between 2% and 10% of German and Belgian elite members see Russia as a threat to EU cohesion. Instead, Belgian and German elite members see the close relationships between some EU countries and the United States as a significant threat to EU cohesion, while for Lithuanian and Polish elites it is not a big threat or not a threat at all. Close to 40% of the Belgian elite members followed by 20% of their German counterparts think that close relationships with the United States pose a big or quite a big threat; in Lithuania and Poland such opinion is shared by a minuscule share of between 5% and 10% of the elite members. In contrast, perception of the enlargement of the EU to include Turkey as a threat to the cohesion of the EU is not distributed along the same lines of the divide between old and new EU member states. On this issue the Belgian and Lithuanian elites form one group and the German and Polish another group: for 20% of Belgian and 15% of Lithuanian elite members Turkish membership constitutes a big threat, and for 40% for each country quite a big threat, while for 45% of German and 40% Polish elite members it is not a big threat and for 25% of the German and 18% of Polish elites it is only a slight threat or no threat at all.

Having observed these differences in the views of national elites concerning the external threats to EU cohesion, we turn to the description of how political ideologies and other social and political preferences shape the elites' perception of the external threats (see Table 1).

It appears that, across the countries, elite members identifying themselves with the political right (on a scale from extreme left, coded as 0, to extreme right, coded as 10) consider EU enlargement to include Turkey as a bigger threat: the mean value of political self-placement among those who think that Turkey is a big threat is 6.72 compared to 5.35 among those who think that it is not a threat at all. Similarly, elite members who perceive the interference of Russia in European affairs as a big threat also tend to espouse right-wing views, compared to those who place themselves more to the left, and think that Russia does not present that big a threat. The mean values of political self-placement for these two groups are respectively 6.68 and 5.66. Finally, those elite members who view close relationships between some EU countries and the United States as quite a big threat to EU cohesion systematically place themselves towards the political left compared with those who think that it is not a threat at all. The mean value of political self-placement for the first group is 5.14 compared with 6.42 for the second.

As to the selected attitudinal variables, we find that elite members, strongly supporting the emergence of a common EU foreign policy toward outside countries

TABLE 1

THE RELATION OF ELITES' POLITICAL IDEOLOGIES AND SOCIAL AND POLITICAL PREFERENCES WITH THEIR PERCEPTIONS OF EXTERNAL THREATS TO EU COHESION (BELGIUM, GERMANY, POLAND, LITHUANIA, 2007)

Threat to the cohesion of the EU		Left–right self identification (mean)[a]	Attitude towards the future of the EU: favouring a single foreign policy (mean)[b]	Importance of having national parents for being true national (mean)[c]	The main aim of the EU (proportion)[d]	
					Making the European economy more competitive	Providing better social security for all its citizens
Close relationships between some EU countries and the USA	Not a threat at all	6.42			0.50	0.22
	Not that big a threat	5.44			0.39	0.48
	Quite a big threat	4.97			0.10	0.22
	A big threat	5.14			0.01	0.08
Enlargement of the EU to include Turkey	Not a threat at all	5.35		2.36		
	Not that big a threat	5.44		2.70		
	Quite a big threat	5.87		2.85		
	A big threat	6.72		2.73		
Interference of Russia in European affairs	Not a threat at all	5.66	3.38			
	Not that big a threat	5.06	3.32			
	Quite a big threat	6.02	3.33			
	A big threat	6.68	3.46			

Notes: [a]Mean on a scale from 0—extreme left, to 10—extreme right.
[b]Mean on a scale from 1—strongly against, to 4—strongly in favour.
[c]Mean on a scale from 1—not important at all, to 4—very important.
[d]Proportion of respondents choosing the indicated answer.

over the next 10 years (measured from 1—strongly against, to 4—strongly in favour) are more inclined to perceive the interference of Russia in European affairs as a big threat. Interestingly, elite members' support for a single EU foreign policy in general is rather high and the mean value of support for a single EU foreign policy of those who perceive Russia as a threat to EU cohesion is 3.46, compared to 3.38 for those who do not perceive Russia as a threat.

The relationship between the importance of having ethnic (Belgian, German, Lithuanian and Polish) parents in order to be a truly national citizen (measured from 1—not important at all, to 4—very important) and elite members' perception of the threat posed by the eventual enlargement of the EU to include Turkey, reveals that elite members who base citizenship primarily on ethnic criterion perceive Turkey as a bigger threat than those for whom this 'primordial' characteristic of citizenship is not that important. Elite members who perceive Turkey as a threat to EU cohesion exhibit the mean value of 2.73 on the scale of importance of having ethnic parents in order to be a true national. Among those who do not see any threat posed by the EU enlargement to include Turkey, the respective mean value is 2.36.

Finally, we observe that almost all of the elite members (89%) who prefer making the European economy more competitive across the countries analysed here tend to perceive close relations between some EU countries and the United States as not a threat at all, or not that big a threat to EU cohesion. However, those elite members who support provision of better social security for citizens tend to be more sceptical of close relations between some EU countries and the United States. Half of the elite members for whom making the European economy more competitive is a clear priority (over provision of better social security for all EU citizens) do not see any threat in close relations between some EU countries and the United States. Meanwhile, only about a quarter of those who prioritise social security do not see any threat in close relations between some EU countries and the United States. Alternatively, only about 10% of elite members who value market competition see quite a big or a big threat in close relations between some EU countries and the United States, while this proportion is 30% in the case of those who are in favour of increasing social security provisions.

Thus, descriptive analysis confirms our hypotheses: elites' political ideologies, other social and political preferences and attitudes contribute to their distinct perceptions of external threats to EU cohesion. However, we must now turn to a more sophisticated analysis in order to discern to what extent and how different factors shape elites' perceptions of external threats to EU cohesion and therefore constitute the grounds for the formation of distinct European identities. The influences we consider are political ideologies, different visions of the role and future of the EU, preference for particular understandings of national identity (achieved or ascribed), and the socio-political experiences of a country. Therefore, we turn to generalised ordered logit regression analysis (Williams 2006)[2] and test our three major hypotheses formulated in

---

[2] We did not use a usual regression model for ordinal outcomes, since in two of the three models some coefficients of the independent variables did not conform to the parallel regression/proportional odds assumption.

the 'Hypothesis' section. As we shall see, the results of the analysis convincingly confirm all of our hypotheses (see Table 2).

The chances of considering close relationships with the United States to be a big threat to the cohesion of the EU among the elites in the two founding EU member states (Belgium and Germany) are significantly larger statistically than among elites in the new EU member states. Moreover, the elites of the old EU members are especially likely to hold strongly negative positions on this issue. Further, the chances of elite members expressing greater concern about close relationships between some EU countries and the United States are more than twice as great for those who consider that the main aim of the EU is to provide better social security for all its citizens than for those who think that its aim is to make the European economy more competitive in world markets. Also, the odds of believing that close relationships with the United States pose a threat to the cohesion of the EU are related to elite members' political self-identification. Elites with leftist political views tend to underscore that this issue is a big threat. Conversely, their counterparts on the right of the political spectrum tend not to consider it to be a threat at all.

Turning to the elites' opinion on whether the enlargement of the EU to include Turkey poses a threat to the cohesion of the EU we see that the chances of considering this issue to be a bigger threat among the elites of the founding EU member states are 43.5% greater than among the elites of the new EU member states.[3] Also, the chances of considering this issue to be a bigger threat are greater (by 17.3%) for more politically right-oriented elite members compared to more left-oriented elite members and similarly greater (by 24.7%) for those who consider it important to have ethnic parents to be a fully-fledged national citizen, compared to those who consider this factor to be less important.

Finally, the likelihood of considering Russia's interference in European affairs to be a greater threat for the cohesion of the EU by the elites of the new EU member states is almost five times greater than for the elites of the founding EU member states. Further, the odds of considering this issue to be a bigger threat are greater (by 25.4%) for the elite members who are in favour of developing, over the next 10 years, a single EU foreign policy toward outside countries, compared to those who are against it.[4] Also, the chances of believing that the interference of Russia in European affairs poses a threat to the cohesion of the EU are related to elites' political self-identification: elites with values on the political right are especially likely to hold strongly negative positions on this issue.

In order to consider the significance of our findings from the regression analysis for the inter-relations between different factors, we have constructed 'ideal typical characters' of the elites and compared their perceptions of the threats. It appears (see Figure 2) that the probability of considering that relationships between some EU countries and the United States do not pose any threat for the cohesion of the EU is much higher (0.73) among extreme right elite members from the new EU member states, for whom the main aim of the EU is to make European economy more competitive in world markets, than among extreme left elite members from the

---

[3] We note that this relationship is significant only at a 0.1 confidence level.
[4] We note again that this relationship is significant only at a 0.1 confidence level.

TABLE 2
Generalised Ordered Logit Regression of Elites' Perceptions of External Threats to the EU Cohesion on Their Political Ideologies and Social and Political Preferences (Belgium, Germany, Poland, Lithuania, 2007)

Threat for the cohesion of the EU: close relationships between some EU countries and the United States (base outcome = a big threat, N = 398)

			Outcome = not a threat at all	
Explanatory variables	β	z-score	p-value	$e^β$	%
New versus old EU member state[a]	0.526	2.440	0.015	1.692	69.2
Left–right self identification[b]	−0.215	−3.560	0.000	0.807	−19.3
The main aim of the EU: making the European economy more competitive versus providing better social security[c]	0.882	3.660	0.000	2.415	141.5

			Outcome = not that big a threat	
Explanatory variables	β	z-score	p-value	$e^β$	%
New versus old EU member state	1.647	4.970	0.000	5.194	419.4
Left–right self identification	−0.047	−0.670	0.502	0.954	−4.8
The main aim of the EU: making European economy more competitive versus providing better social security	0.882	3.660	0.000	2.415	141.5

			Outcome = quite a big threat	
Explanatory variables	β	z-score	p-value	$e^β$	%
New versus old EU member state	2.610	2.460	0.014	13.605	1,260.5
Left–right self identification	0.038	0.310	0.760	1.039	3.9
The main aim of the EU: making the European economy more competitive versus providing better social security	0.882	3.660	0.000	2.415	141.5

Threat for the cohesion of the EU: enlargement of the EU to include Turkey (base outcome = a big threat, N = 447)

			Outcome = not a threat at all	
Explanatory variables	β	z-score	p-value	$e^β$	%
New versus old EU member state	0.361	1.770	0.078	1.435	43.5
Left–right self identification	0.160	3.560	0.000	1.173	17.3
Importance of having national parents for being true national[d]	0.221	2.020	0.043	1.247	24.7

(continued)

TABLE 2
(Continued)

Explanatory variables	β	Outcome = not that big a threat		e^{β}	%
		z-score	p-value		
New versus old EU member state	0.361	1.770	0.078	1.435	43.5
Left–right self identification	0.160	3.560	0.000	1.173	17.3
Importance of having national parents for being true national	0.221	2.020	0.043	1.247	24.7

Explanatory variables	β	Outcome = quite a big threat		e^{β}	%
		z-score	p-value		
New versus old EU member state	0.361	1.770	0.078	1.435	43.5
Left–right self identification	0.160	3.560	0.000	1.173	17.3
Importance of having national parents for being true national	0.221	2.020	0.043	1.247	24.7

Threat for the cohesion of the EU: the interference of Russia in European affairs (base outcome = a big threat, N = 449)

Explanatory variables	β	Outcome = not a threat at all		e^{β}	%
		z-score	p-value		
New versus old EU member state	−1.624	−8.310	0.000	0.197	−80.3
Left–right self identification	−0.014	−0.180	0.859	0.986	−1.4
Attitude towards the future of the EU: a single EU foreign policy[e]	0.226	1.940	0.053	1.254	25.4

Explanatory variables	β	Outcome = not that big a threat		e^{β}	%
		z-score	p-value		
New versus old EU member state	−1.624	−8.310	0.000	0.197	−80.3
Left–right self identification	0.278	5.060	0.000	1.321	32.1
Attitude towards the future of the EU: a single EU foreign policy	0.226	1.940	0.053	1.254	25.4

(continued)

TABLE 2
(Continued)

Explanatory variables	Outcome = quite a big threat			
	β	z-score	p-value	e^β	%
New versus old EU member state[a]	−1.624	−8.310	0.000	0.197	−80.3
Left–right self identification[b]	0.302	3.980	0.000	1.353	35.3
Attitude towards the future of the EU: a single EU foreign policy[e]	0.226	1.940	0.053	1.254	25.4

Notes: [a]New EU member states coded 0 and old EU member states coded 1.
[b]On a scale from 0—extreme left, to 10—extreme right.
[c]Making the European economy more competitive coded 0, and providing better social security coded 1.
[d]On a scale from 1—not important at all, to 4—very important.
[e]On a scale from 1—strongly against, to 4—strongly in favour.
β = raw β coefficient; z-score = z-score for test of $\beta = 0$; p-value = p-value for z-test; e^β = exp(β) = factor change in odds for unit increase in explanatory variable; % = percent change in odds for unit increase in explanatory variable.

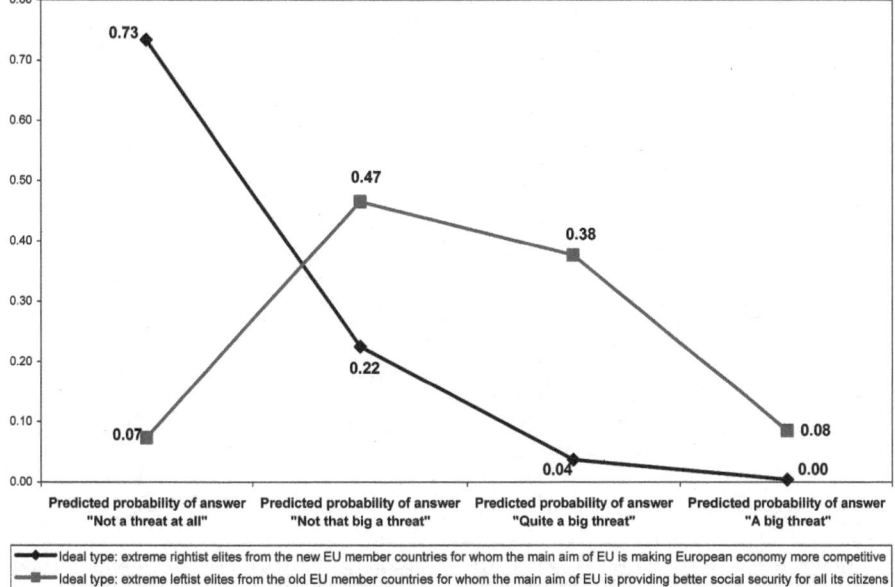

FIGURE 2. PREDICTED PROBABILITIES OF ELITES' PERCEPTION OF EXTERNAL THREATS TO EU COHESION: CLOSE RELATIONSHIPS BETWEEN SOME EUROPEAN COUNTRIES AND THE UNITED STATES (CALCULATED FROM THE RESULTS OF GENERALISED ORDERED LOGIT REGRESSION; BELGIAN, GERMAN, POLISH AND LITHUANIAN ELITES, 2007)

founding EU states for whom the main aim of the EU is to provide better social security for all its citizens (0.07; difference 0.66). However, the probability of considering relationships between some EU countries and the United States to be a big threat is only slightly higher (0.085) among the extreme left elite members from the old EU member countries, for whom the main aim of the EU is to provide better social security for all its citizens, than among the extreme right elites from the new EU member countries for whom the main aim of the EU is to make the European economy more competitive in world markets (0.004; difference 0.081). This is mainly due to the fact that close relationships between some EU countries and the United States are considered as a big threat by only a tiny minority of elite members.

Similarly, it appears (see Figure 3) that the probability of considering Turkey's accession as a big threat for the cohesion of the EU is considerably higher (0.35) among extreme right elite members from the founding EU member states, for whom having ethnic parents is a very important criterion of being a true national, than among the extreme left elite members from the new EU member countries who regard having ethnic parents as not important at all in determining a person's true national identity (0.04; difference 0.31). Also, the probability of not considering Turkey's accession to the EU at all as a threat for the cohesion of the EU is considerably higher (0.35) among the extreme left elite members from the new EU member countries for whom parents' ethnicity is not at all important in determining the true nationality of a

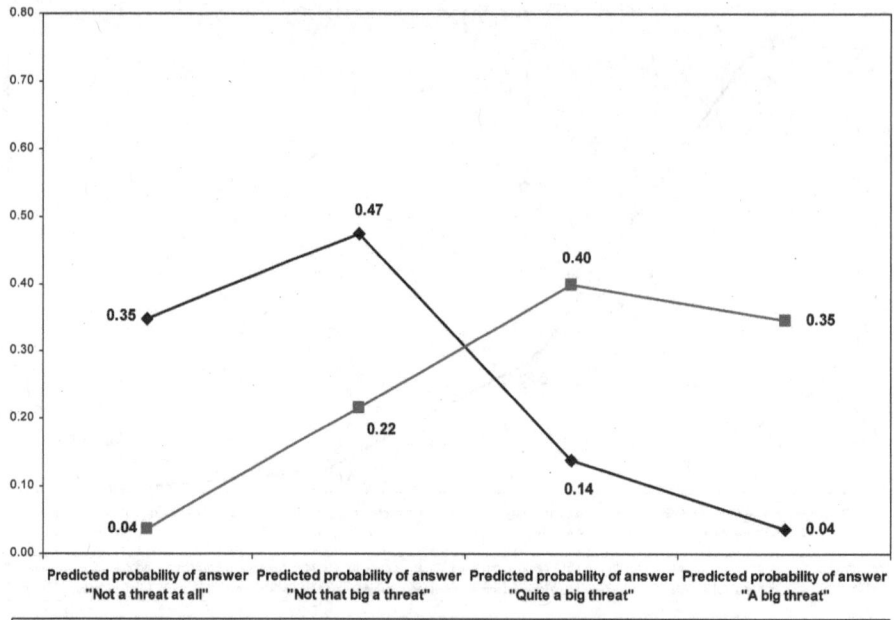

FIGURE 3. PREDICTED PROBABILITIES OF ELITES' PERCEPTION OF EXTERNAL THREATS TO EU COHESION: ENLARGEMENT OF THE EU TO INCLUDE TURKEY (CALCULATED FROM THE RESULTS OF GENERALISED ORDERED LOGIT REGRESSION; BELGIAN, GERMAN, POLISH AND LITHUANIAN DATA, ELITES)

person, than among the extreme right elite members from the old EU member countries who see having ethnic parents as a very important criterion for being a true national (0.04; difference 0.31).

Finally, the probability of considering the interference of Russia in European affairs (see Figure 4) as a big threat for the cohesion of the EU among the extreme right elite members from the new EU member states who are strongly in favour of a single EU foreign policy towards outside countries is much higher (0.57) than among the extreme leftist elite members from the founding EU member states who are strongly against a single EU foreign policy toward outside countries (0.01; difference 0.56). Conversely, the probability of considering the interference of Russia in European affairs not to be a threat at all for the cohesion of the EU is considerably higher (0.23) among the extreme left elite members from the old EU members who are strongly against a single EU foreign policy towards outside countries than among the extreme right elite members from the new EU member countries who are strongly in favour of a single EU foreign policy toward outside countries (0.03; difference 0.20). Interestingly, the difference is much higher (0.66) if we consider the probabilities of the same groups of elite members regarding the interference of Russia in European affairs in only moderately negative terms (as not that big a threat). This result indicates that only a minority

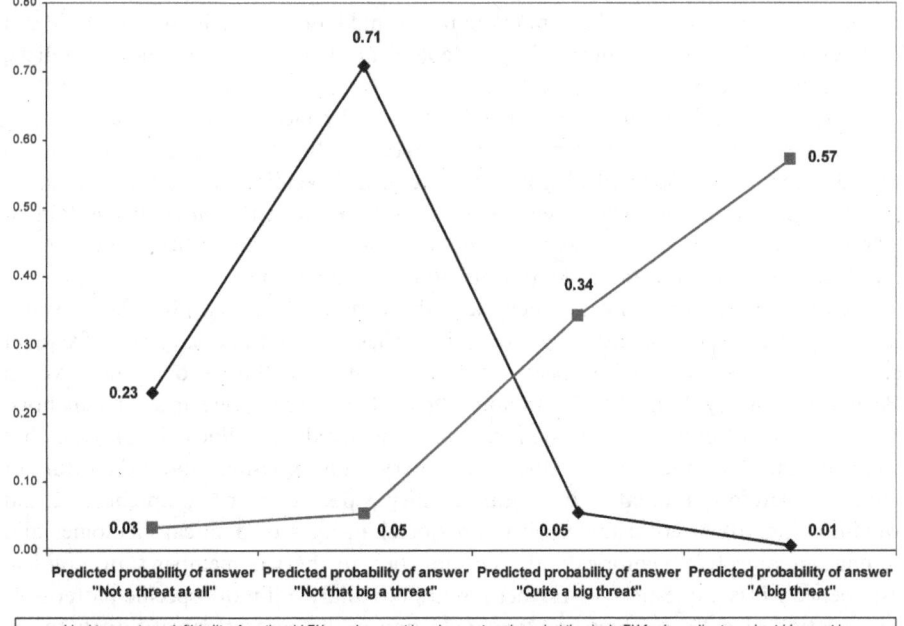

FIGURE 4. PREDICTED PROBABILITIES OF ELITES' PERCEPTION OF EXTERNAL THREATS TO EU COHESION: THE INTERFERENCE OF RUSSIA IN EUROPEAN AFFAIRS (CALCULATED FROM THE RESULTS OF GENERALISED ORDERED LOGIT REGRESSION; BELGIAN, GERMAN, POLISH AND LITHUANIAN ELITES, 2007)

of the elites does not perceive any threat coming from the interference of Russia in European affairs.

Conclusions

The most general theoretical conclusion of our study is that social constructivism provides a useful lens for European studies, since it emphasises the positive role played by political and cultural traditions and conventions in shaping the content of social experiences and their conceptualisations, while also implying that all social and political practices are products of choices informed by contingent meanings and values.

Our main empirical conclusion is that the national elites survey data of spring 2007 show that there are clear divisions in what constitutes a European identity for the elites of our four chosen countries and that the main dividing factors are elites' political ideology, political and social preferences and attitudes, as well as the recent sociopolitical experiences of their countries. In general, if we believe that identity is (at least partly) grounded in the common perception of threats, European identity on the level of national elites is rather divided at the moment. Among national elites of the EU member states different visions of the European Union coexist, nurture and support each other. Adhering to the view that the collective national and supranational identities are consensual (constructed collectively by means of a longitudinal process of trial and error) and that they are taken for granted and internalised, we should not underestimate the importance of the ideological debates and political conflicts, engaged in the construction of the EU.

We should also keep in mind that individual and collective identities are context bound. Measuring the elites' perceptions of external threats to the EU, we revealed how different components of identities are invoked depending on the public issue or policy area in question. The observed parallelism between the elites' perception of external threats and political ideologies, political preferences and attitudes once again highlights how the process of identity building is context-bound.

Even though the idea of multiplicity and the variability of collective identities has led many authors to conclude that social identities are fluid and subject to frequent changes, our research on European identity formation at the national elite level in Belgium, Germany, Poland and Lithuania shows that there are certain strong anchors, embedded in a country's socio-political past and fixed in political ideologies, that compel seeking out the 'other' to the EU, and crystallising visions about the future of the EU. Therefore, ultimately European identity is deemed to be comprehensive and wide-ranging, albeit consistent with the major challenges of political ideologies and resonating collective memories and identities, tied to the EU member state political experiences. It is a question for further research to analyse if more specific patterns of socialisation of national elites find their reflection in the perceptions of threats to the EU cohesion and therefore shape European identity itself. Here, along with the study of country histories which might yield valuable insights about national isomorphisms of the European identity, we also have in mind potential differences in the perception of the threats to EU cohesion to be found among the national and supra-national sub-elites (political, economic, cultural, media and academic) as well as among different cohorts of elites and elites split by variables of gender or nationality.

In keeping with the ideas of those researchers who underline the importance of institutions, myths and symbols, as well as cultural understandings, which help fix collective identities, we claim that the importance of the old–new EU member state divide in the European identity building process—vividly illustrated by the results of our analysis—demonstrates that the EU enlargement was and is a major critical juncture, propelling revisions, alterations and amendments of collective (national and supra-national) identities within the European context and beyond. Therefore, it is important to study carefully the prospective shifts in threat perception articulated around the themes of possible EU enlargement to the east and to the south and in the discussion of the role of the EU in globalisation.

Institute for Social Research, Vilnius

References

Aberbach, J. D., Putnam, R. D. & Rockman, B. A. (1981) 'The Compass of Elite Ideology', in Aberbach, J. D., Putnam, R. D. & Rockman, B. A. (eds) (1981) *Bureaucrats and Politicians in Western Democracies* (Cambridge, MA, Harvard University Press).
Budge, I., Klingemann, H. D., Volkens, A., Bara, J. & Tanenbaum, E. (2001) *Mapping Policy Preferences: Estimates for Parties, Electors, and Governments 1945–1998* (Oxford, Oxford University Press).

Davis, J. W. (2000) *Threats and Promises: The Pursuit of International Influence* (Baltimore, MD, Johns Hopkins University Press).

Jupille, J., Caporaso, J. A. & Checkel, J. T. (2003) 'Integrating Institutions: Rationalism, Constructivism, and the Study of European Union', *Comparative Political Studies*, 36, 1/2, February/March, pp. 7–40.

Mörth, U. (2003) 'Framing an American Threat. The European Commission and the Technology Gap', in Knodt, M. & Princen, S. (eds) (2003) *Understanding the European Union's External Relations* (London, Routledge).

Noreen, E. & Sjostedt R. (2004) 'Estonians' Identity Formation and Threat Framing in the Post-Cold War Era', *Journal of Peace Research*, 4, 6, pp. 733–50.

Radaelli, C. (2000) 'Whither Europeanization? Concept Stretching and Substantive Change', *European Integration Online Papers EIoP*, 4, 8, available at: http://eiop.or.at/eiop/texte/2000-008a.htm, assessed 12 March 2008.

Risse, T. (2001) 'A European Identity? Europeanization and the Evolution of Nation-State Identities', in Cowles, M. G., Caporaso, J. & Risse, T. (eds) (2001) *Transforming Europe. Europeanization and Domestic Change* (Ithaca, NY & London, Cornell University Press).

Rousseau, D. L. & Garcia-Retameo, R. (2007) 'Identity, Power, and Threat Perception. A Cross-National Experimental Survey', *Journal of Conflict Resolution*, 51, 4, October, pp. 744–71.

Sherif, M. (1966) *Group Conflict and Co-operation: Their Social Psychology* (London, Routledge & Kegan Paul).

Williams, R. (2006) 'Generalized Ordered Logit/Partial Proportional Odds Models for Ordinal Dependent Variables', *The Stata Journal*, 6, 1, pp. 58–82.

The Nation State and the EU in the Perceptions of Political and Economic Elites: The Case of Serbia in Comparative Perspective

MLADEN LAZIĆ & VLADIMIR VULETIĆ

AT THE TIME OF THE COLLAPSE OF COMMUNISM in Central and Eastern Europe (CEE), the political and economic elites (and the majority of the population for that matter) of each of these countries were faced with very different situations, which resulted in different positions *vis-à-vis* the European Union (EU). There were, of course, several basic common points which made the EU an attractive proposition: in economic terms it offered integration into the European capitalist market economy (which would guarantee systemic change, higher growth rates and abundant donations and investments from the EU); in political terms it provided a 'fast-track' accession process to EU membership (which would secure not only the best way to achieve the first (economic) goal but also would guarantee a radical break with the 'danger from the East');[1] in cultural terms it facilitated interpenetration with the Western value system (which would instantly confirm that these countries 'have always belonged' to the West). Whilst being drawn to the EU by these attractive prospects, the elites of these various countries faced starkly contrasting situations across all spheres of social life: unequal rates of modernisation (relatively early modernising countries such as the Czech Republic as compared with latecomers such as Bulgaria or Serbia); historical experiences of different legal systems (the Austrian and the Ottoman traditions); and religious diversity, combining a range of Catholic, Protestant, Orthodox, Muslim, or multi-faith populations.

Within the political sphere, it is of particular interest to our study that the collapse of communism came about with the dissolution of the Soviet empire, and of two other federal states (Yugoslavia and Czechoslovakia), which led to the emergence of new

---

We would like to thank José Pereira, Slobodan Cvejić and Mladen Ostojić for comments regarding the contents of the essay, and Romy Danflous for correcting our numerous English mistakes.

[1] In this way, the 'classical' argument is confirmed: '... the attribution of the superiority of European states to the liberty incorporated in their administration of the *res publica*, which stood in opposition to the arbitrary disposal of power typical of despotism, whether oriental or not' (Woolf 1991, p. 7).

states formed along ethnic lines. This process of post-communist state-building brought an interesting paradox to light: on the one hand, the (re-)making of nation states based itself on a strong upsurge of nationalism, as the tool through which secession or liberation from the former federal states was legitimised (and which consequently elevated the nation state into a sacrosanct entity); on the other hand, it appeared very early on in the process that the safest way of securing state independence was, as mentioned, through integration into the EU, which erodes state sovereignty both at the institutional and attitudinal levels (and therefore puts into question the ethnic basis of the state). A similar paradox arises when considering the fact that secessionist movements have started to grow in strength in several 'old EU member' multi-ethnic states (Belgium, Spain, Great Britain), which appears to work against the continuous process of institutional, cultural and other forms of integration of the Union.

Post-communist transformation and EU integration: the case of Serbia

Serbia holds a distinct position with regard to the processes of systemic transformation and European integration. From the very beginning the process of post-communist transformation was accompanied by the civil wars for Yugoslav succession, which meant that the dismembering of the federative territory was only completed very recently. There is too little space here to analyse, at a historical-descriptive or analytical-causal level, the complex historical web through which systemic transformation in the context of civil war has taken place in Serbia.[2] It will suffice here to enumerate several points which are important for our argument.

Serbia represents the only CEE country in which the old political elite won the first multi-party elections in 1990 and subsequently stayed in power until 2000. This does not mean that post-communist transformation was completely frozen for a decade: elections (which were not free, but where the opposition could challenge Milošević's power) were held on a regular basis; and privatisation was very slow, but a multitude of new private firms were set up and occupied a growing share of the Serbian economy. This process may be described as 'blocked transformation' to represent how the former communist elite used political power in order to convert its resources into its own private capital (Lazić 2000a). Once this 'transformation' away from the communist system was successfully completed and a new economic elite was formed (made up of the former political and managerial elite, as well as new entrepreneurs), the Milošević regime was brought down and a new political elite came to power. This was achieved by a combination of a middle-class mass movement, the finally united opposition parties, and the new economic elite, with pressure from the USA and the EU.

Another consequence of this 'blocked transformation' (which took place during—and was largely facilitated by—conditions of civil war) was that during the 1990s

---

[2]For detailed discussion on this process which we call 'blocked transformation', see Lazić (2004) and Lazić and Cvejić (2007).

the Serbian political elite operated a policy of isolationism towards the USA and the EU in particular. This policy was adopted at the time of the UN sanctions against Serbia, and reached its peak during the NATO intervention in 1999. Even if in practice the regime's isolationist policy occasionally went hand in hand with a pro-EU rhetoric, one of the most important tools for mobilising the population used by the opposition parties at the time was the promise to bring Serbia into the process of European accession as soon as they came to power. It is both important and pertinent to note that the majority of the population accepted this mixed message: on the one hand people blamed 'the West' for their anti-Serbian policies, while on the other hand they expressed the wish to join the EU as soon as possible.[3]

The third point that should be mentioned is the evolution of nationalist tendencies. Nationalist sentiment grew rapidly amongst the Serbian population (and more widely across the former Yugoslavia) in the late 1980s. This became extremely prevalent during the 1990s at the time of the civil wars, and is still very pronounced today as a consequence of the unresolved issue of Kosovo.[4] Again, people's perceptions of the policies of the USA and the EU have been very negative in relation to this particular issue. The question of whether EU membership should be paid for with the secession of Kosovo has been debated in public many times. It is not so surprising that in these circumstances the nationalist rhetoric, by focusing on territorial issues, gives European integration a bad name.

This becomes even more important if we take into consideration the fact that political parties that held power throughout the 1990s still play a very important role in the parliament today.[5] The strong public presence and widespread influence of political parties, whose policies brought Serbia into international isolation and even confrontation with the EU, is closely connected with the nationalist sentiment of large parts of the population (and these have been mutually supportive). On the other hand, it is necessary to recall that these political parties have continuously produced ambivalent messages with regard to Serbia's potential EU membership. They have stated many times that membership would be acceptable to Serbia only if the EU stopped its anti-Serbian policies (in Kosovo and Bosnia & Herzegovina today, or during the civil wars in the 1990s). Even the two parties that belonged to the ruling coalition at the time of our survey—the Democratic Party of Serbia (*Demokratska stranka Srbije*, DPS), together with its coalition partner, New Serbia (*Nova Srbija*,

---

[3] In a survey carried out a few months after the war with NATO it was found that the majority of the population was still pro-EU. The explanation for such a seemingly contradictory situation was that they blamed 'politicians'—Milošević and NATO leaders—for the war, and not 'the people' of EU countries. For further discussion, see Lazić (2000b).

[4] A 2004 survey shows that relatively high levels of nationalism persist among all strata except professionals and parts of the economic and political elite. For further details, see Lazić and Cvejić (2007).

[5] The Serbian Radical Party (*Srpska radikalna stranka*, SRP) represents the strongest individual party in Serbia, and together with the Socialist Party of Serbia (*Socijalistička partija Srbije*, SPS), had the support of one third of voters at the parliamentary elections in 2007. Recently, after the parliamentary elections in 2008, the SPS entered the coalition government as a minority partner of the pro-European Democratic Party (Demokratska stranka, DP), by declaring also to be a supporter of Serbia gaining EU membership.

NS)—have very often adhered to such ambivalent messages. And such messages have found a clear resonance among the population since, in parallel with nationalist attitudes, support for Serbia in joining the EU has been constant and extremely high. (According to different public opinion polls, approximately 70% of the population supports membership.)

Thus, the main factors influencing the attitudes of different groups of population in Serbia towards the EU would include the following. First of all, throughout recent history, and still today, several different factors have contributed to producing ambivalent attitudes amongst the Serbian population with regard to joining the EU. Perhaps the most important factor which has led to this ambivalence is the internal division of the political elite. As mentioned above, while part of the elite (that came to power in 2000) is very much pro-EU, those who represent the anti-EU policies of Milošević's regime remain very influential (enjoying the support of a large part of the population). The unresolved territorial issue—the status of Kosovo—has further nurtured nationalist attitudes in Serbia, and has thus increased the political strength of anti-EU parties. Finally, EU policies during the wars for Yugoslav succession, including present-day policies on the status of Kosovo—which has continuously been interpreted by the vast majority of the political elite and population as contrary to Serbian national interests—has continued to fuel the nationalist rhetoric. On the other hand, the idea that EU membership is vitally important for the long-term economic and political interests of the country (in particular for economic growth and political stability) still rings true for the vast majority of the Serbian population.

Hypotheses and methodological remarks

On the basis of our previous discussion, we may formulate a number of hypotheses concerning the influence of several key factors in determining the attitudes of members of the Serbian political and economic elite towards the EU. First, we will assume that there are internal divisions within the political elite, so that members of the parties who have formed governments since the year 2000 are generally in favour of the EU, whereas parties who represent the 'old regime' express anti-EU (or ambivalent) attitudes. (The recent change of policy towards the EU by SPS demonstrates this ambivalence.) In addition, we presuppose that members of the economic elite are pro-EU, since they should profit from the economic prosperity and political stability which is expected to follow a country's accession to the EU. Since Serbian attitudes towards the EU are heavily determined by recent state-territorial problems (the wars for Yugoslav succession, and Kosovo) and by a powerful nationalism which is causally, and reciprocally, connected to these issues, we will limit our analysis of attitudes towards the EU to issues where the EU and the nation state provide two alternative solutions.

Through our hypotheses, we seek to examine the overall perceptions of Serbian political and economic elites of the EU, and the impact of these perceptions, whilst taking into account the specific historical circumstances which have caused them. (The dismemberment of Yugoslavia has been in process for nearly two decades.) In order to test these hypotheses, we will compare findings about the attitudes of the members of

Serbian elites with those of other EU-country elites. Since the relationship between the nation state and the EU is the focus of our research, we have chosen to compare Serbia with countries that have recently experienced problems affecting their territorial sovereignty.

With regard to these problems we may differentiate two typical sub-groups of countries suffering from 'endangered sovereignty'. The first group is represented by countries whose territorial sovereignty is in danger because of the existence of a relatively strong secessionist political movement—supported by a significant share of the population—in the part of their territory. (Such movements seek to establish a new sovereign state, or to join another already-existing state.) Serbia clearly belongs to this sub-group; but Spain, Great Britain, Belgium, Bosnia & Herzegovina and other countries all also come into this category, which we call 'countries facing a secessionist threat'. The second sub-group is represented by recently internationally recognised sovereign states, established through secession, which face issues in terms of state independence as a result of a (real or perceived) threat *vis-à-vis* the state from which they seceded. All post-Soviet countries such as the Baltic states and Ukraine come under this category which we will call 'countries facing an irredentist threat'.

We assume that in both cases—the experience of a (potential) secessionist or irredentist threat—the same dynamic is at play with regard to defending the state's sovereignty. Namely, their political elites and large parts of the population become increasingly sensitive to, and ready to oppose, any policies (internal or external) aiming at reducing state sovereignty[6] and transferring national sovereignty to a larger political unit, even if membership in this unit is voluntary, as in the EU. In this respect, we will analyse the attitudes of members of the elites in two countries where the issue of 'secessionist or irredentist threat' has been raised (currently, or very recently): Spain, where the Basque secessionist movement has been active for decades, as well as the Catalan and other autonomist movements; and Lithuania, which recently seceded from the USSR and in which anti-irredentist policies have played an important role. On the other hand, we will look at the attitudes of elites in Portugal and Hungary, where territorial problems affecting the very existence of the nation state (at least in their existing borders) have not arisen for a relatively long time.

Our analysis will be driven by the following hypotheses. We generally expect that the acute problem of a threat of secession or irredentism is directly connected to increased concerns about state sovereignty (therefore leading to a strengthening of pro-nation-state attitudes, to the detriment of pro-EU attitudes) and to an increase in nationalism (with the same consequences). However, we have to bear in mind other possible factors, such as the fact that integration into the EU may be interpreted as a process which 'softens' the importance of nation-state sovereignty, and thus tames the problem of secession or irredentism, leading to the assumption that pro-EU politics curbs the secessionist or irredentist threat (even if the contemporary experiences of Belgium and Great Britain do not confirm such expectations). An additional

---

[6]Such policies would include lessening state control over its territory and population, over the national defence and law and order apparatus, and over the collection and redistribution of taxes. For further discussion on the constitutive elements of the state, see Tilly (1990).

hypothesis related to this aspect is that in the case of prominent secessionist and irredentist issues, divisions amongst the elites might occur as a result of the erosion of state sovereignty. Therefore, we can expect that the attitudes of the Serbian elite will be more similar to the attitudes of elites in Lithuania and Spain than those in Hungary and Portugal.

However, the problem of state sovereignty has been closely linked with the process of post-communist transformation during the last two decades, which as mentioned above, has led people—and elites—in all CEEC countries (except for Serbia during the 1990s) to believe that EU accession would ensure economic growth and political stability (democratic stability). In this respect, since Serbia still remains outside the Union, we can expect attitudes of the elites here to be more in favour of the EU, if it is to follow the pattern of other post-communist countries prior to their inclusion into the Union. In Hungary and Lithuania we can expect the 'remnants' of such attitudes, so that here we presume that the following hierarchy exists: strongest support for the EU in Serbia, moderate criticism in Hungary and Lithuania, and stronger criticism in Spain and Portugal.

Finally, we suppose that the duration of membership in the EU also plays a key role in determining the elites' attitudes towards the Union with possibly ambivalent consequences. A longer (real) 'experience' of the Union may at the same time both increase trust in its institutions (in the case of positive evaluations of its effectiveness) and criticism (based on concrete observations of specific shortcomings). A brief experience might also produce similar ambivalences, which could be founded on exaggerated expectations on the one hand, and early disappointments on the other. Therefore, we might expect here that the Serbian elite, with its very limited practical experience with everyday policies of the 'external' EU institutions and of their internal consequences, will evaluate the EU more positively than its counterparts in either the 'old' or 'new' member states. Naturally, we have to remember here that the duration of EU membership and the experience of post-communist transformation overlap, so that separating out the influence of each factor might be quite difficult.

Our study is based on the analysis of data collected under the Intune research programme. In the case of Serbia, our sample consisted of 80 members of the political elite[7] and 40 members of the economic elite.[8] The elite samples in other countries are approximately of the same size and were formed using the same procedure, which makes the comparison possible.

In order to test our hypotheses on the basis of a comparative analysis, we constructed an 'Index of orientation toward the EU or the nation-state' (IOEU).[9] All

---

[7]These included 17 members of the government and 63 members of the parliament; 48 respondents belong to parties that formed the majority in the parliament and made up the government, while 32 belonged to opposition parties.

[8]These included top managers or majority owners, selected among the 250 largest Serbian firms, in the public and private spheres and across all sectors, including industry, finance and services.

[9]We constructed the Index using the following 10 variables: attachment to a country (variable id01c); attachment to the EU (id01d); scale of unification (rp08); whether 'the member states should remain the central actors of the European Union' (rp08_a); whether 'the European Commission should become the true government of the European Union' (rp08_b); whether 'the powers of the European Parliament should be strengthened' (rp08_c); single European Army or national armies (rp08_2); the

questions (variables) in the questionnaire, to which respondents answered by choosing between 'the nation state' and 'the EU' as alternative policy actors, were included in the construction of the index. Since in most of the questions four possible answers were offered (completely agree, mostly agree, mostly disagree and completely disagree), we adjusted the rest of the variables to this scale by recoding the existing 11 positions into four (for example, 0–2 into 1: 'strong national orientation'; 3–5 into 2: 'weak national orientation'). In the original IOEU, whenever there were missing values in any of the 10 variables, the case was eliminated. In the Serbian sample, members of one particular party family represented the majority of cases with missing values (since this party family represents the main power holders under Milošević's regime, one of our hypotheses with regard to internal divisions among the political elite has been confirmed). In order to avoid systematic errors we decided to construct a new Index (IOEU_2).[10] In the next step, we recoded values of IOEU_2 into a new variable: orientation toward the nation state or the EU (O).[11]

Relationship of Serbian elites towards the EU and the nation state

We will start our analysis with an overview of the attitudes of the Serbian political and economic elites towards the EU and the nation state as two competing frameworks through which to resolve different political and economic problems. If these attitudes are reduced to a simple dichotomy, according to our survey data summarised in the two indexes (IOEU_2 and O_2), a fifth (21.7%) of the members of the Serbian elite is oriented towards the nation state, and only 8.3% display a strong national orientation. On the other hand over three-quarters (78.3%) of the members of the Serbian elite are oriented towards the EU, with two-fifths (43.3%) of the total having a strong EU orientation. It therefore becomes apparent that our general expectation—of the clear dominance of pro-EU orientation among the elite members in Serbia—is strongly supported by these figures.

We now need to test this conclusion in a comparative perspective to see if such a trend has been observed in other countries and in similar proportions. However,

character of the European Union in 10 years—unified tax system (sg03_1); common system of social security (sg03_2); and single foreign policy (sg03_3). Reliability analysis showed that Alpha = 0.7201.

[10] IOEU_2 is actually an adapted and upgraded IOEU. In fact, we replaced missing cases with the average of existing values in existing variables. The procedure is not quite correct, but in our opinion the resulting error is significantly less than if we eliminated the missing cases (only cases where five or more variables had missing values were excluded from the analysis). New computing gives us IOEU_2 which we use in the analysis.

[11] Values of IOEU_2 have a distribution from 10 to 40. Cases with values between 10 and 24 we defined as national oriented cases; cases with values between 25 and 40 we defined as EU oriented. Alternatively, we made a variable (O_2) with four values: strong national orientation, weak national orientation, weak EU orientation and strong EU orientation. Cases with values between 10 and 20 were defined as 'strong national oriented' (value 20 was defined as the upper line, because in a hypothetical case it meant that respondents gave an answer at each selected question with maximum value of 2). Cases with values between 30 and 40 were defined as strong EU oriented. Weak state oriented cases were defined by values between 21 and 24, and weak EU oriented cases were defined by values between 25 and 29.

before we try to test our findings comparatively, we must also examine if there are any structural factors which might explain the division of the Serbian elite.

First of all, we analyse whether there is a significant difference between members of the political and business elites, regarding their attitudes towards either the EU or the nation state as competing frameworks for solving different policy-level issues. Our data clearly indicate that such differences do exist. Namely, while practically all members of the economic elite (97.5%) demonstrate pro-EU attitudes, among members of the political elite slightly more than two-thirds (68.8%) support the same orientation, while almost one-third (31.1%) favour a nation state orientation.[12] In this way our initial hypothesis about the economic elite being more strongly in favour of the EU is confirmed. An additional explanation for this observation which emerges from these findings might be that businessmen express the attitude of one specific social stratum, whereas politicians' opinions tend to represent a wider spectrum of public opinion. Certainly, it does not mean that the attitudes of politicians simply reflect the general view of the population; what seems obvious, however, is that politicians have to be much more sensitive to public opinion than businessmen. It is also of great interest that the huge majority of businessmen not only express a pro-EU attitude, but also that none of them have a strong nation-state orientation. On the other hand, almost 15% of the members of the political elite hold a strong nation-state orientation.

Next, we seek to investigate whether there is any correlation between the attitudes of politicians towards the EU or the nation state and the position of the political party they belong to along the left–right axis. Here we find a very strong connection between orientation towards the EU or the nation state and party allegiance. As our data show, in the Serbian case, orientation towards the EU decreases from the left to the right side of the spectrum of the party family. Namely, while 88.0% of socialists and social democrats, 92.9% of liberals and 81.3% of right liberals express pro-EU orientations, the same attitudes are only displayed by 5.3% of the respondents who belong to the far right parties.[13] Another very important finding is that members of ethnic minority parties (although there are only a few parties representing them) are the strongest supporters of EU integration (100% of them expressed such an opinion).

Conversely, the greatest number of supporters of the nation state are to be found on the far right of the political spectrum. It might seem that social democrats and liberals hold very similar orientations to one another towards the EU. However, if we look at strong supporters of the EU (using our more detailed breakdown of attitudes—variable O_2), we can conclude that liberals are closer to right-wing liberals than to social democrats, who express the highest level of pro-EU orientation (35.7% of liberals, 37.5% of right liberals and 64.0% of social democrats show strong support for the EU).

---

[12] T-test value sig. $= 0.001$, $t(df) = -3.085(118)$; political elite mean $= 26.8606$; economic elite mean $= 29.6910$.

[13] It is interesting that a clear link between self-orientation on the left–right axis and orientation toward the EU does not exist. The main reason for this lies, in our opinion, in a very confused interpretation of the political left and right in contemporary post-socialist countries, and particularly in Serbia (in view of the fact, for example, that during Milošević's regime, the closest coalition party to his Socialist Party was the extreme-right Radical Party (*Srpska radikalna stranka*, SRS)).

We have also sought to examine the relationship between IOEU_2 and the socio-demographic characteristics of respondents. Here we find strong connections between the level of education and age of respondents and their attitudes toward the EU or the nation state. However, it seems that there is no strong connection between gender and religious affiliation and attitudes towards the EU or the nation state in our index IOEU_2.

If we start the analysis with the level of education, it appears that there is a very strong connection between this variable and IOEU_2 in the sense that orientation towards the EU increases together with the level of education in a linear regression model ($B = 1.097$, sig. $= 0.013$, $R^2 = 0.051$). Namely, pro-EU attitudes are supported by 87.0% of respondents with complete university education, 42.9% of those with incomplete university and 0.0% with secondary education only, while the rest opt for pro-nation-state orientation. On the other hand, although EU orientation is strongly supported by respondents who belong to all age groups, the middle-aged population (83.6%) is more strongly oriented towards the EU than the younger (71.4%) and the older categories (75.7%).[14]

We also expected to find a strong connection between IOEU_2 and the life experience of respondents, but the data did not show any. With the exception of variable ev07 (having close relatives or friends who live in any of the EU countries (T-test: sig. $= 0.006$, $t(df) = 2.988(117)$)), other variables—experience of living in a European country, use of foreign media, working abroad—did not show any significant correlation with our index.

According to our expectations, however, we found strong or medium connections between attitudes of our respondents towards the EU and each of the forms of contacts they had with interest groups (T-test sig. $= 0.000$, $t(df) = 1.179(116)$), NGOs (T-test sig. $= 0.000$, $t(df) = 4.064(117)$) and political parties from EU countries (T-test sig. $= 0.018$, $t(df) = 949(117)$). Networking is obviously a very important determinant of EU orientation, unless it is simply understood as the result of such orientation.

Attitudes of Serbian elites towards the EU and the nation state in a comparative perspective

If we want to assess the inclination of Serbian elites towards the EU or the nation state in more detail, we must compare the data that we have analysed so far with the same data in other countries. For this purpose, we picked four EU member states: Spain, Portugal, Hungary and Lithuania. These countries were chosen on the basis of our initial theoretical assumptions about the significance of particular factors in determining EU and nation-state orientation. More specifically, as explained above, we took into account the existence of a potential 'separatist or irredentist threat', experience of post-communist transformation and the duration of membership in the EU as crucial structural factors which might determine the attitudes of the respective national elites towards the EU or the nation state. We used these countries in different

---

[14] We did not find statistically significant difference between those two variables. In the linear regression model $B = -3.97\text{E}-02$, sig. $= 0.320$, $R^2 = 0.008$.

combinations of pairs so that they represent the characteristics of the above-mentioned structural factors.

We will start our analysis with the question of whether there exists any significant difference between these countries regarding IOEU_2. In other words, we will try to test whether members of these countries' elites have similar means in their EU and nation-state orientation scores. A one-way ANOVA shows a 0.05 level, meaning that differences are significant between Hungary and both Lithuania and Portugal; Lithuania and all countries; Portugal and both Spain and Hungary; Serbia and both Spain and Lithuania, and Spain and all countries with the exception of Hungary.

If we now look at the Mean column in Table 1, we can conclude that the elite in Spain is most strongly in favour of the EU as opposed to the nation state, whereas the Lithuanian elite shows the weakest pro-EU preferences among the observed countries. Attitudes of the Serbian elite are in the middle: below Spain and Hungary, but above Portugal and Lithuania.

Also, in Table 1 we see that the standard deviation is lowest at the poles of the spectrum and highest in the middle (in the case of Serbia). It means that the Serbian elite has the most divided opinion on this issue of support for the EU as opposed to the nation state. The differences between these countries' elites' orientation towards the EU and the nation state are also observable if we look at the data represented in our recoded index (orientation toward the nation state or the EU—IOEU_2). Namely, even if a pro-European orientation is dominant in each of the countries analysed, the level of support of this orientation is different, starting with 64.2% of elite members in Lithuania and 68.3% in Portugal, going up to 78.3% in Serbia and 82.0% in Hungary, and reaching 90.6% in Spain.

Each country's ranking remains the same if we look at a more detailed breakdown of attitudes (Index O_2), with one interesting finding that deserves to be mentioned: a comparison of Hungary and Serbia shows that in Serbia there are more supporters of strong nation-state orientation (8.3% as opposed to 2.5% in Hungary) as well as supporters of a strong EU orientation (43.3% as opposed to 37.7% in Hungary). This finding is consistent with our previous conclusion on the more divided attitudes of the Serbian elite about the choice of nation state or the EU.

At this point we might want to conclude that the orientation of the Serbian elite towards the EU and the nation state, when compared to several other EU countries, does not significantly differ in its direction (a vast majority is pro-EU oriented, while a

TABLE 1
BASIC STATISTICAL INFORMATION ABOUT THE ORIENTATIONS OF THE ELITES OF SELECTED COUNTRIES TOWARDS THE EU AND THE NATION STATE

	N	Mean	Standard deviation	Min	Max
Spain	149	29.3886	3.4682	18.00	37.00
Hungary	122	28.3549	3.9966	17.00	38.00
Serbia	120	27.8041	4.9038	13.00	36.00
Portugal	120	26.6892	4.6587	14.00	37.00
Lithuania	120	25.6491	3.6810	16.00	35.00
Total	631	27.6629	4.3415	13.00	38.00

significant minority opts for pro-nation-state attitudes). However, the question still remains whether factors are at work which we think might influence the direction of these orientations, and how strong they might be. In particular, we have seen that the 'order' of countries according to their elites' preferences of the EU or the nation state does not seem to support our hypotheses about the influence of the experience of a separatist or irredentist threat or of post-communist experience or the duration of EU membership. The reason for the absence of clarity might certainly be linked to the fact that we have analysed too small a number of cases. Therefore, in order to test these hypotheses more thoroughly, we need to increase the number of cases to include most of the countries where the survey was conducted.

Do countries with and those without the experience of a (potential) separatist or irredentist threat[15] have similar mean IOEU_2 scores? We used a T-test to answer this question. The result was a t-value of -3.582 with 2,023 degrees of freedom, and sig. $= 0.000$. On the basis of this finding we can conclude that the two groups of countries do not have similar mean orientations towards the EU and the nation state (generally speaking, the experience of a potential separatist or irredentist threat increases nation-state orientation and decreases pro-EU attitudes; see Table 2).

Do post-communist countries and countries which have not experienced a communist regime have a similar mean IOEU_2? The result is similar to the previous one (t-value of -14.721 with 2,023 degrees of freedom, and sig. $= 0.020$), so that we can again conclude that former membership of the 'Socialist Bloc' (economic and politico-military) decreases a pro-EU orientation and orients the elites towards pro-nation-state attitudes (see Table 2). In other words, both factors, experience of a potential separatist or irredentist threat and of post-socialist transformation, could be significant in determining the inclination of the elites towards either the EU or the nation state.

We tested the significance of the third factor—duration of EU membership[16]—through a one-way ANOVA analysis. In this case, we found again significant differences between 'newcomers' and both 'establishers' and 'followers' (sig. $= 0.000$). Contrary to our expectation, however, there was no difference between 'establishers' and 'followers' (sig. $= 0.896$; see Table 2).

The above analysis shows that both the experience of a potential separatist or irredentist threat and of post-communist transformation are very important factors which significantly influence the level of IOEU_2. Nonetheless, explaining such

---

[15]This included Belgium, the Czech Republic, Estonia, Great Britain, Italy, Slovakia and Spain on the one hand, and Austria, Bulgaria, Denmark, France, Germany, Greece, Hungary, Poland and Portugal, on the other. We put the Czech Republic and Slovakia into the first group on the basis of the assumption that the recent dissolution of a common state makes them closer to countries with a secessionist experience even if their sovereignty has not been threatened by any external or internal actor (data in Table 3 below, corroborate our decision).

[16]In this case we divided countries into four groups: 'establishers' (Belgium, France, Germany and Italy, and Denmark which became a member in the 1970s); 'followers' which became members in the 1980s (Greece, Spain, Portugal and Austria), 'newcomers' (the Czech Republic, Slovakia, Estonia, Lithuania, Hungary and Bulgaria) and non-members (Serbia). The division between the 'old' and 'new' members would simply repeat the division between post-socialist and older capitalist countries. We excluded Great Britain, which joined in the 1970s because it is an outlier with exceptionally low levels of EU-orientation.

TABLE 2
Elites' Orientations towards the EU and Nation State with Regard to the Experience of Separatism or Irredentism, Post-communist Transformation and the Duration of EU Membership (Whole Sample without Serbia)

%	Nation-state orientation	EU orientation	Total
With separatist/irredentist experience	38.0 (359)	62.0 (585)	100.0 (944)
Without separatist/irredentist experience	26.1 (282)	73.9 (799)	100.0 (1,081)
Post-communist countries	44.7 (410)	55.3 (507)	100.0 (917)
Non post-communist countries	20.8 (231)	79.2 (877)	100.0 (1,108)
'Establishers'	21.4 (128)	78.6 (469)	100.0 (597)
'Followers'	20.2 (103)	79.8 (408)	100.0 (511)
'Newcomers'	41.1 (348)	58.9 (498)	100.0 (846)

variations between the attitudes of these different countries' elites towards the EU and the nation state solely on the basis of these factors is not possible. If we only look at the initial selection of countries, the Spanish and Lithuanian examples provide evidence of the fact that the experience of a potential separatist or irredentist threat may influence attitudes towards the EU and the nation state differently, depending upon which direction the risk to sovereignty is coming from: whether this is an internal or external threat.

If a country has acquired its independent status by seceding from another state (like Lithuania did, for example), its elite and the majority of its population are probably more drawn to support the nation state, and at the same time to decrease potential external threat by seeking protection through EU membership. If on the other hand a state continuously faces the threat of internal separatism from some of its provinces or minority groups (exemplified by the case of Spain), it might try to minimise the threat from within by decreasing the perceived value of state sovereignty and advocating deeper EU integration. This makes the cases of Spain and Serbia seem more similar, and demonstrates in what way such an experience of separatism strengthens the pro-EU-orientation of the elites. Namely, if integration into the EU is stronger (and elements of sovereignty are transferred from the nation state to the Union), the pressure of provinces or ethnic minorities towards independence might seem more controllable. On the other hand, elites in new or renewed independent national states might view the EU as the defender of independence, but only if the EU does not push its sovereignty too far (if the EU does not move too much beyond economic integration, towards a strong political union). This might explain the relatively high proportion of nation-state oriented elites in all new or renewed states. For example, Slovakia, the Czech Republic and Estonia are at the bottom of the list of countries in which elites support the EU more strongly than the nation state. In particular, in each of these countries more than half of elite members prefer the nation state over the EU. Similar attitudes can be found in the older (Western) EU members, but only among the elites of Great Britain and Denmark (Table 3).

To sum up, our findings show that the very high position of Spain regarding the pro-EU orientation of its elite is a consequence of the threat of separatism coming from within (produced by internal political forces), and of the absence of post-communist transformation. The much higher levels of orientation towards the nation

TABLE 3
ELITES' ORIENTATIONS TOWARDS THE EU AND NATION STATE: % (N) OF THE WHOLE SAMPLE

Country	Nation-state oriented	EU oriented	Total
France	8.1 (10)	91.9 (114)	100 (124)
Greece	8.7 (11)	91.3 (115)	100 (126)
Belgium	8.9 (11)	91.1 (113)	100 (124)
Spain	9.4 (14)	90.6 (135)	100 (149)
Italy	13.5 (17)	86.5 (109)	100 (126)
Bulgaria	15.6 (20)	84.4 (108)	100 (128)
Hungary	18.0 (22)	82.0 (100)	100 (122)
Serbia	21.7 (26)	78.3 (94)	100 (120)
Germany	27.6 (34)	72.4 (89)	100 (124)
Portugal	31.7 (38)	68.3 (82)	100 (120)
Austria	34.5 (40)	65.5 (76)	100 (116)
Lithuania	35.8 (43)	64.2 (77)	100 (120)
Poland	41.8 (51)	58.2 (71)	100 (122)
Slovakia	52.5 (63)	47.5 (57)	100 (120)
Denmark	56.0 (56)	44.0 (44)	100 (100)
Czech Republic	61.5 (75)	38.5 (47)	100 (122)
Estonia	66.1 (74)	33.9 (38)	100 (112)
Great Britain	87.3 (62)	12.7 (9)	100 (71)
Total	31.1 (667)	1,478 (68.9)	100 (2,145)

state among the Lithuanian elite could be the combined effect of post-communist transformation and of the external risk to state sovereignty (the irredentist threat).

The Serbian median position is the result of contradictory influences. On the one hand there is the influence of the internal threat of separatism (Kosovo), on the other hand post-communist transformation processes have also been at work. Following this type of explanation, we could say that the absence of both these factors in Portugal creates a space for other factors to influence elites' orientations. Finally, the Hungarian case creates a problem in this kind of analysis. If we take into account the hypothetical influence of our two factors, we would expect to find less supporters of the EU in Hungary than in Serbia. However, this is only true if we focus on the 'strong supporters of the EU' category.

There are undoubtedly several other cases that cannot be explained by these two factors alone and would require a much wider scope of analysis.[17] We have in mind here, first of all, the case of Great Britain where it was not possible to find any respondent who demonstrated a strong pro-EU attitude. Simultaneously, almost two-thirds of them (63.4%) declared holding strong pro-nation-state orientations, which reinforces its traditionally distant position *vis-à-vis* integration into supra-state structures. On the other hand, in the case of Lithuania, the orientations of the elite are clearly more similar to those of the Austrian elite than to the Estonian one (another Baltic state, in which the elite perhaps perceives the potential irredentist threat to be much stronger, because of the combined influences of being a small country and of the presence of a large Russian minority).

---

[17] Some unexpected values in Table 3 obviously need further explanation.

Finally, we should bear in mind that Serbia also represents a very special case, if one takes into account the issues regarding its sovereignty, the course of post-socialist transformation and its experience with the EU (Lazić 2004; Vuletić 2003). Contrary to seemingly obvious expectations, a one-way ANOVA test shows that Serbia has more similarities with countries which have not experienced the threat of separatism or irredentism (sig. = 0.229), are not in transition (sig. = 0.893) and are old members of the EU (sig. = 0.990), than with countries that have experienced separatism (sig. = 0.004), are in transition (sig. = 0.000) and are newcomers (sig. = 0.000). Explanations for such discrepancies, however, should not be too difficult to find. At the time of the survey, the majority of the Serbian political elite considered the EU to represent an instrument capable of diluting the secessionist threat coming from Kosovo, and a source of financial, technical, administrative and other resources necessary to boost the process of capitalist transformation (a stage which other post-socialist countries have already gone through, so that they might at least pretend to be more independent from the Union). Naturally and finally, we did not expect the three selected factors to fully explain all of the cases in our survey. Nonetheless, it seems that they do go some way to explaining the middle position of the Serbian elite's orientation towards the EU and the nation state.

University of Belgrade

References

Arts, W., Hagenaars, J. & Halman, L. (eds) (2003) *The Cultural Diversity of European Unity: Findings, Explanations and Reflections from the European Values Study* (Boston, MA, Brill).
Aspinwall, M. (2002) 'Preferring Europe: Ideology and National Preferences on European Integration', *European Union Politics*, 3, 3.
Castells, M. (2003) *Kraj tisućljeća* (Zagreb, Golden Marketing).
Delanty, G. (2002) 'Models of European Identity Reconciling Universalism and Particularism', *Journal of European Public Policy*, 3, 2.
Giddens, A. (2007) *Europe in the Global Age* (Cambridge, Polity Press).
Harris, E. (2003) 'New Forms of Identity in Contemporary Europe', *Perspectives on European Politics and Society*, 4, 1.
Hooghe, L. (2003) 'Europe Divided?—Elites vs. Public Opinion of European Integration', *European Union Politics*, 4, 3.
Hug, S. (2003) 'The State That Wasn't There: The Future of EU Institution and Formal Models', *European Union Politics*, 4, 1.
Lazić, M. (2000a) 'Serbia: The Adaptive Reconstruction of Elites', in Higley, J. & Lengyel, G. (eds) (2000) *Elites after State Socialism: Theories and Analysis* (Lanham, MD, Rowman and Littlefield Publishers).
Lazić, M. (ed.) (2000b) *Račji hod* (Beograd, Filip Višnjić).
Lazić, M. (2004) 'Les obstacles sociaux et institutionnels au processus de transformation en Serbie', *Revue d'Etudes Comparatives Est-Ouest*, 35, 1–2.
Lazić, M. & Cvejić, S. (2007) 'Class and Values in Postsocialist Transformation in Serbia', *International Journal of Sociology*, 37, 3.
Llobera, J. R. (2001) 'What Unites Europeans?' in Guibernau, M. (ed.) (2001) *Governing European Diversity* (Open University, Sage).
Smale, V. (2003) *Istorija evropske ideje* (Beograd, Clio).
Spence, J. (1997) 'The European Union: "A View from the Top"—Top Decision Makers and the European Union', *European Union Politics*, available at: http://ec.europa.eu/public_opinion/archives/top/top.pdf, accessed 18 December 2007.
Spiering, M. (1999) 'The Future of National Identity in the European Union', *National Identities*, 1, 2.
Tilly, C. (1990) *Coercion, Capital and European States AD 990–1990* (Oxford, Basil Blackwell).

Velikonja, M. (2007) *Evropa: kritika novog evrocentrizma* (Beograd, XX vek).
Vossing, K. (2005) 'Nationality and the Preferences of the European Public toward EU Policy Making', *European Union Politics*, 6, 4.
Vuletić, V. (2003) 'Between the National Past and (an) European Future', *Sociologija*, 44, 3.
Woolf, S. (1991) *Europe and the Nation-State*, EUI Working Papers in History, No. 11 (Florence, European University Institute).

Explaining the Attitudes of Parliamentarians towards European Integration in Bulgaria, Greece and Serbia: Party Affiliation, 'Left–Right' Self-placement or Country Origin?

SPYRIDOULA NEZI, DIMITRI A. SOTIROPOULOS & PANAYIOTA TOKA

IT IS COMMONLY ARGUED THAT EUROPEAN INTEGRATION is a project of elites, but a project challenged by the masses whenever they find the opportunity to express themselves. The negative results of the Dutch and French referenda on the Constitutional Treaty of the European Union (EU) in 2005 and the similar result of the Irish referendum on the Reform Treaty in 2008 are cited as examples of this discrepancy between the elites and the masses. But what do European national elites, namely the decision makers in individual EU member states, believe about European integration? While it is probably easy to register and evaluate the attitudes of EU elites, as expressed in the official statements of Commissioners and other European Commission (EC) officials, as well as the public speeches of members of the European Parliament (EP), the opinions of national political elites, and particularly of politicians whose parties are not in power, are neither well known nor adequately researched. While a general trend of Euroscepticism is widely perceived among European publics, the specific opinions of European national elites and the differences and similarities among them on the basis of country origin and political party affiliation are not as well known. The attitudes of members of national parliaments (MPs) are a case in point.

As is well known, Greece is a comparatively old member state of the EU, since it joined the EU in 1981. Bulgaria is a new member state (since it joined the EU in 2007) and Serbia is not a member state of the EU, but has signed a Stabilisation and Association Agreement with the EU in the prospect of becoming a member state at some time in the future. Accordingly, a hypothesis can be constructed that the MPs of a country who are more familiar with European institutions, such as Greece, would trust these institutions more than the MPs of a country that became acquainted with these institutions only recently (which is the case with Bulgaria), and far more so than MPs of a third country not familiar with the institutions (such as Serbian MPs). With regard to Serbia, our hypothesis is that a possible lack of familiarity with EU institutions is reflected in a lack of trust towards such institutions. This tripartite, graded scale of declining trust as we move from an older EU member state to a state that has not yet joined the EU is our overall research hypothesis. We will introduce variations to the hypothesis, taking into account the political party families to which the interviewed MPs belong (see the Appendix) and the individual self-placement of MPs on the left–right scale (0.0 for extreme left, 10.0 for extreme right). Do national politicians trust the EU and specifically some of its main institutions, such as the EC and the EP? To what extent do they believe that the powers of these institutions should be strengthened? And do politicians believe that some European policies, apart from the already existing ones, such as agricultural policy or regional development policy, should be formulated commonly at the EU level? These are a few of the questions asked in 2007 in Greece, Bulgaria and Serbia, where interviews were conducted with 86 Greek MPs, 83 Bulgarian MPs and 80 Serb MPs. In all cases, quota samples were drawn so that all parties participating in each parliament were included in the three samples.[1]

In the remainder of the essay we first present a brief description of the political systems of Greece, Bulgaria and Serbia. Then we will present the political party families to which the interviewed MPs belong. We will then discuss their responses on questions of trust towards EU institutions; the relative strength of EU institutions; the attitudes of MPs towards furthering EU integration; and the responses of interviewed parliamentarians to questions related to common European policies.

The three countries under study

Greece

Greece is a multi-party democracy that made the transition from authoritarian rule in 1974, after the fall of the Colonels' regime. Since the late 1970s, the Greek party system has been dominated by two parties, the conservative New Democracy party (*Néa Dimokratía*, ND) and the Panhellenic Socialist Movement (*Panellinio Sosialistikó Kínima*, PASOK). Greece was admitted to the then European Communities in 1981 and since then has prospered, owing to economic modernisation and to incoming EU funds.

In early 2007, during the time when the interviews for the Intune survey were conducted, the Greek party system comprised five parties with representation in parliament. The conservative New Democracy party has always been pro-European. The centre-left and left parties used to be very critical of the EU, but PASOK made

---

[1] For each country all interviews were conducted from February to June 2007. In all cases quota sampling was applied based on the following quotas: age, gender, number of years in the parliament, political party affiliation, and MP's experience (back-benchers versus the rest of the MPs). For all participating countries face-to-face interviews were conducted. All interviewers were previously trained by the project leaders on how to conduct interviews with members of parliament. On average each interview lasted for about 30 minutes. The questionnaire was divided in to three main sections: identity, representation and scope of governance. Closed format questions where applied.

an about-face on this issue in the mid-1980s. Of the two parties of the left, the left liberals ('Coalition of the Left', *Synaspismos*) used to be more pro-European than the communists (*Kommounistiko Komma Elladas*, KKE) who have rejected the EU project right from the start. The socialist party (PASOK) ruled for most of the period between Greece's accession in 1981 to the then European Community until 2004—with a short interval of New Democracy rule in 1990–1993. Since 2004 the conservatives have been in power and in fact were returned to power in the elections of 2007.

Bulgaria

Bulgaria is a multi-party democracy which made the transition from communist rule in 1989, following the overthrow of Communist Party leader Todor Zhivkov by other members of the party leadership (Bell 1997; Drezov 2000; Kolarova 2002; Spirova 2008). Transition to democracy was cautious and engineered through round table talks. The Communist Party, revamped as the Bulgarian Socialist Party (*Balgarska Sotsialisticheska Partia*, BSP), won most electoral contests until 1997 when power was transferred to non-communist elites for the first time since the end of World War II. In the 1990s, Bulgarian politics was dominated by two parties, the BSP and the centre-right Union of Democratic Forces (*Sayuz na Demokratichnite Sili*, UDF), while the Turkish minority party Movement for Rights and Freedom (*Dvizhenie za prava i svobodi*, MRF) was always present in every parliamentary period. In 2001 the appearance on the political scene of the ex-tsar Simeon II changed the party system. His party, the National Movement Simeon II (*Natsionalno Dvizhenie Simeon Vtori*, NMSS), won the elections of 2001, but failed to be returned to power in 2005. In the elections of June of that year, the BSP was the frontrunner, but no party won an absolute majority of parliamentary seats. After long negotiations, in August 2005 the BSP formed a coalition government with the NMSS and the MRF under the leadership of the socialist Sergei Dmitrievich Stanichev who became the prime minister.

In early 2007, when the Intune elite survey took place, the Bulgarian party system, which is fragmented but stable, comprised six parties represented in parliament (see the Appendix). Generally, Bulgarian parties are pro-European. This was also shown in the presidential elections of October 2006, in which the pro-European socialist Sergei Dmitrievich Parvanov won a second five-year term, defeating nationalist Volen Nikolov Siderov, who opposed EU entry. In contrast to Serbia, no party has followed the path of nationalist populism (Kanev 2005, pp. 65–67). Also one has to take into account that the old rift of the 1990s between the UDF and the BSP has ceased to be a salient cleavage in Bulgarian politics.[2] Bulgaria witnessed economic decline in the 1990s which culminated in a severe crisis in 1997. Since then, under the monitoring of international organisations such as the International Monetary Fund (IMF), the Bulgarian economy has recovered and

---

[2]This cleavage is no longer relevant because of the appearance of the NMSS party and its rise to power in 2001–2005, the economic crisis which hit Bulgaria in the late 1990s, and accusations of corruption which have undermined the legitimacy of the party system as a whole.

political and administrative institutions have been modernised. There are still problems with corruption, public administration and the judiciary system, which however, did not prevent Bulgaria from joining the EU along with Romania in 2007 (Noutcheva & Bechev 2008).

Serbia

Serbia underwent many changes following the disintegration of the Federal Republic of Yugoslavia (FRY) in the early 1990s. The rise of Slobodan Milosevic to the leadership of the League of Yugoslav Communists in 1987 meant the start of a long period of his personal rule and nationalist fervour (Miller 1997; Vejvoda 2000; Pappas 2005). The transition to democracy took longer than in other South East European countries, and Milosevic did not fall from power until the end of 2000. In the meantime, he ruled over his party, the Socialist Party of Serbia (*Socijalisticka partija Srbije*, SPS), and his country, winning successive federal and national elections. His long period of power was probably the result of a number of factors including the manipulation of his adversaries, strong control of the mass media, the close monitoring of public organisations and civil society associations, dependence on the army, the police, security forces and the judiciary as his bases of political power, and his resort to populist and nationalist ideology and rhetoric with which a large share of the electorate identified, the 'skilful forging of elections' (Brussis 2006, p. 105), and the diffusion of corruption (Fatic 2005).

After 2000, parties of the opposition gained strength, such as the Democratic Party of Serbia (*Demokratska stranka Srbije*, DSS), under Vojislav Kostunica and the Democratic Party (*Demokraticheska partia*, DS), under Zoran Djindjic, who became prime minister but was assassinated in 2003. Since the early 2000s, there has been a tension between the DS and the centre-right Democratic Party of Serbia (DSS) of Kostunica. The latter had formed the DS in 1989 with Zoran Djindjic, but went on to create his own party (DSS) which is more nationalist than the DS. Party conflicts in Serbia evolve around cultural and historical issues, the fate of Kosovo and Serbia's relations to the West. The legacy of the nationalism of the 1990s continued into the current decade which witnessed the rise of the Radical Party of Serbia (*Srpska radikalna stranka*, RPS). This party is on the right wing of the party system; it is strongly nationalist and caters to popular anti-Western sentiments.

Owing to its radical nationalism, the RPS is not invited to participate in coalition governments. The centre of the party system, consisting of DS, DSS and G17PLUS, is quite fragmented as a result not only of political disputes but also personal feuds among party leaders, as most parties have a personalistic character and a weak organisational structure. On the left, the SPS (the party of former communists renamed the Socialist Party following the fall of communism) previously played the nationalist card, but in July 2008 the party made an about-face and joined the Democratic Party in forming a coalition government with the aim of achieving Serbia's integration into the EU. This may mean a shift away from the government instability which has plagued the Serbian political system since the fall of Milosevic's regime in late 2000. More concretely, a coalition government was formed under Kostunica in May 2007 after a four-month period of negotiation. Except for his party (the DSS), the coalition included the pro-European DS and the reform-oriented G17PLUS party. SPS and the electorally strong RPS were left in opposition. The coalition government did not last long, as a government crisis erupted in February 2008, after Kosovo declared its independence from Serbia. Meanwhile, in April 2008 Serbia signed a Stabilisation and Association Agreement (SAA) with the EU. The elections in May of the same year were inconclusive. Finally in July 2008, after a long period of negotiations, a new coalition government was formed with the participation of the SPS, the DS and G17PLUS, thus signifying the victory of the pro-European camp over a nationalist alliance with the RPS.

Political party families

The purpose of classifying political parties into party families is to allow for comparisons of responses among MPs who come from different countries but have similar political affiliation. To this effect, we use the classification of parties and the coding scheme of the Intune project, which groups parties into the following nine families or categories of parties: communists; left liberals; socialists; liberals; right liberals; conservatives; Christian democrats; extreme right; and ethnic minority or regionalist parties. For each of the three countries, the country experts participating in the Intune team classified every party into one of these nine party families. Despite their differences, some parties of a certain country fell into the same party family. For example, in Serbia the Democratic Party, which has a social democratic profile, and the former communist Socialist Party of Serbia were both placed in the socialist party family. On the other hand, parties of different countries which at first sight have little in common were classified into the same party family. For example, the Bulgarian National Movement Simeon II and the Greek New Democracy party were classified as conservative parties, because of their comparable political profiles and programmes.[3] The classification of each Bulgarian, Greek and Serbian party into one of the nine party families is shown in the Appendix.

Trust in European institutions

Generally, the European Parliament is the most trusted institution. Compared to the European Parliament, the European Commission scores lower on the 11-point scale from 0.0 to 10.0 (Table 1). This is true for MPs from Greece and Serbia, but not for their colleagues from Bulgaria. The latter trust both institutions equally. Significantly, Bulgarian MPs, whose country joined the EU only in 2007, trust these EU institutions less than Greek MPs who come from an old member state;

---

[3]Obviously there are limits to this exercise of classification, since the criteria on the grounds of which a political party has been assigned to this or that family were the political programme of a party and the personal judgment of country experts participating in Intune.

and Serbian MPs whose country is not an EU member state, and which signed a Stabilization and Association Agreement only in 2008, trust the institutions under study even less.

In all three countries there are families of parties of the centre-right or the centre-left, such as the conservatives, the Christian democrats and the socialists, that fall close to the middle of the left–right political scale. Compared to the parties of the extreme-right or the extreme-left, MPs of these parties show much higher trust in EU institutions.

The pattern of relative pro-Europeanism shown by parties of the centre, in contrast with the parties of the left or right ends of the scale, is clearly borne out by the average scores for all party families presented in Table 2. In Bulgaria, the conservatives and the left liberals trust the EU institutions most. More concretely, the Bulgarian conservative party Democrats for a Strong Bulgaria (*Demokrati za Silna Balgaria*) is the party whose deputies trust the EU institutions more than those of any other Bulgarian party. In Greece, the conservatives and the socialists, and in Serbia the socialists and the liberals, show the same tendency. Specifically,

TABLE 1
TRUST IN EUROPEAN INSTITUTIONS (MEAN SCORES)

	European Parliament	European Commission
Greece	7.11	6.03
Serbia	4.73	4.66
Bulgaria	5.76	5.78

Source: Intune sample survey of parliamentary elites, first wave, 2007.

TABLE 2
TRUST OF GREEK, BULGARIAN AND SERBIAN MPs IN SELECTED EUROPEAN INSTITUTIONS, BY PARTY FAMILY

	European Parliament			European Commission		
	Mean score			Mean score		
	Greece[a]	Bulgaria	Serbia	Greece[a]	Bulgaria	Serbia
Socialists	6.95	5.21	6.80	5.41	5.46	6.44
Liberals	–	–	5.64	–	–	6.00
Left liberals	7.33	6.30	–	3.66	7.00	–
Right liberals	–	6.22	4.56	–	5.66	4.66
Christian democrats	–	7.00	–	–	7.00	–
Conservatives	7.41	6.42	–	6.95	6.06	–
Extreme right	–	3.50	0.72	–	2.66	0.72
Ethnic minority, regionalist, other	–	–	6.50	–	–	6.00

Note: [a]Only one interview was obtained from among Greek Communist MPs. Therefore, no scores are reported in any of the tables for the corresponding party family.
Source: Intune sample survey of parliamentary elites, first wave, 2007.

in Greece deputies of the New Democracy, a conservative party, trust the EU institutions the most, whereas the left liberal party *Synaspismos* (along with the only interviewed Communist Party deputy) trust them the least. In Serbia, deputies of the two parties close to the socialist camp (the Democratic Party and the Socialist Party of Serbia) as well as the parties of ethnic minorities trust the EU institutions more than their colleagues of any other party family. By contrast, the extreme right deputies in Bulgaria, the deputies of the left in Greece and the extreme right in Serbia trust the EU institutions the least. Notably, the nationalists of the Serbian Radical Party, who belong to the extreme right, do not trust the EU institutions at all, scoring 0.72 in the scale 0.0–10.0.

In sum, MPs trust EU institutions, even though they come from countries that are not among the most influential in terms of decision making within the EU. In fact, strong nationalist undercurrents in the recent history and political culture of Bulgaria, Greece and Serbia could have surfaced in the form of mistrust towards EU institutions among parliamentarians of these countries. Nationalist sentiments and populist politicians were popular in Greece in the 1980s and early 1990s and in Bulgaria and Serbia in the 1990s. According to the Intune survey data, these trends are still reflected in the attitudes of contemporary parliamentary elites. The data show that it is correct to hypothesise the following: MPs of the older member state (Greece) trust EU institutions more than their counterparts from a younger member state (Bulgaria) and from a state which is still on the road to possible, but uncertain accession to the EU (Serbia). However, a focus on the national origin of the MPs does not tell the whole story. Their political party affiliation is another interesting dimension, especially as it seems that parties of the centre are more pro-European than parties of the extreme right or left, or the nationalist parties.

Self-placement on the left–right scale

The question of the left–right cleavage is of particular interest since studies of the democratic deficit in EU politics have claimed that it is a salient issue, to the extent that it determines attitudes towards the EU. Further, as shown in the previous section of this essay, parties occupying positions at the left and right extremes are much more sceptical towards the EU, compared to parties located near the centre of the party system. In different countries, parties that belong to the same party family have significantly more in common than parties of the same country who belong to different families. We may examine this hypothesis by referring to the self-placement of the interviewed parliamentarians on a left–right scale.

All MPs on the average locate themselves close to the middle point of the left–right scale (Table 3). On the 11-point scale (0.0–10.0), members of the Greek parliament on average locate themselves at 4.57, the Serbian MPs at 4.91 and the Bulgarian MPs at 5.1.

Even though at this aggregate level we do not see much differentiation among MPs from the three countries, a look at the average self-placement of MPs of different nationality who belong to the same party family indicates diversity. For the socialists, the average self-placement point ranges between 1.87 for Bulgaria to 3.32 for Greece (it is 2.96 for Serbia). We hypothesise that MPs of parties located on the left will be less supportive of the EU and will not trust EU institutions as much as MPs of parties located on the right (with the exception of the generally anti-European radical right parties). This hypothesis sounds plausible if one takes into account that the left has accused the EU of being a project of elites and of serving more the improvement of the competitiveness of European economies than the social cohesion of European societies. If that is correct, then the left-wing should generally be less supportive than the right-wing of EU institutions.

We test our hypothesis by correlating the level of trust in the European institutions and self-placement on the left–right scale in all three countries. Our hypothesis holds true for Greece, where MPs who place themselves on the left have very little trust in the European Commission. However, it is refuted for Bulgaria, as in this country trust in European institutions is not correlated with the self-placement of MPs on the left–right scale (Table 4).

In the case of Serbia, our hypothesis is also refuted: Serbian MPs who place themselves on the left trust the European institutions. By contrast, Serbian MPs who place themselves on the right do not trust these institutions. In all three countries, self-placement at the centre of the left–right scale is not significantly correlated with higher or lower trust in EU institutions. The variation in the above findings may be interpreted as reflecting differences between the political systems of the countries under study, their varied experiences with the European Union and the different political conjunctures at the time of the interviews with MPs (early and mid-2007).

Greek left-wing MPs have been sceptical towards the EU for a long time. Up to 20 years ago even the Greek centre-left (the socialists under the leadership of Andreas Papandreou) were opposed to the country's further integration into the EU and they remained opposed for a long while. Despite the influx of EU funds into Greece, particularly in the context of Community Framework Programmes, Euroscepticism has remained strong among left-wing voters and their representatives over the last 20 years. Left-wing criticism of the EU in Greece has not so much developed along the lines of the EU's democratic deficit, but more in terms of the argument that either the

TABLE 3
COMPARATIVE SELF-PLACEMENT OF GREEK, BULGARIAN, AND SERBIAN MPS ON THE LEFT–RIGHT SCALE (0–10), BY PARTY FAMILY

	Left–right scale (0–10)		
	Greece	Bulgaria	Serbia
Socialists	3.31	1.86	2.95
Liberals	–	–	4.43
Left liberals	2.00	5.92	–
Right liberals	–	8.89	6.63
Christian democrats	–	8.67	–
Conservatives	6.18	6.59	–
Extreme right	–	6.20	7.62
Ethnic minority parties	–	–	3.50
Overall	4.57	5.10	4.91

Source: Intune sample survey of parliamentary elites, first wave, 2007.

TABLE 4
THE IMPACT OF SELF-PLACEMENT ON THE CENTRE (IN THE LEFT-RIGHT SCALE) ON TRUST SHOWN BY BULGARIAN, GREEK AND SERBIAN MPS TOWARDS SELECTED EU INSTITUTIONS

	Self-placement on the left			Self-placement on the centre			Self-placement on the right		
	Greece	Bulgaria	Serbia	Greece	Bulgaria	Serbia	Greece	Bulgaria	Serbia
Trust in the European Parliament	−0.1344	−0.2082	0.3940**	0.1159	0.0316	0.0505	0.0546	0.2041	−0.4182**
Trust in the European Commission	−0.3584**	−0.1213	0.3494**	0.1421	0.0879	0.0643	0.2202*	0.0409	−0.3654**

Notes: *Statistically significant at the 0.05 level; **statistically significant at the 0.01 level.
Source: Intune sample survey of parliamentary elites, first wave, 2007.

EU has not done enough for Greece or that the EU has primarily served the interests of larger European powers and big business enterprises. Things are different in Serbia however, where the right has been heavily imbued by nationalist and anti-European sentiments. These were fuelled in the 1990s by a number of factors: by the bombardment of Serbia's terrain twice by the air forces of Western powers which thus exerted pressure on Milosevic with regard to Bosnia & Herzegovina and Kosovo; by the political strategy of Milosevic who gained and retained power on a tide of anti-Americanism and anti-Europeanism, emphasising Serb traditional values and symbols; and by the widespread perception among Serbs that the West, and specifically major West European powers, should be blamed for facilitating the disintegration of FRY. The Serbian left on the other hand includes MPs who have opposed the semi-authoritarian regime of Milosevic and who have looked to Europe for inspiration and support in order to bring about the democratisation of their country. As a consequence, today Serbian MPs on the left and the centre-left (social democrats and socialists) clearly have a stronger pro-European profile than their colleagues who place themselves on the right. The contrast with Greek MPs who place themselves on the right and have traditionally been more pro-European than their colleagues on the left could not have been starker.

In sum, it would be wrong to believe that the criticism on the part of the left toward the priorities and processes of the EU integration project are reflected in the trust shown by left-wing MPs towards institutions such as the EP and the EC. Depending on the country in question, MPs of the left such as Serbian socialists can be quite pro-European in that respect. Being an MP who places himself or herself at the centre of the left–right scale does not seem to affect whether the MP shows higher or lower trust towards EU institutions. The same general statement can also be made for the right. The extreme right, for example, is associated with anti-European feelings, reflected in our research in the form of low trust of rightists towards the EP and the EC. Thus, self-placement on the right of the left–right scale does not necessarily translate into a pro-European stance.

The relative strength of EU institutions

The above patterns are also corroborated by the findings about the agreement or disagreement of respondents to the following statements: 'the role of the European Parliament should be strengthened'; and 'the European Commission ought to become the real government of the European Union'. As Table 5 shows, with the exception of MPs of the extreme right, the rest of the interviewees from all party families in all three countries are more or less enthusiastic about a possible strengthening of the European Parliament's power. In fact, with the exception of Bulgarian socialists, who are somewhat less enthusiastic about this prospect, the rest of the respondents strongly support the strengthening of the EP. The outliers are Bulgarian extreme right-wing MPs who are split on this question. This is probably a reflection of a particular dilemma which nationalist politicians of EU member states face. Such politicians on the one hand fight for their country's exceptionalism, involving the preservation of national traditions and legislation, even if they go against the integration of their country into the EU; on the other hand they also recognise the primarily financial and diplomatic merits of a country's participation in a supra-national constellation of states such as the EU.

TABLE 5
PERCENTAGE SHARE OF AGREEMENT WITH THE STATEMENT THAT THE EUROPEAN COMMISSION OUGHT TO BECOME THE REAL POWER OF THE EU AND THE POWERS OF THE EUROPEAN PARLIAMENT OUGHT TO BE STRENGTHENED, BY COUNTRY

	Agree that 'The European Commission ought to become the real power of the EU'			Agree that 'The powers of the European Parliament ought to be strengthened'		
	Bulgaria	Greece	Serbia	Bulgaria	Greece	Serbia
Socialists	57.14	50	92	64.29	93.02	100
Liberals	–	–	76.92	–	–	92.31
Left liberals	81.82	33.33	–	91.67	100	–
Right liberals	87.5	–	73.33	100	–	86.67
Christian democrats	85.71	–	–	100	–	–
Conservatives	75	79.07	–	100	93.02	–
Extreme right	20	–	20	50	–	7.14
Ethnic minority, regionalist, other	–	–	66.67	–	–	100

Source: Intune sample survey of parliamentary elites, first wave, 2007.

The pattern is similar regarding whether the EC ought to become the real government of the EU. First, it is noteworthy that the overall trust of MPs in the EC is lower than the corresponding trust in the EP. This difference may be explained by the comparatively stronger wording of the statement about the EC with which respondents were called upon to express agreement or disagreement. The statement did not mention just strengthening the EC, as was the case with the corresponding statement about the EP, but turning the EC into the EU's real power centre. Also the relative lack of enthusiasm among MPs for the prospect of further empowering the EC may be related to the fact that they, in their capacity as members of their country's legislature, felt closer to the legislative rather than the executive branch of the EU's political system.

As far as party families are concerned, MPs of the extreme right in Serbia and Bulgaria strongly disagree with strengthening the role of the EC so that it would become the real power centre of the EU. The opposite is true for Christian democrats and right liberals, a very large majority of whom agree with the prospect of having the powers of the EC strengthened. However, one cannot generalise about the left liberals. In Bulgaria they are in favour of enhancing the power of the EC, but in Greece they are not in favour. This difference may be accounted for by the fact that, comparatively speaking, the Greek left liberals are far to the left of the political spectrum and include former communists who are often reluctant to agree with the idea of an increased role for supra-national organs. A similar argument can be made about the low levels of agreement among Bulgarian socialists (formerly communists), as Table 5 also shows. To sum up, with the exception of the extreme right, MPs from most party families are in favour of strengthening the role of the EP. This does not equally hold for the EC, an increased role for which is not necessarily welcomed by the liberal left and is certainly opposed by the extreme right.

We hypothesise that the higher the level of trust of an MP in EU institutions, the higher the chances that he or she will want to see the role of the EP strengthened and to see that the EC becomes the real power centre of the EU. As Table 6 shows, the bivariate correlations between trusting EU institutions and being in favour of strengthening the roles of the EP and the EC are significant for the cases of Greece and Serbia. Correlations imply that in Serbia the more the MPs trust the EP and the EC, the more they agree that the role of the EP should be strengthened and that the EC ought to become the real government of the EU. The findings are almost the same for Greece (with the exception that among Greek MPs trust in the EP is not correlated with agreement to further empower the EC).

In the case of Bulgaria, there is no statistically significant correlation between trusting the EC and being in favour of strengthening its role. There is some such correlation with regard to the EP, but only at the 0.05 level (Table 6). The difference between Bulgaria and the other two countries may be associated with the difficult experience of the first year of Bulgaria's accession to the EU in 2007. During that year the EC expressed reservations about remaining problems immediately before and after the country joined the EU: first, in Bulgaria's performance in fighting corruption and organised crime; and second in improving its macroeconomic indicators and reforming the judiciary system. Even though Bulgarians rejoiced in the fact that their country became a member of the EU, they obviously understood and probably regretted the fact that their economy, home affairs and justice systems were heavily monitored by the EC, perhaps to a greater extent than in the case of the previous enlargement of 2004, when eight other East European countries along with Cyprus and Malta had joined the EU. Compared to Greek MPs who are long familiar with EU institutions, and whose country is represented in the EC through appointing one Commissioner, and to Serbian MPs for whom the EC is still a distant authority, Bulgarian MPs have probably conceived the EC (and less so the EP) as an intruding collective agent of a larger union, the influence of which they have only recently started to understand.

The future of the EU and its integration process

At the beginning of this essay we hypothesised that the MPs of the three countries under study would be influenced in their opinions about the EU institutions and processes not only by their political affiliation, reflected in their belonging to a certain

TABLE 6
THE IMPACT OF BULGARIAN MPs' TRUST IN SELECTED EU INSTITUTIONS ON THEIR AGREEMENT THAT THE INSTITUTIONS' ROLE SHOULD BE STRENGTHENED

	The European Commission ought to become the real power of the EU			The powers of the European Parliament ought to be strengthened		
	Greece	Bulgaria	Serbia	Greece	Bulgaria	Serbia
Trust in the European Parliament	0.0638	0.0664	0.5094**	0.2987**	0.2507*	0.6677**
Trust in the European Commission	0.4784**	0.2009	0.5346**	0.2108*	0.1286	0.5707**

Notes: *Statistically significant at the 0.05 level; **statistically significant at the 0.01 level.
Source: Intune sample survey of parliamentary elites, first wave, 2007.

political party family, but also by their country's longer or shorter experience and familiarity with the EU. This hypothesis seems to hold in the case of the MPs' stance on the unification of the EU, on whether the process has already progressed too far or if it needs to proceed much further. The participants in the Intune elite survey were asked to place themselves closer to 0.0 in the scale 0.0–10.0, if they thought that unification had already progressed too far or closer to 10.0, if further unification was desirable to them. As shown in Table 7 (in the last row), in all three countries the MPs believe that the unification should be strengthened. Even though the differences among MPs of the three countries are small, overall Greek MPs favour further unification more than Bulgarian MPs who in their turn are more positive than the Serbian MPs in that respect. Longer experience and familiarity with the EU, which is shared by Greek MPs more than their Bulgarian and Serbian counterparts, may indeed result in the socialisation of the participants in the unification process, in this case parliamentarians who favour further unification.

It should also be noted that in Greece MPs of all parties support the further unification of the EU. In Bulgaria the MPs who mostly favour EU unification are the Christian democrats, the conservatives and the left liberals, while in Serbia those in favour of unification belong to socialist and right liberal parties, and also ethnic minority or regionalist parties (for example representing the region of Vojvodina). Thus, in the case of the positive or negative stance towards EU unification on the basis of party families, we see that the picture is not clear. Across countries the picture is clear only about one party family, namely the extreme right: the MPs of extreme right parties clearly distance themselves from the idea of further EU unification. The prospect of unification would be totally alien to the typical nationalist, xenophobic and isolationist profile of extreme right parties.

Focusing more specifically on the impact of trust in EU institutions on other variables however, there is a question concerning how trust is related to opinions of the MPs about certain European policies. The respondents of the survey were asked whether they agreed or not with a common tax system, a common social security system, and a common foreign policy for all EU member states. The results suggest that for respondents from Greece and Serbia the level of trust in EU institutions is

TABLE 7
EXTENT OF MPs' AGREEMENT WITH FURTHERING EU UNIFICATION, BY COUNTRY

	Mean score in the scale 0–10		
	Bulgaria	Greece	Serbia
Socialists	5.57	7.98	7.13
Liberals	–	–	6.31
Left liberals	7.77	7.00	–
Right liberals	7.11	–	6.75
Christian democrats	8.14	–	–
Conservatives	7.75	7.37	–
Extreme right	4.17	–	3.69
Ethnic minority, regionalist, other	–	–	7.83
Overall	6.67	7.56	6.33

Source: Intune sample survey of parliamentary elites, first wave, 2007.

correlated—at a statistically significant level—with a more integrated EU as far as foreign policy is concerned. In contrast, this is not true for Bulgaria (Table 8).

In the case of Greece, the more the MPs trust the EP, the more they support both a common social security system and a common foreign policy; and the more they trust the European Commission the more they support a common foreign policy. However, among Greek MPs, trust in EU institutions is not correlated with accepting or rejecting a common tax system for the EU. It can be suggested that the results concerning foreign policy may relate to the geopolitical position of Greece within Europe. It is commonplace and probably also correct to argue that for Greeks, who live in a country very closely located to the scene of multiple tensions plaguing the eastern Mediterranean, a stable international environment was a main reason for Greece joining the EU in the first place. The need to enhance the country's safety and security internationally probably guides the thinking of Greek respondents on this issue. However, the reason for their supporting a common social security policy may be different. The more Greek MPs trust the EP, the more they are in favour of such a common policy. To understand this tendency, one has to take into account that at the time of the interviews, in early 2007, in Greece there was an open debate about reforming the country's pension system. Greek MPs may have perceived the Greek social security system as inadequate in comparison with the more developed corresponding North or West European systems and thus favoured the emergence of a common EU social security policy, which, once in place, may result in spillover effects for the improvement of their country's ailing social welfare system.

In Bulgaria, among the interviewed MPs, trusting EU institutions is not statistically correlated with being in favour of any common EU policy. Bulgaria is only now taking its first steps in the EU and in fact at the time of the interviews it had just joined the Union, along with Romania. It may then be too early for Bulgarian deputies to have formulated a cohesive image of the EU, linking their own trust in EU institutions with particular EU policies. In other words, Bulgarian MPs are justifiably ambivalent. Paradoxically, such an ambivalent stance is not true for Serbian deputies, whose country is not yet a member of the EU, but who have experienced the negative reaction of the EU and its member states, including the imposition of sanctions on Serbian authorities, during the process of dissolution of Yugoslavia (for example, during the war in Bosnia and the conflict over Kosovo). In the case of Serbia, the more the MPs trust EU institutions, the more they support a common foreign policy and a common tax system. Correlations for both policy domains are quite strong (at the 0.01 level). This pattern may mean that Serbian parliamentary elites, who in the 1990s were bitter about the individual foreign policies of strong EU members (which were accused of having facilitated the disintegration of Yugoslavia), now want to be part of a stronger, more unified EU that will have a common foreign policy of its own. It is an open question whether Serbian MPs are in favour of a common EU foreign policy because they recognise that it would make the Union which they wish to join stronger in the international scene, or because they feel that their own country would be safer and more stable in such a unified environment of common decision making in international affairs after the years of Serbia's exclusion and isolation from international fora.

It is difficult to explain why the more Serbian deputies trust EU institutions, the more they favour a common tax system. Tax harmonisation is a hotly debated issue

TABLE 8
The Impact of Bulgarian MPs' Trust in Selected EU Institutions on Their Agreement that the EU Should Adopt a Common Taxation, Social Security and Foreign Policy

	Common tax system			Common social security system			Common foreign policy		
	Greece	Bulgaria	Serbia	Greece	Bulgaria	Serbia	Greece	Bulgaria	Serbia
Trust in the European Parliament	0.1323	−0.1045	0.3239**	0.2560**	0.0669	0.1249	0.3881**	−0.0677	0.5769**
Trust in the European Commission	0.1546	0.0533	0.3807**	0.1244	0.1364	0.1659	0.2382*	0.0208	0.5673**

Notes: *Level of significance 0.05; **level of significance 0.001.
Source: Intune sample survey of parliamentary elites, first wave, 2007.

across Europe. Serbian respondents may perceive such a harmonisation as a way to streamline the economy of their country and bring it closer to the fiscal standards of current EU member states.

Conclusions

In this essay we discussed the attitudes of Bulgarian, Greek and Serbian MPs towards EU institutions and common policies and tried to interpret their attitudes on the basis of nationality and political party affiliation, as well as on the basis of the level of trust towards EU institutions such as the European Parliament and the European Commission. We have noted that MPs of all countries have a positive view of these two institutions. However, Greek MPs, who come from the member state which is the oldest among the three countries under study, trust the aforementioned institutions more than the rest. Familiarity and experience with EU institutions may breed high trust towards them. However, not all MPs from the same country trust the institutions equally. Notably, MPs of parties of the extreme right or of nationalist parties trust the institutions less than MPs of parties which are conservative, liberal or socialist and generally are closer to the centre of the party system.

Our data however do not corroborate the usual impression that the left is more critical of the EU and its institutions. The data and analysis in this essay show that it is not safe to predict the level of trust in EU institutions on the basis of left or right ideology. Rather, higher or lower trust among the MPs towards the institutions depends on the particular configuration of political parties in each country, namely the record of the attitudes of particular parties towards the EU in general. In Greece and Serbia, MPs of the centre-left (for example, socialists) on average are distinctly pro-European. Similar conclusions can be drawn about parties placed right of centre (for example, conservatives and Christian democrats), while the extreme right, imbued by strong nationalist feelings, is recognisably suspicious of EU institutions.

Comparable conclusions can be drawn in regard to the two possible 'scenarios' according to which in the future the role of the European Parliament could be strengthened or the European Commission could become the real government of the EU. As in the previous battery of questions, in these two cases we saw again that the MPs of the extreme right were the most sceptical about these two prospects. Whether the respondents came from Bulgaria, Greece or Serbia did not seem to matter, as in all three countries there was more or less a majority of positive answers to the two 'scenarios'. What seemed to matter, however, was trust in the two institutions under scrutiny, the EC and the EP. Here national variation surfaced again, as in Serbia there is statistically significant correlation between trusting these institutions and wanting to see their role enhanced. This holds only for the case of the European Parliament in the other two countries, Greece and Bulgaria, while there is some ambivalence towards the European Commission. It could be that in this case the lack of familiarity of Serbian politicians with the EU institutions leads them to think about the institutions in an idealised manner. Greeks have also shown trust in the EP and the EC combined with agreement that the institutions' roles should be strengthened. This may be interpreted in the context of the realisation of long term financial benefits for the Greek economy, flowing from Greece's participation in the EU for over a quarter of a century.

By contrast, some reservations expressed towards the European Commission by Bulgarian MPs, who nevertheless trust it as an institution, may be accounted for by the experience of the indirect but strong influence and leverage the Commission has over national decision making, coupled with the requirements imposed primarily by the Commission on Bulgaria during the latter's journey towards accession to the EU. In the last section of the essay we discussed the opinions of MPs on whether the unification of the EU has already gone too far or if it should proceed further. We also analysed whether trust in EU institutions influences the agreement of MPs over the formulation of common EU foreign policy, taxation policy and social security policy. Confirming our original hypothesis about the more positive stance of older member states toward the EU, we saw that the Greek MPs believe in furthering the process of EU unification more than Bulgarian and Serbian MPs. However, with regard to associating trust in EU institutions with formulating common EU policies, we saw that the only policy area in which higher levels of trust in EU institutions were correlated with accepting the possibility of a common EU policy was foreign policy. And this held true only for Greek and Serbian MPs, but not their Bulgarian colleagues. The levels of trust the latter showed in EU institutions were unrelated to their accepting or rejecting any common EU policy.

The fact that Bulgarian MPs may trust EU institutions but would not make the connection to taking a stance for or against common EU policies in taxation, social security and foreign affairs attests to the formulation of a research hypothesis that may arise from this essay and requires further research. Namely, the hypothesis would be that the political elites of new member states of the EU (for example, Romania) do not have the luxury of believing that EU membership would solve most of their problems as the elites of non-member states (such as Serbia) may think; nor do they have the experience of elites of older member states such as Greece who have seen, so to speak, the good and bad days of EU institutions and European policies. Having just joined the EU, the Bulgarian political elites—or the corresponding elites of any new member state for that matter—remain ambivalent towards EU institutions and processes, and reflect on them more on the grounds of current conjunctures and the political ideology of the party to which they belong. It is probably fair then to conclude that even though the MPs of an older member state are generally more pro-European than the MPs of a new member state (who in their turn are more pro-European than the MPs of a state wishing to become a EU member), in practice the sequence is altered: the neophytes or younger recruits to the Union, who are neither 'seasoned' in EU affairs nor romantic about the distant prospect of joining the EU, are in an ambivalent state of mind reflected—in more than one instance—in the course of the analysis presented in this essay.

University of Athens

References

Bell, J. D. (1997) 'Democratization and Political Participation in "Postcommunist" Bulgaria', in Dawisha, K. & Parrot, B. (eds) (1997), pp. 353–402.
Brussis, M. (2006) 'Serbia and Montenegro: Democratic Consensus Susceptible to Populist Actors', *Southeast European and Black Sea Studies*, 6, 1, pp. 103–23.

Dawisha, K. & Parrot, B. (eds) (1997) *Politics, Power, and the Struggle for Democracy in Southeastern Europe* (Cambridge, Cambridge University Press).
Drezov, K. (2000) 'Bulgaria: Transition Comes Full Circle, 1989–1997', in Pridham, G. & Gallagher, T. (eds) (2000), pp. 195–218.
Fatic, A. (2005) 'Anti-Corruption and Anti-Organized Crime Policy in Serbia: Regional Implications', in Athanassopoulou, E. (ed.) (2005) *Fighting Organized Crime in Southeast Europe* (London, Routledge), pp. 99–108.
Kanev, D. (2005) 'The Bulgarian Party System in the Process of Europeanization: The Case of Parties and the Party System', in Kabaalioglu, H., Dartan, M., Akman, S. M. & Nas, C. (eds) (2005) *Europeanization of South-Eastern Europe: Domestic Aspects of the Accession Process* (Istanbul, Marmara University European Community Institute), pp. 53–68.
Kolarova, R. (2002) 'Democratization in Bulgaria: Recent Trends', in Kaldor, M. & Vejvoda, I. (eds) (2002) *Democratization in Central and Eastern Europe* (London, Continuum), pp. 150–61.
Miller, N. J. (1997) 'Serbia: A Case of Failed Transition', in Dawisha, K. & Parrot, B. (eds) (1997), pp. 146–88.
Noutcheva, G. & Bechev, D. (2008) 'The Successful Laggards: Bulgaria and Romania's Accession to the EU', *East European Politics and Societies*, 2, 1, pp. 114–44.
Pappas, T. S. (2005) 'Shared Culture, Individual Strategy and Collective Action: Explaining Slobodan Milosevic Charismatic Rise to Power', *Southeast European and Black Sea Studies*, 5, 2, pp. 191–211.
Pridham, G. & Gallagher, T. (eds) (2000) *Experimenting with Democracy: Regime Change in the Balkans* (London, Routledge).
Spirova, M. (2008) 'Europarties and Party Development in EU-Candidate States: The Case of Bulgaria', *Europe-Asia Studies*, 60, 5, pp. 791–808.
Vejvoda, I. (2000) 'Democratic Despotism: Federal Republic of Yugoslavia and Croatia', in Pridham, G. & Gallagher, T. (eds) (2000), pp. 219–36.

Appendix

TABLE A1
CLASSIFICATION OF POLITICAL PARTIES INTO POLITICAL PARTY FAMILIES

	Political party	*Political party family*
Bulgaria	Democrats for a Strong Bulgaria	Christian democrats
	Movement for Rights and Freedoms (MRF)	Left liberals
	Coalition for Bulgaria	Socialist
	National Movement Simeon II (NMSS)	Conservatives
	United Democratic Forces (UDF)	Right liberals
	National Union Attack	Extreme right
Greece	Greek Communist Party (KKE)	Communists
	New Democracy (ND)	Conservatives
	Pan-Hellenic Socialist Party (PASOK)	Socialists
	Synaspismos	Left liberals
Serbia	Democratic Party (DS)	Socialists
	Democratic Party of Serbia (DSS)	Right liberals
	G17PLUS (G17)	Liberals
	Liberal Democratic Party	Liberals
	Serbian Radical Party (RPS)	Extreme right
	Socialist Party of Serbia (SPS)	Socialists
	League of Social Democrats of Vojvodina	Ethnic minorities
	Ethnic Minorities Party	Ethnic minorities
	New Serbia and Democratic Party of Serbia	Right liberals
	Serbian Renewal Movement	Right liberals

Identity Formation of Elites in Old and New Member States (with a Special Focus on the Czech Elite)

ZDENKA MANSFELDOVÁ &
BARBORA ŠPICAROVÁ STAŠKOVÁ

The European Union (EU) and the concept of creating a new supranational political institution has been going through an unusually dynamic period of development in recent years. It has to do not only with the admission of a large number of new members in a very short period of time, but also with projects designed to deepen integration. These however have not necessarily been successful as evidenced by the rejection of the European Constitution and the current difficulties in approving the Lisbon Treaty. In light of these processes, in this essay we shall examine whether Europe is united or actually still divided. Some authors postulate the existence of an 'old Europe' and a 'new Europe'; the pretence of unity on the eve of expansion appears to have disappeared and one can only anticipate further fragmentation with the 10 new members of the 2004 enlargement each possessing different social, political and economic conditions (Ichijo & Spohn 2005, p. 1). The various EU member states have gone through different processes of state formation, nation building and democratisation, and, as a result, they have developed different forms of national identity. At the same time, membership of the EU, including the association phase, presupposed the existence of shared European values, norms and goals and the creation of a supranational, European identity. Whether this new identity is embraced by the member states and citizens of the various countries in the same way or differently remains questionable, as does the extent of difference between the content of European identity and national identity.

The question of national and European identity is not new at all. It emerged during the 1950s when the process of European integration was set in motion. After a radical EU expansion and the entry of post-communist countries into the community this question has become more and more appealing to researchers due to the different backgrounds the new members possess in comparison to the previous waves of EU expansion. In the existing body of literature there are three main attitudes toward the development and coexistence of a national and European identity (Ichijo & Spohn 2005).

We would like to thank our colleague Pat Lyons for his consultations and helpful comments.

First, national identity, derived from the national state, is the central core of collective identity, whereas European identity is weak and will remain so for some time. Second, European identity, albeit weak, is becoming stronger thanks to the process of European integration and will gradually weaken or even replace national identity. Third, the national and European identities should not be treated as irreconcilable because the process of unification will bring about a mix of national and European identities.

The ambitions of this essay are modest. We believe that the examination of identity, its components, and the relationship between national and European identities are essential to be able to understand what shapes policy and policies, what the possibilities and limits of the 'European project' are, and how the concept of 'us' and 'them' is formed in the ever deepening integration of a somewhat borderless Europe after the expansion of the Schengen zone. Unlike other essays that concentrate on the mass level, we examine the perception of national and European identities from the viewpoint of the elite only. Our study is based on the assumptions of cognitive mobilisation theory (Inglehart 1970; Schauer 1997), namely that an educated group of persons is more aware of the contexts, strengths and weaknesses of politics at the EU level, and that it is easier for them to form an opinion on distant and often more abstract institutions than for the average population.

In the following we shall focus on the question of what creates the national and European identities of political and economic elites in the old and new EU member states, whether there is a connection between the two and between the understanding of identity and the level of support for European integration. We shall devote special attention to one of the new member states, the Czech Republic, which we shall compare with the old and new EU member states. Beyond the Intune survey[1] we have additional Czech survey results at our disposal to help our interpretation. The Czech case is particularly interesting because, using the definition of Euroscepticism from Kopecký and Mudde (2002), the Czech Republic is known as one of the extreme 'Eurosceptics' in the post-communist region.

The analysis will develop around the following hypotheses. First, we contend that the elites in old EU member states have greater experience with a shared common destiny and for this reason are more strongly attached to Europe than their counterparts from new member states. Second, new member states are still searching for their position in the new make-up of Europe and therefore put greater emphasis on national components than on European identity. Third, the economic elites are familiar with supranational capital which makes them more cosmopolitan than the political elites, including in their understanding of a national and European identity. Fourth, positive experience with EU membership influences one's position on European integration and EU policy in a positive manner. Finally, we argue that identity is made up of various components that are more or less similar and can be put into concrete groups based on their degree of similarity. The grouping of components is similar for national and European identities.

In the first part of the essay we shall outline the multiple nature of identity, the different forms of territorial attachment and the bonds between them. In the next

---

[1] Integrated and United: A Quest for Citizenship in an 'ever closer Europe' (INTUNE), 6FP, No. CIT3-CT-2005-513421, available at: http://www.intune.it.

section we shall examine the positions of elites on European integration, their intensity and further direction, and the possible relationship between these positions and the declared identity of the elites. The third part analyses the components of national and European identities. This is followed by an exploration of the interdependencies between the aspects of both identities and their basic components with the help of factor analysis.

For the sake of analysis, the countries have been divided into two groups, of old EU member states and a new EU member states.[2] The sample consists of 2,025 respondents: 65.9% of them are members of the political elite—deputies of national parliaments (1,335), and 34.1% are members of the economic elite (690).[3] A total of 1,179 respondents came from old member states and 846 came from new member states. We have singled out the Czech elites to be considered both separately and—for comparative purposes—within the new member states group.

The sample of the Czech political elite (as with the samples of the other countries) consists of 80 MPs—selected through quota sampling, which corresponds to 40% of the Chamber of Deputies of the Czech Parliament (the entire Chamber has 200 members). The average age of the members of the political elite is 47.4; they are overwhelmingly males (the Chamber of Deputies is comprised of only 15% female deputies), with university education (83.8%). The typical member of the Czech economic elite could be profiled as follows: a man in his forties (the average age is 43.8), holding a university degree in business, with prior experience in the private or public sector, who came to his current position from a previous post in a company.

The multiple nature of identity

The selection of research questions explored multiple territorial identities from local to global with special focus on the understanding of national and European identities. As a rule, people operate within an intersection of multiple identities. They were born and grew up somewhere, they live and work somewhere and belong to a number of social groups and geographic entities to which they are connected by tighter or looser bonds. We based our study on the idea that there are multiple territorial identities from local to global, and asked the question on four levels of territorial identity: attachment to locality to one's town or village, to region, to one's country, and to Europe. These identities are, in our opinion, not mutually exclusive but they are characterised by varying intensities at the individual level, which can provide some testimony toward identification with the idea of European integration and support for the European project.

For our analysis the relationship between sub-national, national and European identity is the central focus and differences between local and regional identity will not

---

[2]Old member states include Austria, Belgium, Denmark, France, Italy, Germany, Greece, Portugal and Great Britain; new member states include Bulgaria, the Czech Republic, Estonia, Lithuania, Hungary, Poland and Slovakia.

[3]The sample for the economic elite survey includes the leaders of both the main business associations and the major bank groups and companies. Respondents were selected from the presidents, CEOs, general managers and eligible deputies of the biggest companies listed in 'TOP 500' or 'TOP 100'. The Czech TOP 100 and Czech TOP 500 is an ordered scale of 100 (500) companies, composed every year according to their economic indicators by the association Sdružení Czech Top 100.

be considered in further analysis. Concerning the formulation of the question on attachment to Europe, a certain degree of doubt can be cast as to whether the elites always identified Europe with the EU. Still, on the basis of academic literature we can assume that people generally have more of a tendency to identify with the EU (which is definable) than with Europe (Optem 2001; Lengyel & Göncz 2005). They have experience, whether shorter or longer, with membership in the EU, and they can evaluate the gains and losses that European integration has brought their country. We also lean toward the opinion that national and European identities do not compete with each other but complement or strengthen each other (Bruter 2004).

When we look at the intensity of attachment to individual territorial identities (see Table 1), the strongest attachment is found for one's own country, followed by one's town or village, region and only in last place do we find attachment to Europe. This ranking can be observed in both groups of elites in both the old and new member states.

The political elites expressed a much greater degree of attachment with the local or regional community than the economic elites in both country groups. The economic elites in EU member states are more cosmopolitan, more attached to the EU and open to Europe. One possible explanation might be the continuous contact between the political elite (MPs) and their constituencies, their dependence on the region in which they were nominated and elected, and the interests of the constituency they try to represent. Another possible explanation might be the influence of personal life experience in another EU country; members of the economic elite have more experience with life abroad (41.2%) than members of political elites (7.5%). Attachment to the ever more multinational and globalised business world is more typical for them, as is higher mobility. The surveyed members of the economic elite were selected from the 'Top 100' companies. Therefore we can assume that the surveyed persons have extensive work contacts in the supranational sphere and that their professional experience has shaped their identification with the respective communities.

Aside from intergroup differences, we also find differences among the individual countries, as is demonstrated by the case of the Czech Republic, where the difference in territorial attachment between political and economic elites is more marked than the average values for these two groups in the old member states and new member states. It is interesting to note that overall the Czech economic elites expressed the most lukewarm relationship to each mentioned community and thus are generally different from their national political counterparts in the strength of their attachment. Similarly to their colleagues from other European countries, they are most strongly tied to their own country but, as seen in Table 1, their attachment to Europe is weaker than in other countries. Table 1 demonstrates that the question of whether someone is a representative of business or politics plays a much greater role than whether they come from a new member state. First of all, it is the national and European identity that distinguishes new and old member states and the individual countries from each other.

Views on European integration

In order to evaluate the feeling of attachment with one's own country and with Europe it is necessary to consider how this attachment is connected to satisfaction with a country's membership in the organised supranational community, the European Union. We contend that support for the EU or conversely reservations about the EU are influenced by the evaluation of the gains that European integration has brought to one's own country—not only at the level of public opinion but also at the level of elites. As shown in Table 2, elites in all the countries consider EU membership beneficial for their own country.

In evaluating the benefits of EU membership for their country, the elites from the new member countries are slightly more reserved. Still, more than 90% of them maintain that their country has benefited from membership. The political elites of the new countries are more sceptical than their peers from the old member states. From other answers in the survey we know that the economic elite favour a free market in social security. With this question it is demonstrated that they are more convinced about their country's benefits from membership, which implies that, in their opinion, the desirable economic goals of the EU have been achieved. This is also likely to be related to their stronger attachment to Europe as shown in Table 1. Although the Czech Republic has only a very short experience with EU membership, nevertheless the general evaluation of this period is largely positive; 89% of the political elite and 95% of the economic elite hold the opinion that the Czech Republic has benefited from EU membership. Although this is lower than the evaluation of political elites in other countries, still it is convincingly and surprisingly high in the face of the level of Euroscepticism more widely.

TABLE 1
DIFFERENT LEVELS OF TERRITORIAL ATTACHMENT

Are you attached to: (Very attached/ Somewhat attached—in %)	Czech Republic		Old member states		New member states	
	Political elites	Economic elites	Political elites	Economic elites	Political elites	Economic elites
Your town/village	74/24	24/55	71/24	39/39	74/24	42/43
Your region	55/41	12/51	54/35	29/40	54/36	30/42
Your country	79/21	24/62	70/23	62/32	85/14	66/27
Europe	24/51	27/51	39/47	40/46	34/52	33/48

TABLE 2
BENEFITS FROM BEING A MEMBER OF THE EUROPEAN UNION

Taking everything into consideration, would you say that your country has benefited or not from being a member of the European Union? (in %)	Czech Republic		Old member states		New member states	
	Political elites	Economic elites	Political elites	Economic elites	Political elites	Economic elites
Has benefited	89	95	95	99	94	97
Has not benefited	11	5	5	1	6	3

Globally speaking, the elites agree that their countries have profited from EU membership but differ in their opinions about how their interests are represented in the EU, whether they are represented sufficiently, and whether the interests of all member states are given the same weight, or whether some selected EU members receive preferential treatment. Table 3 shows that the elites from the new member states, and Czech politicians even more so, share the opinion that: 'Those who make decisions at the EU level do not take enough account of the interests at stake for [my country]'. Considering the marked rejection of this claim by the old member states' elites it is clear that it is precisely their weight in the EU, whether real or subjectively experienced, that leads the new member states to criticise the balance of power. It also seems that they still do not feel sufficiently sure of themselves and strong in their new role, nor do they feel equal to their more experienced colleagues and they have the feeling that the interests of their countries are not sufficiently taken into account.

If, however, we ask more generally whether the interests of some member states have more weight at the European level and whether some member states have a greater chance to influence decisions, the old member states' elites are also critical in their evaluation. As can be seen from Table 3, all groups agree that: 'The interests of some member states carry too much weight at the EU level'. That is, equality in the EU is not clear cut and the feeling prevails that, 'we are all equal, but some are more equal than others', which contributes to the explanation of lower attachment to Europe and weaker European identity of the newcomers.

The prevailing agreement on the benefits of EU membership for one's country does not closely correspond to the view on how far unification should or may go. While the majority think that the European integration process should deepen further, support is significantly higher in the original member states than in the new ones. Notably, the attitude toward the deepening of integration is shaped more by the country of origin (or, to be more precise, there are differences between the old member states and the new member states) than by affiliation with the two types of elite. The Czech elites are not particularly in favour of strengthening unification and there is essentially no difference between the political and economic elite in this respect (see Table 4). These views can be explained by Czech Euroscepticism as described by Kopecký.

TABLE 3

REPRESENTATION OF NATIONAL INTERESTS ON THE EUROPEAN LEVEL AND EQUALITY OF OPPORTUNITY

Agreement with the two statements on politics: (Agree/Disagree—in %)	Czech Republic		Old member states		New member states	
	Political elites	Economic elites	Political elites	Economic elites	Political elites	Economic elites
Those who make decisions at the EU level do not take enough account of the interests of [country]	73/28	59/42	33/62	39/58	64/33	62/35
The interests of some member states carry too much weight at the EU level	91/9	95/5	79/19	80/19	89/10	87/11

Note: The replies do not add up to 100% due to 'neither agree nor disagree' replies.

Euroscepticism is understood here as a low level of support for European integration in general (Kopecký 2004, p. 231).

The level of support for deepening European integration (or conversely rejection of further integration) is related to the question of who should be the main actor in the government of a more united Europe. Should it remain the national state or should policy making be transferred to the supranational level? Table 5 shows the difference between elites in the old and new member states concerning this question. The elites, and in particular the political elites, in the new member states emphasise the role of national states, and this is even more marked in the Czech Republic. The Czech political elite believes that states should be the central players within the EU (89% strongly agree or agree). This corresponds with the opinion on the future role of the European Commission. Unlike the elites in other countries, the Czech elites are less enthusiastic about the notion that the European Commission should be the basis of an EU government (only 33% of them agree strongly or agree somewhat with this statement). Strengthening the powers of the European Parliament also attracts only 48% of respondents' support.

According to the Czech MPs the member state itself should definitely remain the most important actor in the European Union. The Czech economic elite shares this view but its support for the national state is significantly weaker than that of the political elite, and in fact, even weaker than their colleagues in the new member states. The views of the Czech elites also differ from those of other countries on whether the European Commission should become the real government of the EU; only every third

TABLE 4
SUPPORT FOR FURTHER UNIFICATION

Support for further unification (from '0' = has gone too far to '10' = should be strengthened)	Czech Republic		Old member states		New member states	
	Political elites	Economic elites	Political elites	Economic elites	Political elites	Economic elites
Mean score	5.5	5.4	7.1	7.2	6.0	6.2

TABLE 5
THE MAIN ACTORS IN THE EU

The main actors in the EU ought to be ... (Agree strongly/Agree somewhat—in %)	Czech Republic		Old member states		New member states	
	Political elites	Economic elites	Political elites	Economic elites	Political elites	Economic elites
The member states ought to remain the central actors of the EU	70/19	38/55	37/33	33/40	52/34	42/41
The powers of the European Parliament ought to be strengthened	18/30	23/30	47/33	29/44	22/40	18/39
The European Commission ought to be the true government of the EU	5/28	13/28	16/35	12/37	12/39	14/37

Czech respondent is in favour of this whereas in the other countries more than half of the respondents accept this view. This is again an expression of Czech Euroscepticism: a preference for the national government as opposed to EU institutions. This may explain their emphasis on national attachment and national identity.

We also asked the elites about the future of the European Union but we did not find much support for common EU policies for the next 10 years. There is stronger support in general for a single foreign policy toward countries outside the EU instead of national policies, as well as for more help for regions suffering from economic and social difficulties. There is much lower support for the idea of a common system of social security, as is the case for a unified tax system. This corresponds to the higher degree of support for a free market and more competitiveness within the EU.

The elites' opinions concerning the goals of the EU as well as concerning national or European jurisdiction over individual policies are linked to the volume of funds available on those levels. Lengyel and Göncz call it a pragmatic aspect of European identity (Lengyel & Göncz 2005). Respondents were asked to distribute €100 (or 100 units of the national currency, CZK in the Czech case) paid by the taxpayers to the regional, national and supranational levels (in other words to divide 100% into three groups). In other words they were asked to present a distribution of taxes that would be desirable from their viewpoint and to determine the division of revenues on the respective levels (see Table 6).

The average values shown in the table indicate that Czech MPs are the most pronounced advocates of a strong state; they would allocate the highest share of the 100 crowns to the national budget, and thus they would maintain the largest influence on the distribution of tax revenues. They would allocate slightly less money directly to the regions and the lowest amount to Brussels. Their more experienced European peers in the old member states have a similar opinion but the amount allocated by them to the supranational Europe would be somewhat larger. The Czech economic elite would send the largest portion of the money directly to the regions and only then to the national budget, and the economic elites of the new member states overall would do the same by a smaller margin. With the exception of the Czech Republic, the economic elite of most countries would like the largest share of tax revenues to end up in national budgets. The biggest advocates of a strong national budget are the political

TABLE 6
DISTRIBUTION OF TAXES AT DIFFERENT LEVELS

Out of €100 of tax money a citizen pays, how much should be allocated on the regional, national and European level? (mean)	Czech Republic		Old member states		New member states	
	Political elites	Economic elites	Political elites	Economic elites	Political elites	Economic elites
Regional level	40.8	47.3	39.4	34.3	43.2	42.7
National level	44.1	38.0	40.9	44.3	42.2	42.1
European level	15.1	14.7	18.7	21.1	14.5	15.2

elites from Great Britain, Lithuania, Austria, Estonia, Denmark and Portugal. They would allocate almost one half of the proposed €100 to the national level and the second highest portion would be sent to regional budgets. This contrasts with the post-communist states like Bulgaria, Poland, Slovakia and the Czech Republic, whose economic elite would send most money to the regions, a large part to the state and the rest to Brussels. No country would allocate more funds to Brussels than to the regional or national levels. Nevertheless, it is once again evident that the old member states' elites prefer the role of the EU more than their new member state EU colleagues. It corresponds with the emphasis on national or territorial identity in new member states.

Understanding national and European identities

The investigation of identity in the Intune survey consisted of two perspectives—the national and the European. Each of them is made up of a whole battery of questions about partial aspects of identity that we call identity components. These are discussed in detail in this section. Classifications of collective identity feature various constitutive elements, ethnic-territorial, cultural-religious, socio-economic and political-legal components. For national identity, the following questions were asked: 'In your view, how important is each of the following to be a true national: to master the language(s) of the country; to respect the (national) laws and institutions; to feel (national); to share (the country's) cultural traditions; to be a citizen (of the country); to have (national) parents; to be born in (the country); and to be a Christian?' For European identity, the following questions were asked: 'For being truly European, how important do you think each of the following is: to master a European language; to feel European; to respect the European Union's laws and institutions; to share European cultural traditions; to have European parents; to be born in Europe; and to be a Christian?'

National identity

For the Czech political elite, a sense of national identity is associated with, in descending order, first, feeling Czech; second, sharing national traditions; third, knowing the Czech language; and fourth having respect for the laws and institutions of the Czech Republic. In contrast, the Czech economic elite's sense of national identity has a different hierarchy: first, knowledge of the Czech language; second, respect for Czech laws and institutions; third feeling Czech; and fourth having been born in the Czech Republic.

The results were similar in other post-communist countries where, unlike the political elite, the economic elite stress knowledge of the national language more than a feeling of mutual belonging. Different attitudes in the new and old member countries with respect to national laws and institutions deserve particular attention: the Western elites, both economic and political, clearly place these first. In the original EU member countries, respect for and compliance with law and order as a factor of national identity dwarfs even knowledge of the national language and a feeling of mutual belonging. Citizenship, too, has been gaining prominence in the eyes of the political elite of those countries to the detriment of sharing national cultural traditions.

Although origin (country of birth) also plays an important role, it is not emphasised as much as the previous factors. The importance assigned to the role of Christianity in national identity attests to Czech atheism; the vast majority of the surveyed members of the elite assert that it is not an important factor in national identity. The link between Christianity and national identity is weak in other countries as well but it is one of the weakest in the Czech Republic. Table 7 shows the differences between the original and the new member countries, as well as the Czech Republic.

European identity

An identical set of questions was asked about European identity. The rank order of replies is similar, at least as far as the first and last positions are concerned. The Czech elites consider knowledge of a European language the most important factor followed by a feeling of European belonging, respect for law and order and the sharing of European cultural values. Both groups of the Czech elite agree on this order. Other East European elites' attitudes concerning the ranking of these components are more similar to the opinion of the Czech elite than to that of the Western European elite. The latter tend to emphasise the need to respect EU norms and institutions. The economic elite from the old member states in fact rank this factor first. For the old member states, to be born in Europe is more important for European identity than having European parents. Detailed results are shown in Table 8.

TABLE 7
COMPONENTS OF NATIONAL IDENTITY

People differ in what they think it means to be a true Czech [or other nationality]. How important is ...? (Very important/ Fairly important–in %)	Czech Republic		Old member states		New member states	
	Political elites	*Economic elites*	*Political elites*	*Economic elites*	*Political elites*	*Economic elites*
To desire to be a (national)	77/22	48/29	59/27	56/35	83/16	68/24
To share (country) cultural traditions	69/28	31/50	38/45	45/42	66/31	48/44
To master the language(s) of (our country)	68/29	52/38	62/30	65/32	72/25	69/28
To respect the (nationality) norms and institutions	64/30	48/40	74/22	72/23	70/26	58/31
To be a citizen of ... (country)	33/46	21/45	47/34	38/40	45/35	39/33
To have parents of (nationality)	29/53	17/38	19/33	19/39	40/38	32/39
To be born in (country)	18/53	12/33	18/30	15/34	32/35	21/39
To be a Christian	3/23	2/5	11/17	7/23	20/29	10/21

National and European identity compared

Overall, different aspects of European identity are attributed a lower weight than those of national identity. Furthermore, the elites in new EU member countries attribute great importance to a higher number of both national and European aspects than their colleagues from the old EU member countries (see Table 9). In the table, we have also summed up all the data, which corroborates our first hypothesis. The new member elites express a greater need for self-identification and the search for their country's identity.

While in the new EU countries it is the political elites in the old member states it is the business elites that emphasise the national aspects more. The difference in the attitudes toward politics between the two country groups manifests itself in the overall score. The tally of positive replies from the economic elite changes this only slightly.

National and European identities, therefore, appear to be much more important for the EU newcomers who need to find their position in the new framework after the demise of the bipolar world. This is also mirrored in their position within the EU; as has been shown in the first part of this article, most of them agree that their country is not represented sufficiently in the EU, or, as it is expressed in the questionnaire: 'Those who make decisions at the EU level do not take enough account of the interests at

TABLE 8
COMPONENTS OF EUROPEAN IDENTITY

For being truly European, how important do you think each of the following is ...? (Very important/Fairly important—in %)	Czech Republic		Old member states		New member states	
	Political elites	Economic elites	Political elites	Economic elites	Political elites	Economic elites
To master a European language	65/29	79/14	56/27	69/25	63/29	75/20
To desire to be a European	63/29	57/24	58/28	64/28	72/25	67/28
To respect the European Union's norms and institutions	43/44	33/50	65/19	74/21	57/36	58/34
To share European cultural traditions	37/49	33/48	30/42	42/40	45/46	46/44
To have European parents	8/44	17/24	16/32	14/36	17/41	17/36
To be born in Europe	6/41	10/36	16/36	17/31	16/36	16/37
To be a Christian	5/28	2/17	10/18	5/21	15/30	5/21

TABLE 9
TOTAL SCORE OF AFFIRMATIVE REPLIES TO THE COMPONENTS OF NATIONAL AND EUROPEAN IDENTITIES

A tally of affirmative replies to the components of national and European identities	Old member states		New member states	
	Political elites	Economic elites	Political elites	Economic elites
National identity	564	577	667	604
European identity	466	486	534	504

Note: The table depicts the sum of all affirmative replies (very important + somewhat important) to all the components of national and European identity (which are considered separately).

stake of [country]'. In this respect, they are very different from their peers in the old member countries.

A comparative perspective on the components of national and European identities

An analysis of individual countries proves that there are substantial differences between them and not necessarily or exclusively on the new versus old member state dividing line. We have ordered the aspects of both national and European identity in various countries by the importance attributed to them by the representatives of the elite and also by the average score in all the EU countries.

As far as national identity is concerned, the highest frequency of 'important' rankings in the old member states group can be observed in the southern European countries: Portugal, Italy, Greece, Spain and also France. The lowest frequencies have been recorded in Belgium, Germany, Great Britain and Austria. In the Eastern group, the highest frequency of important aspects of national identity have emerged in Bulgaria, Estonia, Poland and Lithuania. The elites from Slovakia, Hungary and the Czech Republic, on the other hand, attributed the lowest importance to this component.

The importance attributed to individual country aspects is generally similar, as shown in Tables 7 and 8, which depict aggregate data for the old and new countries. Nevertheless, deviations do appear in some countries, for example the feeling of belonging to one's own nation in Germany is much weaker than other aspects, as is the case in Belgium. In Belgium, the internal division of the country into Flemish and Walloon sections necessarily translates into a lower rate of identification with Belgian nationality as such. In Germany, the most probable cause is the ongoing process of coming to terms with the past. As mentioned by Risse and Grabowsky, German postwar European identity has been constructed in order to overcome the country's own past of nationalism and militarism (Risse & Grabowsky 2008, p. 3; Risse 2001, p. 199). In the Spanish and Austrian cases, being born in the country is more important for national identity than parents' nationality. The largest difference between countries can be observed with respect to these two questions of being born in the country and parents' nationality, along with the role of Christianity, in the formation of national identity.

The same holds true for the elites from Poland, Bulgaria, Greece, Lithuania, Italy, Slovakia and Estonia who perceive the role of Christianity most strongly, whereas it is considered the least important in Great Britain, Belgium, France, Spain and the Czech Republic. Elites from all the countries agree that the component 'To be a (country) citizen' is more important than 'To have (national) parents', with the exception of Poland and Hungary. Thus there are differences between the new and old member states as well as between individual countries. Generally speaking, however, we can argue that new member states support all aspects of identity to a larger degree than the old member states.

Regarding European identity similar connections emerge concerning national identity but some specific results are of even greater interest: in Germany, Hungary and Slovakia, European identity is supported to a somewhat larger degree than the aspects of national identity. These are the countries where individual country aspects of identity have enjoyed the lowest level of importance. We contend that in countries with a low importance attributed to national identity, the feeling of belonging to a superior entity is put in place as compensation. A clear exception here is Great Britain, where the political and economic elites expressed the lowest support for the components of European identity—55% on average, which is 8% lower than support for the components of national identity, which is itself relatively weak. British Euroscepticism was also perceptible in the question concerning the benefits of EU membership: most respondents replied affirmatively but in comparison with other countries, the support was the weakest.[4]

Factors of national and European identity

The responses to the questions analysed above seem to suggest that there are interdependencies between the individual variables examined, and that it might be possible to reduce the number of variables to a smaller number of underlying or latent factors. A preliminary examination of the correlation matrix reveals that there is a reasonably strong level of association among the measures examined, and the correlation patterns have a substantive meaning. On the basis of this evidence it was decided to conduct an exploratory factor analysis. Having estimated a number of models with unrotated solutions, it was decided to see if the factors extracted could be simplified further through the use of factor rotation where variables that load highly on one factor and low on others make interpretation more straightforward. More specifically, two rotation methods were examined: varimax rotation where the factors extracted are treated as being orthogonal or independent of each other; and direct oblimin rotation where the factors are allowed to be correlated with one another. Given the substantive nature of the factors being examined the direct oblimin method proved more appropriate. Our former results concerning the construction of identity within the European Union showed that there are differences between the old member states and the new member states. The analyses reported here will move beyond a focus on the Czech Republic or specific groups of elites. Instead, the focus will be an exploration of to what extent identities exhibit similar features across all EU member states, either old or new.

National identity

The results of the principal components analysis in Table 10 for all of the European Union (the 'All' column in Table 10) reveal three distinct components of national identity in Europe, which are denoted as 'origin', 'civic' and 'cultural'. The origin component of national identity relates to where a person is born or comes from, 'to be born in (country)' and 'to have (national) parents'. In contrast, the civic factor is related to citizenship and consists of the following components: 'to be a (country) citizen', 'to master the language(s) of the country', and 'to respect the (national) laws and institutions'. The last factor, called cultural, refers to attributes generally associated with national history such as traditions and religion: 'to share (country) cultural traditions', 'to feel (national)' and 'to be a Christian'. The cultural component of national identity is the weakest in terms of explained variance (14%) and would

---

[4]The result could be biased due to the fact that a segment of the political elite refused to participate in the project and to grant an interview.

TABLE 10
Principal Components Analysis of the National Identity Items Among European Elites

In your view, how important is each of the following to be a true national? To:	Factors	All components			Old member states components			New member states components		
		Origin	Civic	Cultural	Origin	Civic	Cultural	Origin	Civic	Cultural
Be born in (country)	Origin	0.852						0.824		
Have (national) parents		0.829						0.819		
Be a citizen of (country)	Civic		0.743			−0.870		0.558		
Master the language(s) of the country			0.708			−0.865		0.466		
Respect the (national) laws and institutions			0.657		0.694					
Share (country) cultural traditions	Cultural			0.818	0.678		0.675			0.669
Feel (national)				0.812	0.794		0.885			0.546
									0.835	0.851
									0.774	
Eigenvalues (percentage of total variance explained)		34.9	16.6	14.1	34.4	17.6	13.6	33.9	16.5	15.4
Total variance explained			65.7			65.7			65.9	
Total number of cases (N)			2025			1179			846	

Note: This principal component analysis was undertaken using a direct oblimin rotation. The Kaiser–Meyer–Ohlin (KMO) measure of sampling accuracy is ≥0.70, which indicates no significant problem with partial correlations among the variables. The Bartlett test of sphericity shows that the correlation matrix is not an identity one and factor analysis is appropriate.

seem in substantive terms to be closely related to the origin component. Consequently, it was decided to ignore the component of Christian religion and to construct the cultural component from only two items.

The results presented in Table 10 for the old and new member states demonstrate that the structure of attitudes associated with national identity is not consistent across the European Union. For the elites from the old member states the most important facet of national identity is its cultural component. This explains 34% of the total variance. However, this factor includes a variable that was not present in the overall EU model, the 'respect for (national) laws and institutions' component. It seems that for the elites in the old member states cultural traditions are strongly linked to national laws and institutions although this is not the case in new member states. Moreover, these results suggest that within the EU-15 states attitudes toward national laws and institutions are not seen in the same way as the civic component of national identity, which relates to nationality and knowledge of the local language(s).

For the old member states, Table 10 shows that the second largest component is the origin factor. In contrast to the model for all of Europe the variable loadings for the origin component of national identity are negative. This is an important finding because it indicates that elites within the EU-15 member states do not see the prevailing sources of citizenship, the *jus soli* (place of birth) and *jus sanguinis* (having parents from a country), as a basis for having a sense of national identity. Conversely, among the 10 new accession states (of 2004) national elites see these sources of citizenship as an important pillar of national identity.

For the new member states the factor analysis in Table 10 and the pattern of attitudes associated with national identity among elites are rather different from those observed in the old member states. The first component extracted contains a mix of both origin and civic items, the second factor is made up exclusively of cultural items, and the last factor has only variables associated with the civic aspect of national identity. The first and third components extracted share two civic factor items: to be a (country) citizen and to master the language(s) of the country, and these complex factor loadings persist even if a varimax rotation (which assumes that all factors are uncorrelated) is estimated. In the new member states the 'respect for national laws and institutions' variable is primarily associated with the civic facet of national identity among the elites. The second factor in the new member states' model on the left of Table 10 relates to the cultural component of national identity and the two items making up this factor explain about one in six of the total variation evident in the data.

Overall, the evidence presented in Table 10 suggests that among the elites within the European Union national identity has three distinct facets that are correlated with one another. The origin component of national identity relates directly to attitudes linked with legal definitions of national citizenship based on *jus soli* and *jus sanguinis*. In this respect, there is an important difference between the elites in the old member states and new member states. In the former, national identity is not associated with being born in or having parents from a country while in the latter the legal components of citizenship (along with ability to speak the national language) constitute the most important elements of national identity. Similar patterns are also present in the data presented in Table 7. Likewise, the civic component of national identity among the elites in Europe exhibits different patterns in the old member states and new member states. In the old member states it is mainly linked to citizenship and linguistic ability, while in the new member states the civic facet of national identity is most clearly identified with respect for national laws and institutions. Curiously, what appear to be primary elements of the civic component of national identity among elites in the original EU-15 are also associated with the origin component in the new member states, and this feature is highlighted by the complex factor loadings shown in the centre of Table 10. There is an interesting association between the cultural and civic factors (Pearson correlation = 0.269) and this pattern in the data indicates that respect for legal and cultural traditions implies an important communicative aspect to national identity among elites within the European Union.

European identity

In order to explore the nature of European identity among elites across the EU member states a similar modelling procedure has been used. The main difference between the two sets of analyses is that European citizenship is not present in the evaluation of European identity. The general clustering of variables relating to European identity form a three-factor solution similar to that observed earlier for national identity, based on origin, civic and cultural facets.

Table 11 reveals that the most important factor explaining European identity across the European Union and in the old member states and new member states alike is the origin component, which explains about one third of the total variance in the data. This component of European identity appears to be based on birth in Europe (*jus soli*) and having parents that are Europeans (*jus sanguinis*). In this respect one might argue that European identity replicates a key feature of national identity, the key difference being the higher level of aggregation. Among the elites of the EU the civic component of European identity is less clear cut. Having fluency in a European language is undoubtedly important, but other features such as respect for EU laws and institutions and to feel European suggest a rather complex picture with a certain mixing of variables that have both civic and cultural connotations for the elite respondents. Interestingly, when one considers the importance of the origins components and its citizen basis for European identity the cultural basis of European identity is not as strong as one might expect.

This finding is rather unexpected, although the negative loading on the dimension of 'respect for EU law and institutions' might suggest an anti-EU bias in the sense that European identity for elites does not necessarily mean identification with the European Union. One might speculate that there might be a specific 'priming effect' here in the Intune elite survey.[5] Frequent reference to the EU and a sense of European identity might have led many respondents in the old member states (as the centre of

---

[5]Priming is a concept from cognitive psychology where information used by an individual to answer a question, as in a survey interview, is subconsciously triggered by the context of the interview. For example, it is possible that previous items in a survey will lead a respondent to think about later questions in a particular way because specific pieces of information have been elicited. Had the type of questions asked earlier in the interview been different, so then might the answers to later questions be different (Tourangeau *et al.* 2000, pp. 176–77). Here the argument is that the term 'EU' may lead respondents to think of European identity in a very specific way.

TABLE 11
Principal Components Analysis of the European Identity Items Among European Elites

And for being truly European, how important do you think each of the following is?	Factors	All components			Old member states components			New member states components		
		Origin	Civic	Cultural	Origin	Civic	Cultural	Origin	Civic	Cultural
To be born in Europe	Origin	0.908			0.905			0.891		
To have European parents		0.902			0.912			0.896		
To master a European language	Civic		0.852							0.825
To respect the European Union's laws and institutions			0.636	-0.421		0.886			0.408	0.585
To share European cultural traditions	Cultural			-0.825			-0.792		0.830	
To feel European			0.407	-0.736		0.718	-0.424		0.695	0.453
Eigenvalues (percentage of total variance explained)		*33.5*	*23.1*	*13.8*	*34.3*	*24.5*	*13.3*	*31.6*	*22.2*	*15.0*
Total variance explained		*70.4*			*72.0*			*68.8*		
Total number of cases (N)		*2025*			*1179*			*846*		

Note: This principal component analysis was undertaken using a direct oblimin rotation. The Kaiser–Meyer–Ohklin (KMO) measure of sampling accuracy is ≥0.70, which indicates no significant problem with partial correlations among the variables. The Bartlett test of sphericity shows that the correlation matrix is not an identity one and factor analysis is appropriate.

Table 11 shows) to make a distinction between a general sense of being European and being part of the EU. Additional research on the states that are considered to be Eurosceptic may throw further light on this fascinating aspect of European identity among elites.

Among old member states' elites the origin aspect of European identity is the strongest component, followed by the civic aspect. The cultural component as noted earlier has a rather inclusive meaning where a sense of European identity is not related to knowledge of a European language, sharing European traditions or even feeling European. This suggests that those born outside Europe may identify culturally with Europe even if they may not be European citizens. This represents one of the sharpest contrasts in terms of European identity between the elites in the old member states and new member states, as the left part of Table 11 demonstrates. For the elites of the new member states, respect for EU laws and institutions, a shared sense of European culture and feeling European are strongly associated with each other, that is the civic and cultural bases of European identity are not seen to be distinct as is the case with national identity as shown in Table 10. The final component of European identity for respondents in the new member states is primarily linguistic ability and to a lesser degree respect for the EU's laws and institutions and feeling European.

Overall, the factor analysis demonstrates mutual interdependence of the various dimensions of national and European identity. Both can be divided into three factors: origin, civic and cultural, although this approach works best for national identity. Clearly, there are systematic differences in the constellation of attitudes associated with national identity among elites in the old member states and new member states. While one might argue that such differences are likely to be the product of the different histories of the two regions, one must be careful not to over emphasise this divide. Future research in this respect should explore the degree of heterogeneity within the old member states and new member states and examine the extent to which national environments can explain the variation in the patterns of national identity formation. The three pillars of national identity work imperfectly at the European level. In fact, there is no neat divide of origin, civic and cultural facets as is the case of European identity among elites across Europe. Moreover, the association among attitudes in the old member states and new member states is considerably different, implying different perspectives on what being European actually means. The evidence presented here shows that in the new member states European identity is more strongly associated with the EU than is likely to be the case in the EU-15 member states' elites. This is an important finding because it suggests that long experience of the European integration project among elites does not necessarily lead to a sense of European identity strongly tied to EU institutions. However, such a conclusion must be tempered by the fact that attitudes toward European identity are likely to exhibit significant heterogeneity within the old member states and new member states, primarily on the basis of the degree of Euroscepticism—a factor that exists right across the EU member states.

Overall, we have found that there are significant differences in the structure of attitudes concerning national and European identity and there are significant disparities between the old member states and new member states on these two levels of identity. Moreover, the research results presented here demonstrate the need first, to consider more carefully the country variation within the two groups of old member states and new member states; and second, to explore the degree to which these attitudinal differences have an institutional basis.

Conclusion

The process of European integration, the EU's political development, and the building of European institutions have been characterised by an uncommon breadth and intensity in recent years. In this essay we searched for an answer to the question of whether an 'ever closer Europe' is still divided, or whether it is moving toward deeper integration. We investigated this problem on the level of political and economic elites and focused on their perceptions and concepts of national and European identity. The results of the analysis lead us to the conclusion that a longer experience with European integration influences the feeling of belonging to Europe and identification with Europe in a positive way, albeit with certain differences. The hypothesis that positive experience with EU membership and a country's benefit from it will increase positive attitudes toward European integration and EU policy was not fully confirmed. When they evaluate the benefit to their countries from EU membership, the elites from the new member countries are somewhat more reserved. Nonetheless, the conviction that their countries do profit from membership prevails among them. The economic elites, who have greater experience with supranational capital, international companies, or with integration in the European common market are more cosmopolitan and feel more connected with Europe than the political elites, who are more embedded in the domestic political scene.

National and European identity are made up of a number of components, which can have various weightings and can be put in a hierarchy based on the importance attributed to them. According to our findings the aspects of national identity are given more weight than aspects of European identity. Components of national identity are considered more important than components of European identity. This is true particularly for the new member states, where all factors are emphasised more than in the old member states and the components are not hierarchised according to their importance.

The factor analysis confirmed the assumption that national and European identities are made up of components that can be combined into more or less similar groups. Both the national and European identities are built up of three components (origin, civic and cultural) which are more explicit and clear cut in terms of national identity. The elites from the new member states perceived and evaluated the importance of concrete aspects of identity similarly to their old member state colleagues, but their views were far from identical. The economic elite again proved to be more cosmopolitan. Hence the civic components are more important in their case than either the cultural ones or the origin aspects of their national and European identity. The political elites express more support for the national level, which can be a reflection of their obvious connection with the national level of politics, as well as of the weakening of national parliaments and the transfer of decision making to the European level.

The Czech Republic in comparison with the old member states and new member states confirmed its reputation as a Eurosceptic country, in this case on the level of the elites and in particular the political elites. The make-up of the political elites certainly has a role in this because the strongest party in the governing coalition is markedly Eurosceptic, in contrast with their voters.

Institute of Sociology, Academy of Sciences of the Czech Republic

References

Bruter, M. (2004) 'Civic and Cultural Components of European Identity: A Pilot Model of Measurement of Citizens' Level of European Identity', in Hermann, R. K., Risse, T. & Brewer, M. (eds) (2004) *Transnational Identities: Becoming European in the EU* (New York, Rowman & Littlefield), pp. 186–213.
Delgado-Moreira, J. M. (1997) 'Cultural Citizenship and the Creation of European Identity', *Electronic Journal of Sociology*, available at: http://www.sociology.org/content/vol002.003/delgado.html, accessed 9 April 2009.
Gellner, A. (1993) *Národy a nacionalismus* (Prague, Hříbal).
Holý, L. (2001) *Malý český člověk a skvělý český národ* (Prague, Sociologické nakladatelství).
Ichijo, A. & Spohn, W. (2005) 'Introduction', in Ichijo, A. & Spohn, W. (eds) (2005) *Entangled Identities. Nations and Europe* (Aldershot, Ashgate), pp. 1–18.
Inglehart, R. (1970) 'Cognitive Mobilization and European Identity', *Comparative Politics*, 3, 1, October, pp. 45–71.
Kopecký, P. (2004) 'An Awkward Newcomer? EU Enlargement and Euroscepticism in the Czech Republic', *European Studies*, 20, pp. 225–45.
Kopecký, P. & Mudde, C. (2002) 'The Two Sides of Euroscepticism: Party Positions on European Integration in East Central Europe', *European Union Politics*, 3, 3, pp. 297–326.
Lengyel, G. & Göncz, B. (2005) 'Symbolic and Pragmatic Aspects of European Identity', Paper presented at the International Conference *Contemporary Structural and Value Changes in CEE Societies*, Belgrade, 18–19 November.
Mansfeldová, Z. & Stašková, B. (2007) 'INTUNE Elite Survey in Czech Republic—Final Report 2007', Paper presented at the *International Conference of INTUNE Project*, Budapest, Hungary, 24 November.
Optem, S. A. R. L. (2001) '"Perceptions of the European Union"—A Qualitative Study of the Public's Attitudes to and Expectations of the European Union in the 15 Member States and the 9 Candidate Countries', *General Report—General Report for the European Commission*, June 2001, available at: http://ec.europa.eu/governance/areas/studies/optem-report_en.pdf, accessed 18 April 2009.
Pallant, J. (2001) *SPSS Survival Manual: A Step by Step Guide to Data Analysis Using SPSS for Windows (Version 10)* (Buckingham, Open University Press).
Risse, T. (2001) 'A European Identity? Europeanization and the Evolution of Nation-State Identitites', in Cowles, M. G., Caporaso, J. A., Risse, T. & Rise-kapen, T. (eds) (2001) *Transforming Europe. Europeanization and Domestic Change* (Ithaca, NY, Cornell University Press), pp. 198–216.
Risse, T. & Grabowsky, J. K. (2008) *European Identity Formation in the Public Sphere and in Foreign Policy*, RECON Online Working paper 2008/04 (Oslo, ARENA, Centre for European Studies), available at: http://www.reconproject.eu/main.php/RECON_wp_0804.pdf?fileitem=16662546, accessed 9 April 2009.
Schauer, H. (1997) 'Nationale und europäische Identität. Die unterschiedliche Auffassungen in Deutschland, Frankreich und Großbritannien', *Aus Politik und Zeitgeschichte*, B 10/97, 28 February, pp. 3–13.
Tourangeau, R., Rips, L. J. & Rasinski, K. (2000) *The Psychology of Survey Response* (New York, Cambridge University Press).
Vlachová, K. & Řeháková, B. (2004) *Česká národní identita po zániku Československa a před vstupem do Evropské unie* (Prague, Sociologický ústav Akademie věd České republiky).

Elites' Pragmatic and Symbolic Views about European Integration

GYÖRGY LENGYEL & BORBÁLA GÖNCZ

THIS ESSAY INVESTIGATES THE PRAGMATIC AND SYMBOLIC aspects of elites' views about European integration. The pragmatic aspect includes general support for unification and attitudes to supranational redistribution. By the symbolic aspect we mean how elites conceive their European attachment and identification. Elite members—top decision makers—are approached here in operational terms as members of the national parliaments and leaders of the largest banks and enterprises. First we describe the views of political and economic elites in 18 European countries on support for unification of the European Union (EU), supranational redistribution, attachment and identity formation. Second, we are interested in how these variables are intertwined within and between pragmatic and symbolic aspects of integration. Third, we investigate how symbolic aspects influence pragmatic ones if we control for countries and cultural resources of elites. In other words at this point we are interested in how the symbolic attitudes of elites influence their pragmatic views about integration.

The perception of the European integration process has been researched since the 1970s. Several studies have been conducted focusing on the rationale behind attitudes towards the integration process. Many of the studies in this field consider the European Union primarily as an economic entity and conduct their analysis with a utilitarian, instrumentalist approach supposing that individual attitudes are linked to the perceived benefits of integration either on the micro or on the macro level (Anderson 1998; Gabel 1998). Other studies are based on the assumption of an information deficit related to the EU, and contend that when people evaluate the integration process they use proxies linked to the domestic political arena (Anderson 1998; Gabel & Anderson 2001). Inglehart argues that in order to understand the very complex and abstract information on the EU, special cognitive mobilisation capacities are required (Inglehart 1990).

In the early studies the concepts of support for the EU, perceptions of the European integration process and attachment to Europe were not clearly separated. Since the 1990s however the effect of group membership on attitudes has become the focus of some studies (Hooghe & Marks 2001, 2004). Hooghe and Marks argue that at the beginning of the integration process the political actors shared the view that the process itself would create identity while nowadays the supposed causal path is the opposite, the main question being how multiple identities influence EU support. Others contend that the EU is creating identification by its simple existence (Opp 2005), or that the EU can create affective attachment through the efficient functioning of its institutions (Kritzinger 2005). In this essay we shall claim that attachment to subnational and supranational territorial units is an operational measure of identity as well.

Belonging to communities, real or, as Benedict Anderson argued, imagined ones is an essential part of identity formation and the nation has been probably the most frequently researched entity in this context since the nineteenth century (Anderson 1983; Gellner 1983; Brubaker 1996). The basic distinction in interpreting national identity lies between those who emphasise the civic will of people and those who regard common ethno-cultural characteristics as preconditions of nation formation. This distinction reappears in the understanding of European identity as well.

Authors working in the field offer diverse meanings of European identity. Scholars who share an essentialist approach and emphasise the affective and cultural aspects of identity perceive the concept of European identity as problematic. For example, according to Anthony Smith, European identity does not exist, because identity is rooted in common history, common myths and shared traditions which do not exist at the European level. At the same time Smith admits the existence of common traditions such as Roman law, democracy, renaissance, humanism (Smith 1992). For Horolets also, a European identity is difficult to define, as the direct or common experiences of the people with the EU or Europe are very few and thus they cannot relate to it because the entity remains too abstract. This explains why she introduces the concept of affective deficit which stands for the lack of symbolic attachment. Furthermore she challenges the efficiency of cultural traditions and emphasises the elite-driven character of the European integration process (Horolets 2003).

The constructivist or civic approach to European identity departs from the idea of civic attachment (Delanty 1995; Habermas 1998). European identity is constructed by political participation, a European public sphere and a common lifestyle where the point of reference is a democratic constitution. Habermas describes the two-facet character of national identity (Habermas 1998). He separates voluntary and inherited national identities and argues that nationalism based on citizenship is the source of democratic legitimation while ethnic membership is the source of social integration. In line with Habermas, Bruter (2005) also differentiates between passive and active forms of identification, where passive identity simply accepts an existing form, an objective pattern, whereas active identification means participation in creating new patterns.

According to Haller (2003) there is insufficient empirical evidence to support the distinction between the concepts of civic and cultural approaches. He claims that another distinction has more empirical grounds: one aspect based on rights and language, and another rooted in birth; these are frequently referred to as achieved and ascribed in sociological literature.

There have been efforts to analyse how supranational identity relates to national identity, and whether the two compete with or complement each other. A positive link between the two has been found in several cases showing that national and European identity mutually strengthen each other (Bruter 2004; Haller 2003; Inglehart 1970). Others have found that the expansion of European identity does not influence national attachment but it diminishes local attachment (Duchesne-Frognier 1995). In another study it was found that the cultural aspect prevails in the case of national attachment while European attachment is dominated by instrumentalist characteristics (Ruiz Jimenez et al. 2004). When national pride is involved the picture is even more complex. Carey has found that the higher the level of national pride the more European integration is perceived as a threat to the nation (Carey 2002).

Since integration is largely an elite-driven process (Anderson 1998, p. 570; Haller 2008; Carrubba 2001), in the analysis of elites' perception of the EU some specificities need to be taken into account. On the basis of the above theoretical and empirical remarks we suggest that the relationship of national elites to European integration will vary according to the different aspects of integration. Pragmatic aspects are based on rational evaluation while the symbolic aspect stands for a more affective link which could be approached by territorial attachment and by the underlying components of identification which will be examined below. Furthermore, we will address the question of how support for integration is influenced by attachment, types of identification, political or economic elite position and country specificities as well as by individual social and cultural resources.

Approach and methodology

Drawing on the discussion above, we shall distinguish in this essay between the pragmatic and symbolic aspects of elite attitudes towards the EU. We will explore the idea that these attitudes have a multi-dimensional character, and that they might be inter-related in different countries in different manners. The investigation is based on elite samples within the Intune[1] project collected in the spring of 2007.

In the Intune survey, the pragmatic aspect represents an instrumentalist view and was approached by two questions as already noted. One was the opinion of elite respondents of tax redistribution on the European level. Opinions concerning the share of supranational redistribution of taxes were gathered by means of answers to the third item in the following question: 'Out of one hundred Euro [or the national currency when relevant] of tax money a citizen pays, how much should be allocated on the regional, national and European level?' The other pragmatic question had to do with opinion on whether European unification should be strengthened. In regarding evaluations of unification as part of the pragmatic aspect we are supported by previous research (Gabel 1998; Optem 2001), which demonstrates that support for integration to a large extent is a utilitarian issue. Unification is a special form of integration and support of further unification was measured by the following question: 'Some say European unification should be strengthened. Others say it already has gone too far. What is your opinion? Please indicate your views using a 10-point-scale. On this scale, "0" means unification "has already gone too far" and "10" means it "should be strengthened". What number on this scale best describes your position?'

---

[1] Information on the project and sample can be found in the introductory paper of this collection. No weighting has been applied to the data.

The symbolic aspect is measured by components of identification together with the degree of attachment to different territorial levels such as one's own settlement, region, country or Europe. In our understanding attachment to these territorial levels is an immanent aspect of an individual's collective self-awareness. Attachment was measured on a four-grade scale with the following standard question: 'People feel different degrees of attachment to their town or village, to their region, to their country and to Europe. What about you? Are you very attached, somewhat attached, not very attached or not at all attached?'

While attachment is a relatively simple concept, identification covers several factors, including shared traditions and respect of institutions. Here we follow the arguments of Brubaker and Cooper (2000), who also claim that identification is created as a result of a categorisation process in which its context and situational character are taken into account. This is true in everyday life, as they contend, and it is certainly true in the case of an interview situation, where the respondents are asked to develop their perspective from a definite set of alternatives. The questions used to measure the different dimensions of identification were as follows: 'People differ in what they think it means to be (national). In your view, how important is each of the following to be (national)?' At another place in the questionnaire the same basic question was repeated addressing Europe. The answers included several items, each of them to be evaluated separately on a four-grade scale from very important to not important at all. The possible answers were: 'to be a Christian', 'to share (country)/European cultural traditions', 'to be born in (a country)/Europe', 'to have (national)/European parents', 'to respect (national)/EU laws and institutions', 'to feel (national)/European', 'to master a language of (the country)/Europe', and in the case of national identification also 'to be a citizen'. Questions relating to all of these items were asked in a rotated order except for the latter which was never asked as first option. The components relying on the combination of answers provide an insight to the entitlement regarding individual identification.

In the following sections first we provide an overview of various aspects of European integration: the instrumentalist support for supranational unification and taxation together with European identification and attachment. Identity formation will be further assessed by analysing the different components of national and European identification. In the final part of this essay we will discuss how these aspects are inter-connected with each other and how the different countries can be grouped according to our data on them. Finally, support for unification and supranational redistribution will be treated as dependent variables of attachment and identification.

Pragmatic aspects

Support for supranational redistribution

Support for integration is described by two dimensions in our analysis—both reflecting instrumentalist or pragmatic attitudes to the EU—these are how much tax money the elites would attribute to the different territorial levels, including Europe, and how they perceive the European unification process.

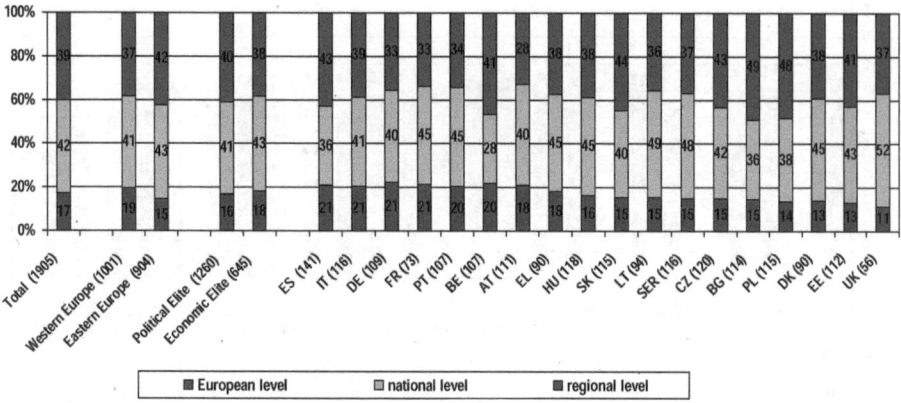

Notes: AT: Austria, BE: Belgium, BG: Bulgaria, CZ: Czech Republic, DK: Denmark, EE: Estonia, FR: France, DE: Germany, EL: Greece, HU: Hungary, IT: Italy, LT: Lithuania, PL: Poland, PT: Portugal, SER: Serbia, SK: Slovakia, ES: Spain, UK: United Kingdom.

FIGURE 1. ATTITUDES TO TAX REDISTRIBUTION

On average the European elites feel it would be fair to distribute a little more than two-fifths of taxes to the national level, another two-fifths to the sub-national level and roughly one sixth to the European level (see Figure 1).

West European elites would allocate slightly more tax to the European level while East European elites give priority to the regional level. The differences are less remarkable, however, between economic and political elites in terms of tax allocation. Interestingly, the average of 17% of tax money that the respondents would allocate to the European level is much higher than the actual share,[2] which implies a latent positive attitude towards the European integration process.

In terms of country differences the elites of the UK, Estonia and Denmark are more Eurosceptical on the question of redistribution to the European level while the elites of France, Germany, Austria, Belgium and the Mediterranean countries are more open toward an above-average supranational redistribution.

Support for unification

Overall, regarding attitudes to further European unification it can be said that European elites support it (see Figure 2). There are no significant differences between political and economic elites in this respect, but Western elites are more supportive than those in the new member states. The proportion of sceptics is very high among the British and Estonian elites, while the Spanish, Italian, Greek, Belgian, German and French elites are in favour of further unification, just as in the case of the tax redistribution. Thus in this regard the two questions dealing with pragmatic aspects of elite opinion towards the EU show very similar patterns across the different countries.

---

[2]The actual share was 2.54% of all EU-27 tax revenues in 2006. Calculation is based on EU-27 tax revenue in 2006 (Lupi 2008) and total commitment appropriation in 2006 (European Commission 2006).

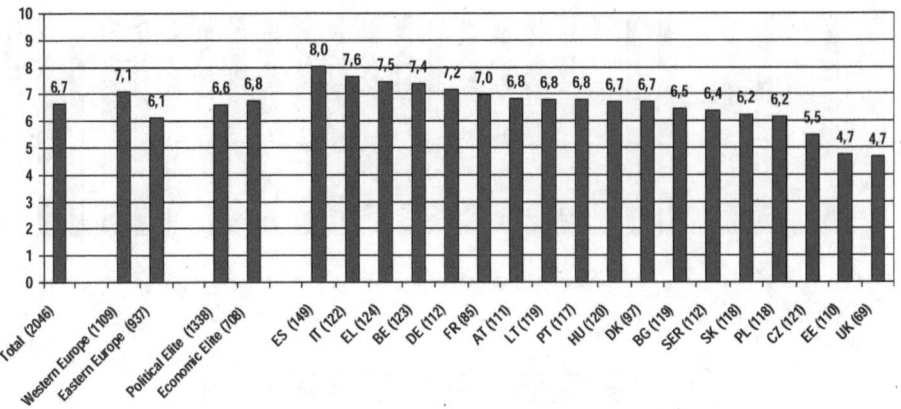

Notes: Country group: $t=9.36***$; elite type: $t=-1.54$; countries (ANOVA) $F=17.39***$ (***: $p<0.01$).
AT: Austria, BE: Belgium, BG: Bulgaria, CZ: Czech Republic, DK: Denmark, EE: Estonia, FR: France, DE: Germany, EL: Greece, HU: Hungary, IT: Italy, LT: Lithuania, PL: Poland, PT: Portugal, SER: Serbia, SK: Slovakia, ES. Spain, UK: United Kingdom.

FIGURE 2. PERCEPTION OF EUROPEAN UNIFICATION (AVERAGES ON 0–10 SCALE, 'UNIFICATION HAS ALREADY GONE TOO FAR' = 0, 'UNIFICATION SHOULD BE STRENGTHENED' = 10)

Symbolic aspects

Attachment to Europe

In terms of attachment to different territorial entities higher levels of attachment can be observed in the case of country and locality, with a somewhat lower level to region and to Europe. Differences between West and East European countries in this respect have to be noted regarding national and European attachment: East European elites are more attached to their respective countries and less attached to Europe than their Western counterparts. There are no differences between political and economic elites in terms of European attachment, but attachment to region, town or country is more important for political than for economic elites. It is worth mentioning that the gradient of difference is gradual, lying between the 'very attached' and 'somewhat attached' categories, because the proportion of those who declare that they are 'not at all attached' to any of these units is below 5% in each case (see Figure 3).

The analysis of territorial attachment by country shows that Polish, French and Hungarian elites represent especially high attachment both to Europe and to their country. Baltic and Bulgarian elites are equally attached to their respective countries, but prove to be more Eurosceptical, together with the British elites who seem to be more sympathetic to their local communities than to the country. An investigation of means, standard deviations and F-statistics shows that country differences are greater concerning national and supranational than the sub-national attachments although attachment to one's own town or region is higher in Great Britain, Spain, Greece and Slovakia than in other countries. In any case, in spite of significant country differences no homogeneous regional groups can be detected except for an East–West difference.

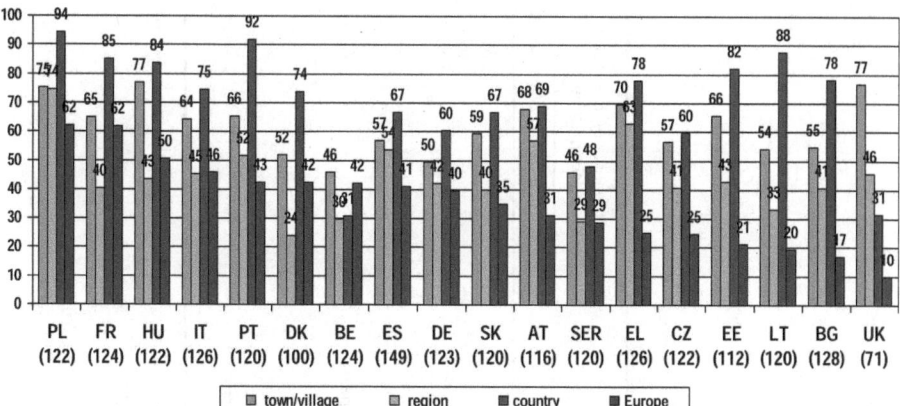

Notes: Cramer's V for attachment (from very attached (5) to not at all (1): 0.142*** (town/village); 0.167*** (region); 0.261*** (country); 0.218*** (EU)) (***: $p < 0.01$).
AT: Austria, BE: Belgium, BG: Bulgaria, CZ: Czech Republic, DK: Denmark, EE: Estonia, FR: France, DE: Germany, EL: Greece, HU: Hungary, IT: Italy, LT: Lithuania, PL: Poland, PT: Portugal, SER: Serbia, SK: Slovakia, ES: Spain, UK: United Kingdom.

FIGURE 3. ATTACHMENT TO DIFFERENT TERRITORIAL LEVELS BY COUNTRY (% OF 'VERY ATTACHED')

Underlying structures of identification

In order to explore the relation between the content and structuring of dimensions of identification with the nation and with Europe we carried out a principal component analysis.[3] The analysis presented here was carried out on the whole sample including all countries and all items of the identification question-set. Two main components, the primordial and decisional ones, can be identified in terms of European identification and, as noted above, there is an additional component, that is Christianity on the national level (see Table 1).

At first glance, on both national and European levels, the first component we used (see 'primordial' component) is very close to what is usually referred to as an ethno-cultural group of characteristics. Indeed, using 'to be born in a given country' or 'to have parents of a given nationality' as a precondition of belonging to a nation seems to lie at the very heart of an ethno-national approach. Interestingly, however, 'having respect for a country's cultural traditions' and 'mastering a country's language' are not tied to these items. Both on the national and the European levels they are tied to citizenship and subjective civic will in the second component (see 'decisional' component). This implies that ethno-cultural as opposed to civic aspects of

---

[3]The questions used were asked on a 1–4 ordinal scale and this compelled us to make a methodological compromise as principal component analysis would require data measured on an interval scale. However, results were straightforward to interpret and all the statistical measures of reliability (Bartlett's test of sphericity and the Kaiser–Meyer–Olin statistic) of the analysis were suitable enough. Compared to other methods we could have chosen (such as cluster analysis) principal component analysis has the advantage that it provides us with individual factor scores which can be used for further analysis. Other scholars have used this methodology for the same purposes with similar conditions, see Bruter (2004), Haller (2003) and Carey (2002).

TABLE 1
COMPONENTS OF BEING TRUE NATIONAL/EUROPEAN (FACTOR LOADINGS)*

	Components of national identification				Components of European identification	
	Primordial	Decisional	To be a Christian		Primordial	Decisional
Variance explained	18.8%	21.9%	12.9%		22.9%	22.6%
To feel (national)		0.653		To feel European		0.699
To share (country) cultural traditions		0.641		To share European cultural traditions		0.589
To master the language(s) of the country		0.593		To master a European language		0.555
To respect the (national) laws and institutions		0.526		To respect the European Union's laws and institutions		0.627
To be a (country) citizen	0.853					
To be born in (country)	0.821	0.519		To be born in Europe	0.855	
To have (national) parents				To have European parents	0.869	
To be a Christian			0.917	To be a Christian	0.296	

Notes: Extraction method: principal component analysis, KMO-test: 0.656 (national) and 0.57 (European). Rotation method: varimax with Kaiser normalisation. Factor loadings below 0.3 are left blank.

identification require some qualification. In our interpretation, based on the principal component analysis, the first component refers to essential dimensions that are not chosen and cannot be influenced by the individual; they are established by birth and thus cannot be changed. These dimensions are by their very nature primordial ones. The other component regroup dimensions that may rely on an individual's decisions—either based on rational or emotional factors. We shall call this component 'decisional'. We prefer to use the distinction between primordial and decisional instead of that between ascribed and achieved because they are more precise. Moreover, achievement sounds artificial in identification processes: components that are concerned with sharing cultural traditions or respecting laws and norms have little to do with achievement. Also, one can decide to learn a language, to share cultural traditions, ask for citizenship and respect laws and norms but cannot decide where and to whom she is born. The decisional component contains the most important elements of cultural and civic components as opposed to the primordial one. Naturally, to be born in a country and to have national parents are closely tied in a principal component analysis, but the fact that the other ethno-cultural components are more closely related to civic dimensions than to the primordial ones seems to be important: the basic difference is not between ethno-cultural and civic, but between primordial and the rest.

To be a Christian represents a special case among the different elements of identification. In terms of national identification it plays an important role but it is separate from either primordial or decisional components (see 'to be a Christian' component). In the case of European identification its role is less important compared to the other elements of identification; however, it appears to be loosely attached to the primordial components.[4]

Thus we argue that the basic difference in conceiving collective identities does not lie between civic and cultural approaches among European elites. Civic and cultural components constitute together a group that is distinct from the components that are primordial in collective identity. These findings are rather in line with what Habermas and Bruter called active and passive aspects of identification (Habermas 1998; Bruter 2005) or what Haller referred to as achieved and ascribed components (Haller 2003).

When the analysis is pursued for each country separately the results show a greater variety both in terms of national and European identification components. Still, the primordial components of both national and European identification seem to be stable across countries. Regarding the components of identification with Europe, the content of the components is similar to the above findings. Interestingly, the importance of European cultural traditions is connected to the primordial components for Lithuanian, British and Italian elites only.

When looking at country specificities of the average of individual factor scores (ANOVA analysis) on the original overall components it is confirmed that there are significant differences among them. In the case of national identification the primordial components are especially important for the elites of some East European

---

[4]According to its very low correspondence with the factor structure of European identification, 'to be a Christian' could be left out of the analysis. However, in order to maintain comparability with factors of national identification we have decided to keep it.

and Mediterranean countries. For some of these (Bulgaria, Estonia, Poland, Greece and Portugal) the decisional components are also relatively more important than for the others. On the other hand German, Austrian, Spanish and Belgian elites attribute less importance to any of these components than to the others (see Figure 4).

In the case of the components of European identification, similarly to national identification, Estonian and Polish elites perceive primordial components as being important. German, French and Danish elites think the same, although they thought differently in the case of national identification. In contrast, Austrian, Czech, Lithuanian and Spanish elites attribute less importance to primordial components regarding European identification, just like their Serbian, Bulgarian and Italian counterparts. The previous group is differentiated from the latter by the decisional components. The Slovak and Czech elites' national identification proved to be very much in line, but they show differences in how they conceive the structuring components of Europeanness. Czech elites attribute below-average importance while Slovakians attribute above-average importance both to primordial and decisional components. Understandably, there are further differences concerning the Christian component: while it is around average in the case of Slovakia, it is less important for the Czech elites than for other European elites when it comes to national self-definition.

Overall, some of the East European (for example Polish, Hungarian and Estonian) elites attribute more importance to primordial components both in the case of national and European identification than other elites. Primordialism has low importance with respect to both national and European identification among Austrian and Spanish elites. Another remarkable phenomenon at this point is that French and German elites attribute below-average importance to primordial components when national identification is taken into account but it is not the case concerning their European identification. These two national elites, of crucial importance from the perspective of European integration, seem to reject primordialism in terms of national identity, but they subscribe to primordial identification criteria when thinking about European identity, at least in comparison with the average of the elites. The same is true for the Danish elite, while the Bulgarian and Lithuanian elites on the other hand, attribute importance to primordial aspects in the case of national, but not in European identification.

Explanations of pragmatic attitudes towards the EU

After having described the pragmatic and symbolic aspects of support for European integration we attempt to explore how these aspects are interconnected with each other and what country groups can be identified in this context. We also try to provide some individual-level explanations for the different aspects of the support, controlling for country characteristics.

To display the inter-relation between the different measures of support for the integration process we have used multiple correspondence analysis (MCA). This is a descriptive method that helps to visualise the structure and inter-relation of the variables (Benzécri 1973). MCA is especially suitable for the analysis of categorical variables; thus its use is suitable here because all the variables included are categorical

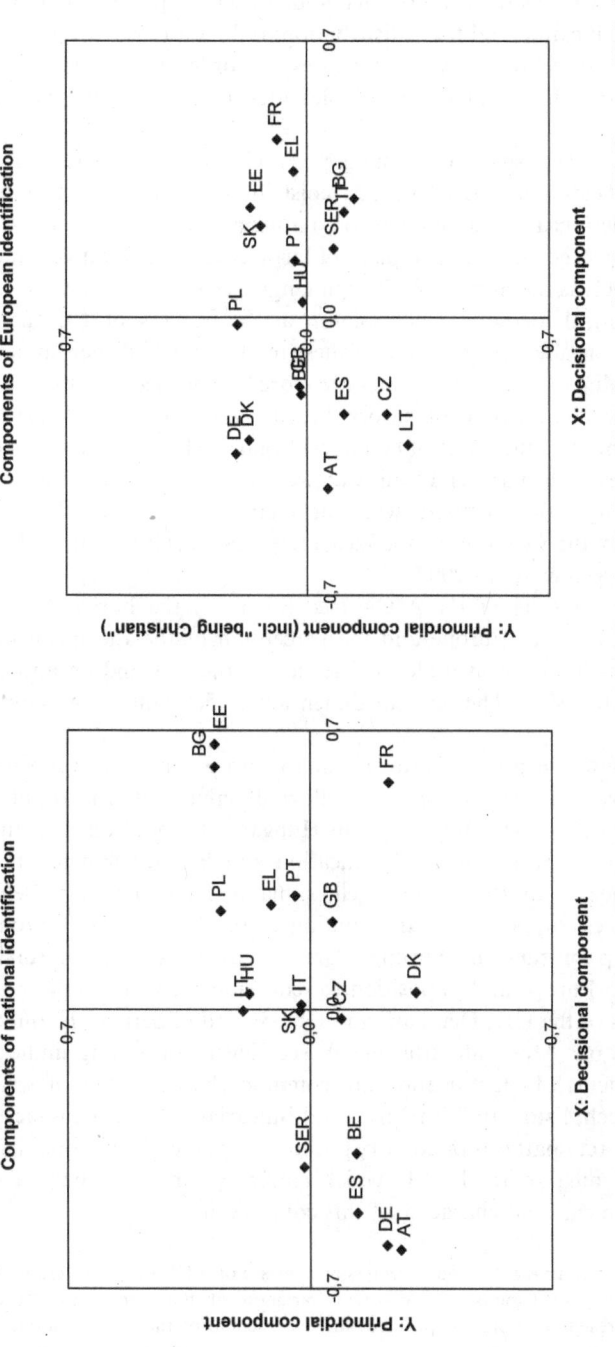

FIGURE 4. IMPORTANCE OF THE DIFFERENT COMPONENTS OF NATIONAL AND EUROPEAN IDENTIFICATION BY COUNTRIES

Notes: AT: Austria, BE: Belgium, BG: Bulgaria, CZ: Czech Republic, DK: Denmark, EE: Estonia, FR: France, DE: Germany, EL: Greece, HU: Hungary, IT: Italy, LT: Lithuania, PL: Poland, PT: Portugal, SER: Serbia, SK: Slovakia, ES: Spain, UK: United Kingdom. Maps show the place of the countries in the factor space based on the average of the individual factor scores.

ones. Attachment to Europe has three categories—very attached, somewhat attached and not attached—whereas the components of identification presented in the previous part—European unification and tax redistribution to the European level—are recoded to above average or below average categories. In order to see which individual components have an influence on these variables, logistic regression will be used on the same variables.[5]

Two models are to be tested corresponding to each one of the dependent variables of support for unification and EU-level tax redistribution. As explanatory factors we test the effect of identification components and attachment as well as of demographic characteristics such as gender, age and place of birth; elite type; cultural characteristics and experiences such as the number of foreign languages spoken and whether one has lived abroad; political ideology; and opinion about benefits of EU membership. Education-related variables were left out of these models, because their impact proved to be insignificant due to the fact that elites are more homogeneous in this respect than the general public. As these explanatory factors might have a different impact according to the country, the effect of country is controlled for by including countries as dummy variables in the models. In this way we can control for the effect of country specificities, although this method will not enable us to provide any further explanation on why the variation of the measured aspects is different in the different countries (Steenbergen & Jones 2002).

According to the results of the MCA (see Figure 5) the horizontal dimension explains the attachment to Europe and the perception of the European unification process with a pro-European attitude on one side of the axis and an anti-European attitude on the other side. The vertical dimension is determined by supranational redistribution.

Overall, the different aspects of attachment to Europe are rather consistent with each other. Different countries seem to follow different patterns of attachment, however. Elites in France, Poland, Italy and Hungary are more open to the idea of strengthening unification, and their identification and EU attachment are built on decisional components. Another group of elites, mainly from Germany, Belgium and the Iberian countries, support tax redistribution to the EU and unification and are unsympathetic to primordialism. Putting a greater emphasis on primordialism, low level attachment to Europe and opposition to redistributing taxes to the EU is more typical of the elites of the UK, Denmark and Greece, and of Serbia, the only non-EU country in the sample. Moderate attachment, scepticism concerning unification and decisional components of identification are common characteristics of some of the post-socialist—Czech, Estonian, Lithuanian and Bulgarian—elites. Thus, according to the MCA four different patterns or country groups can be identified along the different dimensions of the relation to the EU which confirms our preliminary assumption about the multi-dimensional character of this connection.

[5]Logistic regression, contrary to linear regression, does not suppose a structure behind the observations and does not suppose the constant variation of the error term. However, the interpretation of the results is more complicated—the exponential of the regression coefficients are to be interpreted as odds of the probability of occurrence as opposed to the probability of non-occurrence of the dependent variable. Logistic regression estimates the regression coefficients using maximum likelihood estimation.

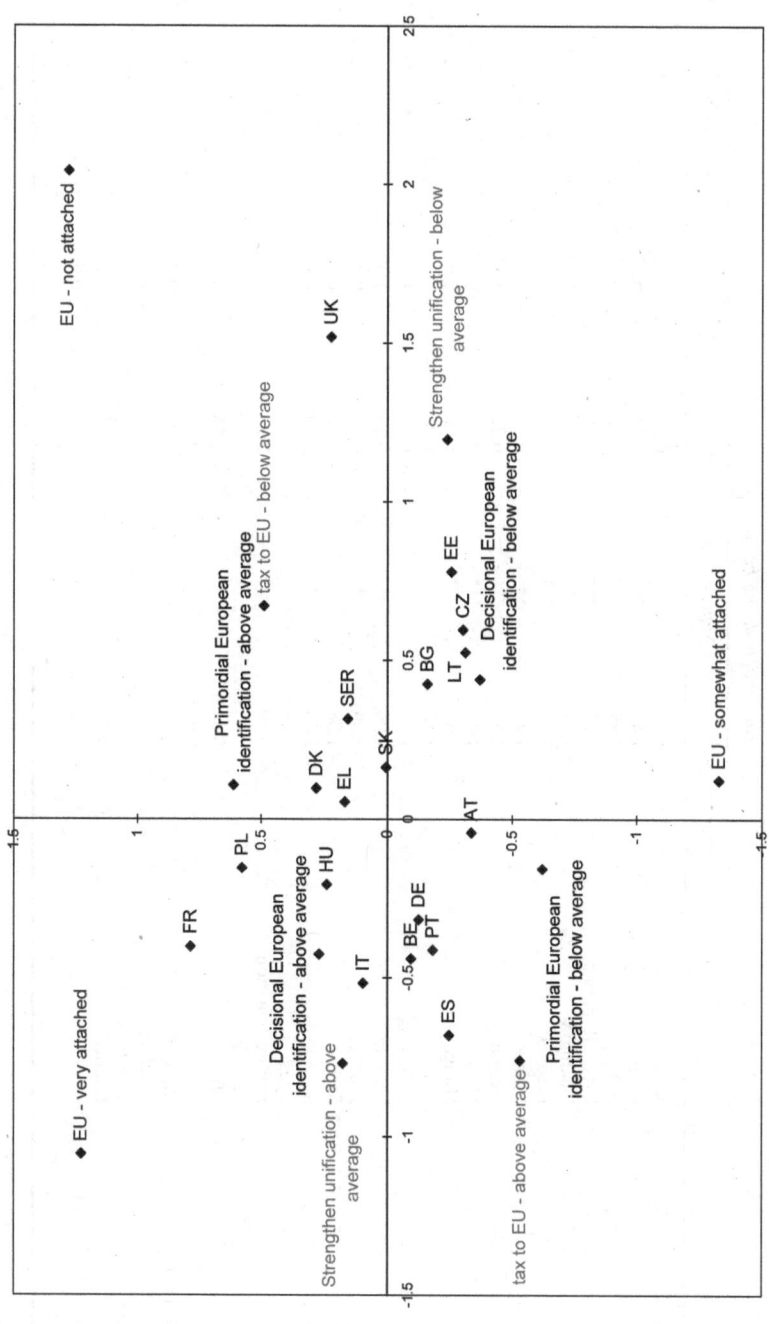

FIGURE 5. DIFFERENT ASPECTS OF SUPPORT FOR THE EU AND FOR EACH COUNTRY (RESULTS OF A MULTIPLE CORRESPONDENCE ANALYSIS)

Notes: AT: Austria, BE: Belgium, BG: Bulgaria, CZ: Czech Republic, DK: Denmark, EE: Estonia, FR: France, DE: Germany, EL: Greece, HU: Hungary, IT: Italy, LT: Lithuania, PL: Poland, PT: Portugal, SER: Serbia, SK: Slovakia, ES: Spain, UK: United Kingdom.

TABLE 2
LOGISTIC REGRESSION MODELS

		Model 1			Model 2		
		Unification should be strengthened			Tax redistribution on EU-level		
		B	Significance	Exp (B)	B	Significance	Exp (B)
Country	Austria	−1.46	***	0.23	−0.53	**	0.59
	Belgium	−1.42	***	0.24	0.11		1.11
	Bulgaria	−1.88	***	0.15	−0.97	***	0.38
	Czech Republic	−2.55	***	0.08	−0.61	**	0.54
	Denmark	−1.64	***	0.19	−1.13	***	0.32
	Estonia	−3.80	***	0.02	−1.46	***	0.23
	France	−1.40	***	0.25	−1.19	***	0.30
	Germany	−1.51	***	0.22	−0.11		0.89
	Greece	−1.03	***	0.36	−0.79	***	0.46
	Hungary	−1.83	***	0.16	−0.61	**	0.54
	Italy	−1.36	***	0.26	−0.26		0.77
	Lithuania	−1.60	***	0.20	−1.08	***	0.34
	Poland	−2.06	***	0.13	−1.37	***	0.25
	Portugal	−1.99	***	0.14	−0.29		0.75
	Serbia	−1.88	***	0.15	−0.78	***	0.46
	Slovakia	−2.43	***	0.09	−0.47	*	0.63
	Spain						
	United Kingdom	−3.40	***	0.03	−1.35	***	0.26
Gender	Female						
	Male	0.04		1.05	0.04		1.05
Age		−0.01	*	0.99	−0.01		0.99
Place of birth	Big city	−0.07		0.93	−0.03		0.97
	Small town						
Elite type	Economic						
	Political	−0.16		0.85	−0.22	*	0.80
Number of languages spoken		0.09		1.09	−0.02		0.98

(continued)

TABLE 2
(Continued)

| | | Model 1 | | | Model 2 | | |
| | | Unification should be strengthened | | | Tax redistribution on EU-level | | |
		B	Significance	Exp (B)	B	Significance	Exp (B)
Lived abroad		0.08		1.09	−0.16		0.85
Political ideology	Centre						
	Left	0.26	*	1.30	−0.04		0.96
	Right	−0.18		0.83	−0.28	**	0.76
Country has benefited from EU membership		0.79	***	2.20	0.83	***	2.30
Attachment to Europe	Very attached	1.07	***	2.91	0.37	**	1.45
	Somewhat attached	0.25		1.28	0.43	***	1.53
	Not attached						
Components of being national	Decisional component	−0.13	**	0.88	−0.07		0.93
	Primordial component	−0.01		0.99	0.02		1.02
	To be Christian component	0.03		1.03	0.04		1.04
Components of being European	Primordial component	−0.04		0.96	−0.05		0.95
	Decisional component	0.15	**	1.16	0.09		1.09
Constant		1.43	***	4.19	0.10		1.11
Correct prediction (%)		70.1			62.9		
Nagelkerke R^2		0.24			0.11		
R^2_{LA}		0.12			0.034		
Adj. R^2		0.19			0.08		
N		1,795			1,742		

Notes: Significance: *** < 0.01, ** < 0.05, * < 0.1.
Reference category in italic.

The regression models where the factors of influence on pragmatic support for integration are analysed also demonstrate that country characteristics have an important effect (see Table 2). The results of these regression models reconfirm our previous conclusions regarding the country differences as shown in the MCA map. In terms of tax distribution, Spanish elites share a similar pattern with Portuguese, Italian, German and Belgian elites while Estonian, Lithuanian, British, French and Danish elites would allocate significantly less tax money to the European level. When it comes to the perception of the European unification process, Spanish elites show a significantly more positive attitude than all other elites. However, here again, Estonian and British elites show the least sympathy for Europe.

Demographic explanatory variables such as gender, age and place of birth have no important influence. Elite type has a significant effect in case of tax redistribution: national political elites support the redistribution of taxes for the European level to a lesser degree than economic elites. This could be a sign of unwillingness on the part of political elites to give up some of the resources that they dispose of.

As opposed to cultural resources such as foreign languages and international experience, political ideology does have a significant effect in the models: other things being equal left-wing views are associated with significantly higher support for unification while a right-wing orientation coincides with below-average support for redistribution of resources to the EU. As for the effect of symbolic factors, attachment to Europe had a highly positive impact: strong attachment to Europe made it significantly more likely to show a positive attitude towards European unification, and being either very or somewhat attached to Europe meant that higher tax share was attributed to that level. The components of identification had no effect on views on the redistribution of taxes to the EU. On the other hand, decisional components of national identification had a negative effect, whilst decisional components of European identification had a positive effect on general support of unification. Pragmatic attitudes towards the EU were interwoven with utilitarianism: the odds of attitudes to strengthen unification or delegate more taxes to the European level doubled in case someone perceived that a country has benefited from the EU membership.[6]

Conclusion

The objective of this essay has been to explore the pragmatic and symbolic aspects of elites' views about European integration. By symbolic aspects we mean how elites conceived their identification and attachment to different territorial levels while pragmatic aspects include the general support for unification and level of supranational redistribution. We described these aspects and analysed the different components of national and European identification in more detail. We were interested in how these variables were connected to each other, assuming that the

---

[6]It should be noted that the logistic regression models presented here do not have a very high explanatory force in explaining between 8% and 19% of the total variance (adjusted R-square), the proportion of explained variance being lowest in the case of the tax redistribution. This implies that although the explanatory variables are significant, other exogenous factors might play a role.

relation to Europe is multi-dimensional where the different dimensions can generate different attitudes. We also provided models of how symbolic and pragmatic aspects are connected if we control for countries as well as for the cultural resources of elites.

Our findings in some respects modify while in other respects enrich the existing literature on EU integration. First, when exploring the different components of identification we found two main components both at the national and the European levels. We called these two components primordial and decisional where the primordial items referred to the origins of parents and the location of birthplace. These aspects have been labelled as inherited, passive or ascribed by other researchers. The decisional items included both civic and ethno-cultural factors of identification. In this respect our findings could not confirm the existence of separate civic and cultural factors of identification. These results are rather in line with former research findings referring to active and passive components.

Regarding the importance of these components we have found that primordial components play a relatively more important role both at the national and the European levels in the minds of some East European elites, for example, the Polish and Estonian elites, while they have low importance on both levels among Austrian and Spanish elites. The French and German elites attribute less importance to primordial components in the case of national identification whereas primordial components of European identification are relatively more important for them.

The analysis of symbolic and pragmatic aspects of views concerning the EU prove that they are consistent with each other. Still, we could identify different country groups that seem to follow different patterns of attachment. A group of elites of old member states is attached both in a symbolic and in a pragmatic way to Europe although their symbolic attachment was rather moderate. Another group of elites, particularly in the new member states and the UK, is against further European unification and less attached to Europe. And finally, a group consisting of French, Polish, Italian and Hungarian elites is more attached to Europe in a symbolic way but less open to a higher level of European redistribution. They are more open toward strengthening unification, and emphasise both the decisional and primordial components of identification.

In terms of explanatory models of how one relates to the EU overall we can state that the distinction between symbolic and pragmatic aspects was useful. Symbolic attachment had a significant positive impact on pragmatic EU support. Even moderate attachment coincides with higher EU-level tax redistribution as compared to non-attachment. Decisional identification components had a significant positive effect on the support of unification at the European level. However, those elites whose national identity-formation was built on decisional components were less ready to support unification. Primordial components of identity formation proved not to be significant after checking for country and cultural factors.

Demographic characteristics and cultural resources seem to play no role in the explanation of the pragmatic aspects. At the same time the difference between political and economic elites is obvious: national political elites are less open to European redistribution of taxes than the economic elite, which implies that political elites might be somewhat reluctant about the idea of delegating more budget resources to the EU level. We should note however that the tax share they feel fair to be allocated on the EU level hugely exceeds its actual share even in their case.

In terms of political self-categorisation right wing self-placement has a negative effect on attitudes to EU-level tax redistribution while a left orientation has a positive impact on support for unification. Our results at this point coincide with what Inglehart has suggested (1970, 1990).

Overall, the attitudes of European elites regarding the EU vary substantially both in individual and country terms. In our essay we mainly focused on the individual level even when we explored the multi-dimensional character of the attitudes towards the EU or different components of European identification. Other things being equal, envisaging Europeanness not in primordial, but in cultural and civic terms, coincides with higher level of European attachment and support for integration.

Corvinus University of Budapest

References

Anderson, B. (1983) *Imagined Communities. Reflections of the Origin and Spread of Nationalism* (London, Verso) (reference is to the 1991 edition).
Anderson, C. (1998) 'When in Doubt, Use Proxies', *Comparative Political Studies*, 31, 5, October, pp. 569–601.
Benzécri, J.-P. (1973) *L'analyse des correspondences* (Paris, Bordas).
Brubaker, R. (1996) *Nationalism Reframed. Nationhood and the National Question in the New Europe* (Cambridge, Cambridge University Press).
Brubaker, R. & Cooper, G. (2000) 'Beyond "Identity"', *Theory and Society*, 29, 1, pp. 1–47.
Bruter, M. (2004) 'Civic and Cultural Components of European Identity: A Pilot Model of Measurement of Citizens' Level of European Identity', in Hermann, R. K., Risse, T. & Brewer, M. B. (eds) (2004) *Transnational Identities: Becoming European in the EU* (Boulder, CO, Rowman and Littlefield Publishers), pp. 186–213.
Bruter, M. (2005) *Citizens of Europe? The Emergence of a Mass European Identity* (Basingstoke, Palgrave, Macmillan).
Carey, S. (2002) 'Undivided Loyalties. Is National Identity an Obstacle to European Integration?', *European Union Politics*, 3, 4, pp. 388–413.
Carrubba, C. J. (2001) 'The Electoral Connection in European Union Politics', *The Journal of Politics*, 63, 1, pp. 141–58.
Delanty, G. (1995) *Inventing Europe: Idea, Identity, Reality* (New York, St. Martin's Press).
Duchesne, S. & Frognier, A.-P. (1995) 'Is there a European Identity?', in Niedermayer, O. & Sinnott, R. (eds) (1995) *Public Opinion and International Governance* (Oxford, Oxford University Press).
European Commission (2006) *General Budget of the European Union for the Financial Year 2006. The Figures*, SEC(2006) 50 (Luxembourg, Office for Official Publications of the European Communities), available at: http://bookshop.europa.eu/eubookshop/download.action?fileName=KVAG06001ENC_002.pdf&eubphfUid=636023&catalogNbr=KV-AG-06-001-EN-C, accessed 18 May 2009.
Gabel, M. (1998) 'Public Support for European Integration: An Empirical Test of Five Theories', *The Journal of Politics*, 60, 2, pp. 333–54.
Gabel, M. & Anderson, C. (2001) *Exploring the European Demos (or Lack Thereof): The Structure of Citizen Attitudes and the European Political Space*, Jean Monnet Centre for European Studies (CEuS) Working Paper no. 2001/4, available at: http://www.monnet-centre.uni-bremen.de/pdf/wp/2001-4-Gabel-Anderson.pdf, accessed 4 April 2009.
Gellner, E. (1983) *Nations and Nationalism* (Oxford, Blackwell) (reference is to the 2006 edition).
Habermas, J. (1998) *The Inclusion of the Other—Studies in Political Theory* (Cambridge, Polity Press).
Haller, M. (2003) 'National Identity and National Pride in Europe. A Study in 9 Member States of the EU', in Nevola, G. (ed.) (2003) *Una patria per gli italiani: La quetione nazionale oggi* (Rome, Editore Coracci).
Haller, M. (2008) *European Integration as an Elite Process. The Failure of a Dream?* (New York, Routledge).

Hooghe, L. (2003) 'Europe Divided? Elites vs. Public Opinion on European Integration', *European Union Politics*, 4, 3, pp. 281–304.
Hooghe, L. & Marks, G. (2001) *Multi-Level Governance and European Integration* (Lanham, MD, Rowman and Littlefield).
Hooghe, L. & Marks, G. (2004) 'Does Identity or Economic Rationality Drive Public Opinion on European Integration?', *PS: Political Science & Politics*, 37, 3, pp. 415–20.
Horolets, A. (2003) 'Conceptualising Europe through Metaphors: A Way to Identity Formation?', *Polish Sociological Review*, 141, 1, pp. 115–29.
Inglehart, R. (1970) 'Cognitive Mobilization and European Identity', *Comparative Politics*, 3, 1, pp. 45–70.
Inglehart, R. (1990) *Culture Shift in Advanced Industrial Society* (Princeton, NJ, Princeton University Press).
Kritzinger, S. (2005) 'European Identity Building from the Perspective of Efficiency', *Comparative European Politics*, 3, 1, pp. 50–75.
Lupi, A. (2008) 'Tax Revenue in the EU', *Eurostat*, Statistics in Focus 47/2008, available at: http://www.eds-destatis.de/de/downloads/sif/sf_08_047.pdf, accessed 18 May 2009.
Opp, K-D. (2005) 'The EU and National Identifications', *Social Forces*, 84, 2, pp. 653–80.
Optem, S. A. R. L. (2001) *Perception of the European Union. A Qualitative Study of the Public's Attitudes to and Expectations of the European Union in the 15 Member States and in 9 Candidate Countries.* Summary of results, available at: http://ec.europa.eu/public_opinion/quali/ql_perceptions_summary_en.pdf, accessed 22 March 2009.
Ruiz Jimenez, A. M., Górniak, J. J., Kosic, A., Kiss, P. & Kandulla, M. (2004) 'European and National Identities in EU's Old and New Member States: Ethnic, Civic, Instrumental and Symbolic Components', *EIOP*, July, available at: http://eiop.or.at, accessed 4 April 2009.
Smith, A. (1992) 'National Identity and the Idea of European Unity', *International Affairs*, 68, 1, pp. 55–76.
Steenbergen, M. R. & Jones, B. S. (2002) 'Modelling Multilevel Data Structures', *American Journal of Political Science*, 46, 1, pp. 218–37.

National Discontent and EU Support in Central and Eastern Europe

GABRIELLA ILONSZKI

AS THE EUROPEAN UNION (EU) IS BEING CONSTRUCTED increasingly as a political entity more attention is being paid to how its institutional evolution corresponds to national demands. It is necessary to understand how political responsibility patterns are structured (MacMullen 1999), and moreover how they are related to accountability, policy and transparency considerations (Bovens 2007). We want to know whether the extension of direct democracy (Binzer Hobolt 2007) challenges the EU polity. Quite naturally, the question of how representation is taking place on the European level is a significant issue, and most importantly, how the party vote at the national level is being transposed to the European level (Reif & Schmitt 1980; Marsh 1998; Hix & Marsh 2006). All these issues and considerations are part of and belong to the democracy deficit debate and they influence the evaluation of European unification.

However, before the question of party stances and participatory or representation opportunities can be addressed, the first question to be asked concerns how the national polity affects citizens' views about the EU—and thus probably about the integration process itself. This essay argues that the opinion of voters of their home country's democratic performance will influence their views about the EU. It asks whether people are more pro-EU when they are satisfied with their national political environment or, on the contrary, whether they are more sceptical about the EU when their own country performs well according to democratic criteria. This question can be raised about citizens' views and indirectly about political elite views as well, and this leads in turn to a further question of whether citizens' and elite views are structured similarly or differently: do mass views and elite views about Europe correspond to the health of the national polity in the same way, or does the elite think more positively about the EU irrespective of the national political scene? Are the political elites in the countries whose performance is undervalued by their citizens more pro-EU?

Views and opinions about the EU appear in more than one dimension. In the broadest sense they express a general sympathy concerning integration. On a 'lower level' they reveal what people think about the operation and about the politics of the EU, and even more concretely they reflect views about EU policies. In the following we shall examine the impact of the national citizens' and elites' evaluations of the polity and the policy dimensions. This will help identify the sources of Euroscepticism or Europhilia as a function of the national polity. We will ask whether the evaluation of the national polity was transformed into general support or scepticism concerning the EU in the broadest sense without affecting the citizens' policy perspectives or whether the polity and policy dimensions are interrelated, so that favourable views about the integration process in general also imply policy consequences. The Intune database provides the opportunity to answer these questions: on the mass and the elite level it has many similar 'polity' and 'policy' questions and enables comparison between (almost) the same set of countries.[1]

The author's interest in this approach was prompted initially by the national and EU experiences of a particular country, Hungary. Formerly a front runner in the democratic transition and consolidation in East Central Europe, after her entry to the EU Hungary became one of the problem children in the European family. By 2006, declining economic performance and rising political dissatisfaction had led to turmoil, and since then even the democratic potentials of the regime have been questioned (Lengyel & Ilonszki forthcoming). However, while in the background of the turmoil a huge gap can be identified between the elite and the masses, and representative linkages between them are weak (Tóka 2006), according to survey data elite and mass views are surprisingly close in terms of positive EU support. For example, we can find only a 4% difference between mass and elite opinion about whether the European unification process should be further strengthened. This difference corresponds to the average difference in all surveyed countries, although it often hides huge mass–elite gaps within countries.

Hopefully the answers to the broad range of questions covered in this study will help reveal country variation as well as mass and elite differences about how EU support is structured on the basis of national satisfaction. In the first section we shall examine what people think about the performance of their own country using the Intune mass survey. Then we shall explore how these opinions are related to views about the EU both on the polity and policy levels. Finally, the relationship between the mass and elite views in these two respects will be examined with the help of the elite part of the Intune database. In the conclusion an attempt will be made to explain the variation between the selected countries.

Country performance—citizens' views

In this first section we shall examine how citizens evaluate their own country. This is based on the Intune mass survey. Four questions may be selected from the survey that reflect the respondents' views about their national political system (see Table 1). The first is a general opinion question: 'On the whole how satisfied are you with how democracy works in your country?' The next two questions are related to confidence in fundamental institutions, in the national government and in the national parliament. The fourth concerns opinions about decision makers: 'Are those who make decisions in your country competent people?' These four questions largely cover

---

[1]For further details of the project, see the editor's introduction to this collection.

the evaluation of a political system from its systemic attributes through to the roles played by concrete actors. Overall, the responses well describe the level of satisfaction with each particular country.

Since 2004 EU developments have often been analysed in terms of comparing old and new member states. Indeed, as Table 1 demonstrates the level of satisfaction—or rather dissatisfaction—with the national polity has a regional divide. The proportion of those who are very dissatisfied with how democracy works in their country is higher in the new member states than in the old ones. Also, having no confidence or a low level of confidence in the national government and in the national parliament are reported in higher proportions in these countries, and respondents also strongly disagree with the statement that decision makers in their country are competent people. But above and beyond this West–East regional divide an analysis of the regions' internal distribution might help us understand the connection between the national and the European more fully. Since the new member states are far from being identical in terms of their performance—whether it be political democracy or simply economic success—we can rightly expect differences in mass opinion in this respect.

On closer inspection two distinct groups can be identified among the new member states.[2] On the basis of three questions there is an obvious divide: respondents in Bulgaria, Hungary and Poland show higher levels of dissatisfaction with their national parliament, their national government and their decision makers than respondents in Estonia, Slovakia and Slovenia. Bulgaria and Hungary also stand out in their generally negative evaluation of their democracy. On this basis, we can identify two groups within Central and Eastern Europe (CEE): Bulgaria, Hungary and Poland on the one hand, and Estonia, Slovakia and Slovenia on the other. Table 1 presents fundamental information that strengthens this argument. First and foremost it includes the proportion of those who express the most dissatisfied views with respect to the four selected questions in the old member states and in the new member states, as well as in each country separately and in the two created country groups. In addition it shows the mean and the standard deviation figures for the responses so that one can observe not only the share of extreme dissatisfaction but the overall picture as well. For example, the average level of satisfaction with democracy is 2.74 (on a four-point scale, four being the lowest): that is people are rather dissatisfied both in the old and the new member states, with a very low level of standard deviation. Average dissatisfaction with leaders' competence also prevails, but in this respect standard deviation is higher in the new member states. Higher levels of standard deviation in the CEE countries concerning each question hint at more polarised opinions in that region. Overall, the table confirms a division between the old member states and the new member states and also provides a basis for a sub-regional typology.

We have to note the 'novelty' of the division since the literature on CEE tends to create different subgroups: the Visegrád four (Poland, Slovakia, the Czech Republic and Hungary), the three Baltic states, and the two latecomers (Bulgaria and Romania)—a divide not merely based on the EU perspective.

---

[2]At this stage we shall not examine the hypotheses in relation to the old member states, that is we shall not identify groups within them.

TABLE 1
LEVEL OF DISSATISFACTION WITH OWN COUNTRY'S POLITICAL PERFORMANCE OR SITUATION ON FOUR QUESTIONS (%)

Countries and country groupings	Question A		Question B		Question C		Question D	
	Very dissatisfied (%)	Means/standard deviation	No or low confidence (%)	Means/standard deviation	No or low confidence (%)	Means/standard deviation	Strongly disagree (%)	Means/standard deviation
Old member states	16.7	2.64/0.903	21.2	5.82/2.778	17.3	6.01/2.644	13.6	2.63/1.103
New member states	23.4	2.90/0.943	32.7	5.22/3.091	34.3	4.89/2.834	17.5	2.90/1.315
Bulgaria	41.8	3.22/0.914	54.4	3.73/2.772	58.3	3.44/2.640	25.1	3.15/1.397
Estonia	12.8	2.64/1.050	10.7	6.74/2.823	12.7	6.34/2.692	8.8	2.56/1.417
Hungary	32.8	2.99/0.918	32.0	5.41/3.273	37.8	4.47/2.584	19.1	2.88/1.326
Poland	17.9	2.89/0.860	55.1	3.70/2.736	54.5	3.72/2.651	29.4	3.26/1.165
Slovakia	13.2	2.77/0.830	19.3	6.02/2.730	19.5	5.77/2.554	7.7	2.82/1.231
Slovenia	22.3	2.78/0.930	25.6	5.63/2.916	24.1	5.49/2.633	15.9	2.74/1.216
Bulgaria–Hungary–Poland	30.9	3.07/0.916	47.2	4.28/3.043	50.2	3.88/2.660	24.5	3.10/1.309
Estonia–Slovakia–Slovenia	16.1	2.73/0.940	18.6	6.12/2.857	18.8	5.86/2.648	10.7	2.71/1.293
Total	19.4	2.74/0.928	25.8	5.58/2.924	24.1	5.56/2.777	15.2	2.74/1.200

Notes: A: 'On the whole how satisfied are you with how democracy works in your country?'—'very satisfied (1), somewhat satisfied (2), not satisfied (3), not at all satisfied (4) (percentage value of 'not at all satisfied' responses).
B: 'Please, tell me on a scale of 0 to 10 how much you personally trust the national government'—0 means that you do not trust it at all, 10 means complete trust (percentage value of responses in the 0–3 range).
C: 'Please, tell me on a scale of 0 to 10 how much you personally trust the national parliament'—0 means that you do not trust it all, 10 means complete trust (percentage value of responses in the 0–3 range).
D: 'Those who make decisions in my country are competent people who know what they are doing'—strongly agree (1), somewhat agree (2), somewhat disagree (3), strongly disagree (4) (percentage value of 'strongly disagree' responses).

Although the essay does not aim to dwell on the causes of this new division, some remarks are appropriate. First, political culture patterns might explain why views are expressed with a different force in different countries, as for example Hungarians are regarded as notoriously pessimistic. This is difficult to measure, however. More concrete political and economic explanations can be found in the background.

Although the question of how national economic performance influences voting behaviour remains controversial (Tilley *et al.* 2006), we can assume that even non-conscious voters or survey respondents react somehow to their country's performance. However, it would be misleading to base an analysis only on such facts as that Slovenia has been closest to EU average economic development figures from the very beginning of democratisation, Estonia has produced the highest level of economic growth in CEE in the past decade, and Slovakia—after a difficult start—became the second CEE country after Slovenia to introduce the Euro in January 2009. Indeed, we can find a connection between general economic tendencies and the level of dissatisfaction. Table 2 shows how GDP per capita figures have changed in the six countries as compared to the EU averages and CEE averages in two years, in 2001 and 2006. It indicates that Poland and Bulgaria have stood still and Hungarian development has slowed down in comparison to the regional dynamic.

In addition to economic performance political developments might also explain different levels of satisfaction with the home country. The political environment of the survey period was highly conflictual in Poland. Between the 2005 elections and the early elections of October 2007 the Law and Justice (*Prawo i Sprawiedliwość*) centre-right party was in power first in a minority government position and then in an alliance with two populist parties, the League of Polish Families (*Liga Polskich Rodzin*, LPR) and the Self-Defence Party (*Samoobrona Rzeczpospolitej Polskiej*, SRP). This period under the 'Kaczynszki twins' as the prime minister and the president, brought about political instability and public discontent. It is also indicative of the political atmosphere of this period that the leader of the SRP was fired and then hired and then again fired from the government as a result of corruption scandals. Public discontent with the governing parties can be demonstrated by the fact that eventually,

TABLE 2
GDP PER CAPITA AT PURCHASING POWER STANDARD, EU-25 = 100

	2001	2006
EU-25	100	100
EU-15	109.6	108
CEE-10	43.7	51.7
Bulgaria	28.0	34.2
Estonia	43.7	65.0
Hungary	56.9	63.6
Poland	46.1	51.1
Slovakia	48.7	59.4
Slovenia	73.9	83.6

Source: http://uninews.unicredito.it, accessed 15 December 2008.

at the early elections in 2007, the two populist parties were virtually eliminated and the Law and Justice Party also suffered severe losses.

As for Hungary, in addition to block politics full of hostilities between the conservative *Fidesz* and the centre-left Socialist Party, from the second part of 2006 the government was under pressure to resign due to the infamous speech by the socialist prime minister Gyurcsanyi in which he admitted 'telling lies' about the economic conditions of the country during the election campaign in 2006, and well before. As a result, the legitimacy of the system and confidence in government reached unprecedentedly low levels. In Bulgaria, the populist National Movement Simeon II (*Nacionalno Dviženie Simeon Vtori*) lost the 2005 election and an extreme nationalist and racist party (ATAKA, Coalition Attack (*Natsionalen Săyuz Ataka*)) was elected to parliament for the first time. All in all, Bulgaria's entry into the EU in January 2007 could not hide the fact that '... corruption, judicial inefficiency, a weak police force and strong organised crime continued to be real problems in Bulgaria' (Spirova 2007, p. 908).

In the other countries group politics was less tense. In Estonia government formation—first in 2005 and then in 2007—proved that political dividing lines can be crossed, and block politics does not necessarily prevail. The liberal Reform Party (*Eesti Reformierakond*) was in government with the leftist Centre Party (*Eesti Keskerakond*) and the agrarian People's Union (*Eestimaa Rahvaliit*), and when it maintained its position at the 2007 March elections its new coalition partners were the centre right Pro Patria (*Isamaaliit*) and Res Publica Union (*Erakond Res Publica*) as well as the Social Democrats (*Sotsiaaldemokraatlik Erakond*). In Slovenia, although the shift towards the centre right of 2004 brought several normative issues to the surface (from the role of direct democracy to media freedom) these were resolved within the environment of public debate, and by 2006 the government had succeeded in having the 'Partnership for Growth' programme accepted by almost all parliamentary parties (Fink-Hafner 2007). In Slovakia after the June 2006 elections a politically dubious coalition was formed by the winning Social Democracy (*Smer—sociálna demokracia*) in alliance with the extremist and xenophobic Slovak National Party (*Slovenská národná strana*, SNS) and Vladimír Meciar's People's Party (*Ľudová strana—Hnutie za demokratické Slovensko*). However, at the time of our survey the more confrontational and nationalistic political style of this government had not yet fully developed and the positive results of the former government were still being enjoyed.

Table 3 shows some of the indicators of good governance for the year 2007 according to the Worldwide Governance Indicators of the World Bank. These indicators are regularly developed on the basis of expert judgement in the given countries. The results largely coincide with the Intune mass data and thus further justify the creation of subgroups. Estonia and Slovenia can be grouped together on the basis of their positive scores on all five indicators while Poland and Bulgaria can be similarly grouped together at the opposite pole on the basis of their negative scores. Hungary and Slovakia are in-between these extreme groups: in terms of political stability and government effectiveness Slovakia lines up with Estonia and Slovenia while in terms of accountability, rule of law and control of corruption Hungary is better placed. In a similar way to the economic rankings, longer-term trends do matter however, and since Hungarian governance rankings have been worsening, at the time of writing (two years after the data in Table 3

TABLE 3
GOOD GOVERNANCE INDICATORS, PERCENTILE RANK (0–100), 2007

Governance indicator	Bulgaria	Estonia	Hungary	Poland	Slovakia	Slovenia
Voice and accountability	66.3	82.7	85.6	71.6	77.4	84.1
Political stability	61.1	69.7	67.8	66.8	80.3	84.1
Government effectiveness	59.2	84.8	73.5	67.3	76.8	83.4
Rule of law	51.4	83.8	72.9	59.0	60.6	75.2
Control of corruption	53.1	80.7	70.5	61.4	65.2	78.3

Source: Worldwide Governance Indicators, available at: www/info.worldbank.org, accessed 15 December 2008.

were collected), more critical views of the Hungarian political situation seem to be justified.

Overall, we can suggest that the level of satisfaction of the mass respondents may be explained for all countries by the economic performance of the country and for some countries by their political performance as well. The Bulgaria–Hungary–Poland group faced a politically more controversial environment and also more economic difficulties than the Estonia–Slovakia–Slovenia group around the survey period. This can be regarded as a sound starting point to connect a country's national performance with their citizens' views about the European Union.

EU support—polity and policy dimensions

How is satisfaction with the national polity reflected in the respondents' views concerning the EU, first in terms of their general opinion about the integration process and then in policy terms? Several studies warn that general survey questions, as opposed to more concrete questions, will bring forward different answers. For example, Schmitt and Thomassen (2000) found differences between the answers given by respondents on political and policy dimensions when they explored the positions of parties and their voters on EU matters. Differences between these two dimensions can be expected on the grounds that one describes a diffuse and the other a more specific support (Kopecky & Mudde 2002). Having these issues in mind it is worth exploring whether the level of national satisfaction has an impact on both the political and policy dimensions, and if so to what degree and in what direction.

Some differences between the CEE countries in terms of public attitudes about the EU were observed well before they entered the EU. Against a background of a general consensus that they should join the EU there was a clear '... variation between states in the scope of the debate on its implications' already from the second part of the 1990s (Grabbe & Hughes 1999, p. 201). After an initial period of very positive attitudes a general decline could be observed. At that time the Baltic countries were the least positive about EU membership while Poland and Romania were the most supportive. In the following we shall contend that this variation has been further enriched, among other things, by experiences within the national polity.

Political views

Let us first examine how the sub-regional divide is reflected in views on European integration in the broadest sense. The following question from the Intune survey provides an insight into the general evaluation of the European Union in each country: 'Has the integration process gone too far or should it be strengthened?'; this was measured on an 11-point scale (0–10). Table 4 shows different levels of support in which the 0–3 values, 4–6 values and 7–10 values are grouped together. Those who offered opinions in the 0–3 range obviously are not in favour of further integration, while those whose opinions were in the 7–10 range can be regarded as supporters of unification. The proportion of these answers is shown with respect to three country groups: the old member states, the Bulgaria–Hungary–Poland group where national discontent was highest and the Estonia–Slovakia–Slovenia group where it was low. The strength of the connection between country grouping and opinion about further unification is shown that it is significant at the 0.000 level with 0.063 Cramer's V value.

A similar approach was adopted in a recent study which is based on data for the period up until the 1999 elections to the European Parliament (Scheuer & van der Brug 2007). The same questions were used as in the Intune survey: 'On the whole are you very satisfied, fairly satisfied, not very satisfied or not at all satisfied with the way democracy works in your country?'; and more specifically, the degree of support for EU integration was measured by the score on a two item additive scale, asking whether 'integration has gone too far or should be strengthened'. In addition a further question was asked in the earlier survey: 'Do you think that your country's membership of the EU is a good thing, a bad thing or neither good nor bad?' Scheuer and van der Brug concluded that the data

> ... demonstrate(s) the existence of a spill-over between attitudes toward the national and European levels of governance. In general, attitudes toward the domestic and the European political system are not compensating each other: negative attitudes toward domestic politics do *not* result in positive ones toward the European system, or the other way round. (Scheuer & van der Brug 2007, p. 111, italics in original)

In addition it is claimed that the 'support for integration is positively affected by length of EU membership and by the recency of non-democratic experiences' (Scheuer & van der Brug 2007, p. 109).

TABLE 4
HAS UNIFICATION GONE TOO FAR OR SHOULD IT BE STRENGTHENED? MASS VIEWS (%)

Country group	Unification			
	Has gone too far (0–3)	*Middle scale (4–6)*	*Should be strengthened (7–10)*	*N*
Old member states	13.3	32.4	54.3	9,024
Bulgaria–Hungary–Poland	9.1	34.0	56.6	3,006
Estonia–Slovenia–Slovakia	13.0	38.3	48.7	3,100
Total	12.0	33.9	54.0	15,131

Because our data cover the new member states, all of which have a communist past, this gives an opportunity to control for length of EU membership as well as length of period under democratic rule. Does our analysis confirm a positive spill-over effect between the evaluation of the national polity and support for the European Union? The Intune findings apparently lead to different conclusions than the analysis of the pre-1999 period in the old member states. As Table 4 demonstrates, the two country groups identified above on the basis of different levels of national satisfaction evaluate the integration process differently: the worse they evaluate their national performance the more open their views are towards the EU polity. Respondents in Bulgaria–Hungary–Poland contained the lowest proportion who answered that the unification process has gone too far and the highest proportion who answered that unification should be strengthened. In contrast, national satisfaction complements lower levels of EU support: less than half of the respondents in Estonia–Slovenia–Slovakia express the opinion that unification should be strengthened. Thus, the new 'fault lines' (Zielonka & Mair 2002) observed above concerning evaluation of the national polity are reaffirmed by views about the EU. The more critical respondents are about their national polity, the more positive they seem to be about strengthening the unification process, at least in the CEE context.

Although personal group characteristics and positions also have an impact on what people think about integration, former studies show that overall it is rather system characteristics and not individual level independent variables that explain EU support (Scheuer & van der Brug 2007). Accordingly, systemic explanations, among which the status and evaluation of the national polity apparently play a role, deserve more attention.

Indeed, the above divide is confirmed by other systemic features. First, different perspectives on nationhood might explain at least some of the divide: Estonia, Slovakia and Slovenia are new nation states and their respondents might express less enthusiasm about strengthening integration because of their precious new statehood. In the other group, the countries' identity as a nation state was not directly threatened in the communist period. As we have seen, the actual differences in good governance indicators between Hungary and Slovakia are more modest than the respondents' evaluations. In these two cases different experiences of nation-building and state-building might have an impact on citizens' views, not only concerning European integration but also national self-evaluation.

The conclusion that there is a reciprocal connection between new statehood and support for integration is a different conclusion than had been envisaged previously about the impact of nationhood on integration. It had been claimed that

> for countries that are also building new nationhood as independent states, such as Slovakia, Slovenia and the Baltic States, acceptance by international organisations is often seen as an affirmation of their independence and sovereignty, as well as their success in transition. (Grabbe & Hughes 1999, p. 185)

The emphasis seems to have changed since then: having been accepted by the 'international organisations' national self-assurance now seems to be more important than enthusiasm about integration. The Intune dataset does not contain a mass survey for the Czech Republic—another old–new state—but the Czech elite survey does reveal levels of Eurosceptic views that are as high as those of the Estonia–Slovakia–Slovenia group.

There have been two main explanations given in the academic literature to explain support for or rejection of the EU: the utilitarian approach, which claims that directly expected gains (in our cases hopes in the face of national underperformance) will increase support for the EU (Gabel 2000); and the symbolic approach according to which ideological or symbolic factors, for example national sentiments, are similarly important (Hooghe & Marks 2005). It is interesting to note that these two approaches converge in our group divide.

In addition to national satisfaction and longevity of statehood still another systemic feature, that is party system characteristics, might also explain positive or negative views about the integration process. Is the party system also 'responsible' for variations in views concerning the EU? First of all, does it matter that parties are structured on the EU cleavage line, or that they place EU issues on the agenda?

The answer is not easy because cleavage lines, and the EU cleavage among them, are still in the process of formation in CEE. Initially, no EU cleavage prevailed among the parties at all (Lewis 2005), and for recent years it is more difficult than in Western Europe to diagnose the roots of the EU cleavage, for example to distinguish between 'economic and cultural opposition to integration ... [that is] defence and/or rejection of the European project on the basis of national sovereignty and national community or on the basis of its neoliberal character' (De Vries & Edwards 2009, p. 9). Nevertheless we contend that signs of the evolution of the EU cleavage can be observed. The mere existence of anti-integration or at least Eurosceptic parties indicates that an EU cleavage line does exist and has some impact on mass views, irrespective of whether this is confirmed by actual voting behaviour on either the national or the European level.

This approach is different from that of the rich party and election literature, which focuses on the linkage between the national and the European and the mass and the elite by analysing figures for the party identification of voters and their actual voting behaviour. In the old member states it was found that vote choice on the European level is influenced by the domestic concerns of voters (Reif & Schmitt 1980; van der Eijk & Franklin 1996); moreover, due to the second-order nature of the European elections, small and often anti-system and opposition parties tend to win in larger proportions (Marsh 1998). This literature claims that these tendencies, prevalent in the old member states, apparently are not present in the new member states: on average government parties do not perform worse at the European Parliament elections than at the national elections and even the impact of party size is not as robust as expected (Hix & Marsh 2006, p. 43 ff). While from the electoral perspective this conclusion is justified, from the perspective of the party system it has to be revisited.

Amongst the conditions in which cleavages are still being formed the mere presence of anti-EU parties deserves attention. We argue that even if anti-EU parties do not achieve much electoral success, they can be 'a decisive force in swaying popular opinion against Europe by mobilising the growing uncertainties about the future of European integration ...' (De Vries & Edwards 2009, p. 22). Having said that, are party system characteristics connected to the evaluation of European unification in a systematic way?

At the 2007 Bulgarian European Parliament elections, GERB (Citizens for European Development in Bulgaria, *Grazhdani za evropeysko razvitie na Balgariya*), a party which was established only at the end of 2006, won the largest proportion of the vote on an anti-EU basis; its anti-corruption, anti-crime and family values slogans also brought them votes. In Poland, the two extremist parties that have been already mentioned, the League of Polish Families and the Self Defence Party, managed to put the EU on the agenda (Markowski & Tucker 2005); and after gaining around 30% of the vote they sent 10 and six deputies respectively to the European Parliament (out of the 54 seats available). In Slovenia two anti-EU parties also succeeded in winning a seat in the European Parliament.

In contrast, in Hungary the anti-EU party was hardly heard in the campaign and did not have any electoral success (Bátory 2008). Also, in Slovakia, in the context of the lowest ever turnout for European Parliament elections (17%) and a low key campaign, the small anti-EU parties were unable to make any impact (Gyárfásová 2006). However, both in Estonia and Hungary soft Euroscepticism can be observed among the mainstream parties: the Centre Party and the *Fidesz*, respectively (Taggart & Szczerbiak 2008a). Thus, in terms of partisanship and political discourse concerning the EU the country groups are not homogenous. The EU cleavage is strongest in Poland and Bulgaria, two countries out of the three that are in favour of further integration and are also highly dissatisfied with their country's performance. Paradoxically, the presence and even some success of anti-EU parties does not inhibit general and above average support for European integration.

Overall therefore, we can claim that with respect to systemic explanations, citizens' views about European integration are strongly structured by national satisfaction, they are confirmed by the time of nation-state formation, and they are also connected—although more weakly—to the presence of an EU cleavage among the parties. This last observation has to be handled with care however, and can only be confirmed at a later date when the cleavage lines are fully settled in CEE.

The policy dimension

While systemic causes have clearly emerged to explain the general support for integration, can we find a similar connection in the policy field as well? Table 5 shows the proportion of respondents who are 'strongly in favour' that certain policies appear (or are reinforced) on the European Union level: a unified tax system for the EU, a common system of social security, a single European foreign policy and more help for EU regions in social or economic difficulties. The share of the 'strongly in favour' answers are shown according to the same country groups as used above, that is in the old member states and in the two sub-regional CEE country groups.

In each and every question the Bulgaria–Hungary–Poland group has the highest proportion of 'strongly in favour' answers. Thus already at first glance we can confirm that national discontent is positively connected to supporting policies on the EU level. Nevertheless, a more subtle analysis of the answers requires us to differentiate between the four policy areas. The first three—a unified tax system, a common social security system and more regional help—can be regarded as pragmatic issues, while the single

TABLE 5
SUPPORT FOR DIFFERENT POLICIES BY COUNTRY GROUPS (%)

Country group	Question A	Question B	Question C	Question D
Old members states	23.5	28.8	35.2	27.1
Bulgaria–Hungary–Poland	24.8	40.2	52.0	29.5
Estonia–Slovakia–Slovenia	18.0	30.4	48.8	28.4
Total	22.6	31.4	41.3	27.8

Notes: A: A unified tax system for the EU—strongly in favour, somewhat in favour, somewhat against, strongly against (percentage value of strongly in favour responses).
B: A common system of social security in the EU—strongly in favour, somewhat in favour, somewhat against, strongly against (percentage value of strongly in favour responses).
C: More help for EU regions in social or economic difficulties—strongly in favour, somewhat in favour, somewhat against, strongly against (percentage value of strongly in favour responses).
D: A single European foreign policy towards other countries—strongly in favour, somewhat in favour, somewhat against, strongly against (percentage value of strongly in favour responses).

European foreign policy question has strategic implications about the direction of integration. Does the group divide prevail in all policy fields to the same degree?

The difference between the two CEE country groups is highest concerning the support for a common social security system and a unified tax system. National discontent goes hand in hand with a higher level of support of these policies on the EU level. Although more than 50% of respondents in the Bulgaria–Hungary–Poland group are also strongly in favour of more regional support, in this case the divide sharpens between the old member states on the one hand and the two groups of the new member states on the other hand. The distribution of the answers to these questions provides arguments for the utilitarian understanding of EU support: it is national interests and regional interests that seem to structure the answers the most. The fourth strategic policy question creates a different image. The share of supportive answers about a single European foreign policy is very close in the three country groups. In this case, broader and not concrete policy considerations are at stake: for example how respondents understand European identity or what they think about potential threats against Europe.

Altogether we can conclude that the country group divide is consequential in the policy field but it depends on the nature of the policy issue. The group division built on the level of national satisfaction makes most sense in the pragmatic policy questions. National discontent increases the level of general support of integration as well as the demand that pragmatic policies are dealt with on the European level.

Comparison of mass and elite views

In this section we shall compare mass and elite views on European integration on the basis of the above findings. Does the level of national satisfaction have an impact on elite views as well, and if so in what direction? Are elite and mass views closer to each other concerning EU issues when the country is thought to perform well, or is this condition irrelevant? Does satisfaction with the domestic scene bring mass and elite views closer to each other or pull them apart?

These questions are interesting at least for two reasons. From the 'European' perspective their relevance flows from the fact that elites have always been found to be more supportive of integration than citizens. However, is this the case irrespective of region, and more importantly, irrespective of country performance? From the theoretical perspective the question is important because the distance between elite and mass responses tells us about the representative linkage. We can assume that if these views are closely linked this strengthens representation on the national level and might also contribute to the success of the European project.

The Intune elite survey contains a representative sample of 80 political elite members (members of national parliaments) in addition to 40 economic elite members in each country, but only the political elite answers are used in the analysis here because we wish to explore how their views are directly connected to mass views via the representative linkage. Since Slovenia is not included in the elite part of the survey it has been excluded from the further steps of the comparative analysis. In a rerun of all the previous tables without Slovenia the statistical correlations remain valid however, and so the group division does not have to be revised. In the following we shall analyse the connections between mass and elite views in the two groups: Bulgaria–Hungary–Poland on the one hand and Estonia–Slovakia on the other.

Table 6 uses the same question as before in Table 4, 'Has the integration process gone too far or should it be strengthened?' to show the views of mass respondents and political elite respondents in terms of their broad support for the EU in terms of polity. The table contains the two 'extreme' views: those in the 0–3 range on one side and in the 7–10 range on the other, on a 0–10 point scale.

With respect to the old member states the figures confirm the findings of previous studies, namely that the elites are more supportive of the integration process than the public. This is confirmed both in the negative and the positive sense: the proportion of those who think that unification has gone too far is higher among the mass respondents while the proportion of those who support unification is higher among the elite respondents.

CEE shows a different picture however. Citizens' and politicians' views correspond most in the countries that underperform economically and politically, and where the

TABLE 6
'Has Unification Gone Too Far or Should it be Strengthened?'—Elite and Mass Views Compared (%)

Country group	Unification			
	Has gone too far (0–3)		Should be strengthened (7–10)	
	Mass	Elite	Mass	Elite
Old member states	13.3	10.5	54.3	61.5
Bulgaria–Hungary–Poland	12.2	13.1	58.7	54.7
Estonia–Slovakia	7.4	19.5	47.8	36.2
Total	11.9	12.0	54.3	57.5

public is the most dissatisfied. There is merely a 1% difference in the least supportive answers concerning integration, and a 4% difference in the most supportive answers between mass and elite views. Moreover, the mass respondents are in favour of further unification in somewhat higher proportions than the elite. Interestingly, this reverse connection prevails in the Estonia–Slovakia group as well: one fifth of the elite members in these two countries think that unification has gone too far and one third think that it should be strengthened, while in the mass answers the same figures are one in 12 think that unification has gone too far and one in two think that it should be strengthened. The countries that perform well on the national level show lower levels of Europhilia, the views between the elite and the public are further apart with respect to the EU, and the elite are considerably more Eurosceptic than the citizens. Overall, the Bulgaria–Hungary–Poland group is closer to the figures for the old member states than Estonia and Slovakia; they are more supportive of unification and the representative linkage is also tighter there.

Our earlier conclusions, namely that national performance will have an impact on views concerning the EU and that some pragmatic—or as it is more often called utilitarian—considerations play a role in this, now are confirmed on the elite level. The exceptionally high level of Euroscepticism among the elite answers in the Estonia–Slovakia group strengthens the opinion that new statehood also has a decisive impact on EU views. The reverse connection between mass and elite views in both CEE regions, that the public is more pro-integration than the elite, might give a new impetus to the widely debated issue in the academic literature over whether the formation of views on the EU is a top down or a bottom up process. Probably this finding will add to a recently demonstrated argument that—in terms of party elites and their supporters—'these linkages run in both directions: party supporters influence elites and the reverse is also true' (Steenbergen *et al.* 2007, p. 29). It would go beyond the space limitations of this essay to attempt to reveal some further causes of this reverse connection. However, further research should clarify, for example, the potential impact of the level of information, that is how support for the EU or rejection of it is influenced by knowledge about the EU.

Was the connection between mass and elite views established in the same way in the more concrete policy questions as well? In Table 7 the same questions are applied as in Table 5, the percentage figures show the share of those who are 'strongly in favour' of certain policies on the EU level in the given country groups.

In the more pragmatic policy areas (a unified tax system and a common system of social security in the EU) in the Bulgaria–Hungary–Poland group, mass and elite respondents are again very close to each other with a mere 1% difference or less between them. In Estonia and Slovakia mass respondents are more supportive of these policies than the elite, which is not surprising in the face of Table 6. The elite support of these policies is exceptionally low in Estonia and Slovakia, both in comparison to the 'dissatisfied' CEE group and to the old member states. In general, the elites in the old member states 'keep to the standards', that is, they are more supportive of integration than the citizens in the realm of policies.

We have seen that support for more help to EU regions in social and economic difficulties (question C) (see Tables 5 and 7) was very high among the mass respondents in the new member states irrespective of the sub-regional divide. This is

TABLE 7
SUPPORT FOR DIFFERENT POLICIES—ELITE AND MASS VIEWS COMPARED (%)

Country group/question	Question A		Question B		Question C		Question D	
	Mass	Elite	Mass	Elite	Mass	Elite	Mass	Elite
Old member states	23.5	28.3	28.8	31.5	35.2	57.0	27.1	53.4
Bulgaria–Hungary–Poland	24.8	23.8	40.2	40.4	52.0	71.0	29.5	51.7
Estonia–Slovakia	14.0	6.7	28.3	18.7	42.7	51.3	27.3	51.3
Total	22.4	25.2	31.1	31.6	39.9	58.8	27.6	52.9

Notes: A: A unified tax system for the EU—strongly in favour.
B: A common system of social security in the EU—strongly in favour.
C: More help for EU regions in social or economic difficulties—strongly in favour.
D: A single European foreign policy towards other countries—strongly in favour.

further strengthened by the elite answers in the Bulgaria–Hungary–Poland group: somewhat more than half of the mass respondents and nearly three-quarters of the elite respondents in these countries are strong supporters of this policy, which would clearly serve the interest of countries that are falling behind in their economic performance. In the final question concerning a single European foreign policy (question D) (see Tables 5 and 7) the answers are very similar among the public and among the elite respondents irrespective of the country group: the elite are much more in favour of this strategic area. It seems that in this respect, where the status of the national polity might be at stake—particularly in the case of countries with problematic national sovereignty—strategic advantages rooted in a common foreign policy are stronger than more pragmatic policy considerations.

Conclusions

The future of European integration increasingly depends on the views and opinions of its citizens and therefore it is imperative to identify the sources behind attitudes of support or rejection of the EU. The Intune database has provided evidence that beyond the divide between the old and new member states regional groupings of countries can be identified with respect to EU support. Our hypothesis was that systemic characteristics will explain the variation. Foremost, it has been found that satisfaction with the national polity has a strong explanatory force. In CEE the mass respondents in the countries that show the highest level of national discontent tend to support European integration both in general terms and in a more concrete policy perspective. In contrast, countries with better national performance tend to be more Eurosceptic. This finding in the CEE context is different from what has been found about old member states (Scheuer & van der Brug 2007). We have also found a reverse connection between recent state formation and an absent or weak EU cleavage on the one hand and EU support on the other. New–old states tend to be more Eurosceptic, as well as those where the EU cleavage is relatively weak.

These findings on the mass level have been largely confirmed by the elite views in the given countries. On the elite level the divide between old and new member states and, within the latter group, satisfaction with the national polity seems to matter most. We have found most support for the EU among the elite in the country group where satisfaction with the national polity was low, and also, it was in these cases that the mass and elite views were closest to each other. This is paradoxical because their underperformance is explained by national commentators—and also by mass respondents—partly by the weakness of the representative linkage between the elite and the masses. This is certainly not the case concerning the European project. A utilitarian approach might explain why the mass and elite respondents in these countries think in similarly positive terms about integration but, in contrast, we cannot find evidence of a 'spillover' of national satisfaction to satisfaction with the EU. However, the utilitarian explanation is confirmed by the fact that similar tendencies can be observed in the polity and policy dimensions.

Some connection between the evaluation of one's country and EU support has been found in some old member states, particularly comparing Germany and France (Milner 2000). Our analysis also supports a way of thinking about the EU in which cultural and societal patterns (national sentiments, historical experiences about independence or lack of it, and political culture) are considered. EU developments cannot be possibly understood without broader and deeper knowledge of the national level. The current crisis should provoke further questions about the connection between the national and the European levels. Would it strengthen the view that the integration process might be an escape route? It remains questionable. In the light of the strong impact of national conditions on support or rejection of the EU, national solutions, including economic protectionism might also emerge as new–old strategies. Nevertheless, small or medium size countries are rarely in a position to survive difficult times by themselves. We strongly contend that the national context does matter in understanding the views about the EU and the elite and mass views alike will decide whether unification has gone too far or if it should be strengthened.

Corvinus University of Budapest

References

Bale, T. & van Biezen, I. (eds) (2007) 'Political Data Yearbook 2006', *European Journal of Political Research*, 46, 7–8.
Bátory, Á. (2008) 'Euroscpetism in the Hungarian Party System. Voices from the Wilderness?', in Taggart, P. & Szczerbiak A. (eds) (2008b).
Binzer Hobolt, S. (2007) 'Taking Cues on Europe? Voter Competence and Party Endorsements in Referendums on European Integration', *European Journal of Political Research*, 46, 2.
Bovens, M. (2007) 'New Forms of Accountability and EU-Governance', *Comparative European Politics*, 5, 1, pp. 104–20.
De Vries, C. E. & Edwards, E. E. (2009) 'Taking Europe to Its Extremes: Extremist Parties and Public Euroscepticism', *Party Politics*, 15, 1.
Fink-Hafner, D. (2007) 'Slovenia', in Bale, T. & van Biezen, I. (eds) (2007).
Gabel, M. J. (2000) 'European Integration, Voters, and National Politics', *West European Politics*, 23, 4, pp. 52–72.
Grabbe, H. & Hughes, K. (1999) 'Central and East European Views on EU Enlargement: Political Debates and Public Opinion', in Henderson, K. (ed.) (1999) *Back to Europe: Central and Eastern Europe and the European Union* (London, UCL Press).
Gyárfásová, O. (2006) 'A 2004-es EP-választás Szlovákiában az Európai Unió közmegítélésének kontextusában', in Tóka, G. & Bátory, Á. (eds) (2006).

Hix, S. & Marsh, M. (2006) 'Az európai parlamenti választások üzenetei: büntetés vagy tiltakozás?', in Tóka, G. & Bátory, Á. (eds) (2006).
Hix, S. & Marsh, M. (2007) 'Punishment or Protest? Understanding European Parliament Elections', *The Journal of Politics*, 69, 2. [This is a translation into English of Hix, S. & Marsh, M. (2006).]
Hooghe, L. & Marks, G. (2005) 'Community, Calculation and Cues', *European Union Politics*, 6, 4, pp. 419–43.
Ilonszki, G. (2008) 'A képviselet-felfogás és az EU-ról alkotott vélekedések. Okok és következmények', in Lengyel, Gy. (ed.) (2008) *A magyar politikai és gazdasági elit EU-képe* (Budapest, Új Mandátum Kiadó).
Kopecky, P. & Mudde, C. (2002) 'The Two Sides of Euroscepticism. Party Positions on European Integration in East Central Europe', *European Union Politics*, 3, 3, pp. 297–326.
Lengyel, Gy. & Ilonszki, G. (forthcoming) 'Hungary between Consolidated and Simulated Democracy', in Higley, J. & Best H. (eds) (forthcoming) *Democratic Elitism: Comparative and Evolutionary Perspectives* (Leiden & Boston, Brill).
Lewis, P. G. (2005) 'EU Enlargement and Party Systems in Central Europe', *Journal of Communist Studies and Transition Politics*, 21, 2.
MacMullen, A. (1999) 'Political Responsibility for the Administration of Europe: the Commission's Resignation March 1999', *Parliamentary Affairs*, 52, 4, pp. 703–18.
Markowski, R. & Tucker, J. (2005) 'Political Representation and EU Accession: Evidence from Poland', Paper presented at the annual meeting of APSA, Washington DC, 1–4 September, available at: http://www.allacademic.com/meta/p40466.index.html, accessed 15 December 2008.
Marsh, M. (1998) 'Testing the Second-Order Election Model after Four European Elections', *British Journal of Political Science*, 28, 4, pp. 591–607.
Milner, S. (2000) 'Euroscepticism in France and Changing State–Society Relations', *Journal of European Integration*, 22, 1.
Reif, K. & Schmitt, H. (1980) 'Nine Second-order Elections', *European Journal of Political Research*, 8, 1, pp. 3–44.
Scheuer, A. & van der Brug, W. (2007) 'Locating Support for European Integration', in van Der Brug, W. & van der Eijk, C. (eds) (2007) *European Elections and Domestic Politics. Lessons from the Past and Scenarios for the Future* (Notre Dame, IN, University of Notre Dame).
Schmitt, H. & Thomassen, J. (1999) 'Distinctiveness and Cohesion of Parties', in Schmitt, H. & Thomassen, J. (eds) (1999) *Political Representation and Legitimacy in the European Union* (Oxford, Oxford University Press).
Schmitt, H. & Thomassen, J. (2000) 'Dynamic Representation: The Case of European Integration', *European Union Politics*, 1, 3, pp. 318–39.
Spirova, M. (2007) 'Bulgaria', in Bale, T. & van Biezen, I. (eds) (2007).
Steenbergen, M. R., Edwards, E. E. & de Vries, C. (2007) 'Who's Cueing Whom? Mass–Elite Linkages and the Future of European Integration', *European Union Politics*, 8, 1, pp. 35–49.
Taggart, P. & Szczerbiak, A. (2008a) 'Introduction: Opposing Europe? The Politics of Euroscepticism in Europe', in Taggart, P. & Szczerbiak, A. (eds) (2008b).
Taggart, P. & Szczerbiak, A. (eds) (2008b) *Opposing Europe? The Comparative Party Politics of Euroscepticism*, Vol. 1 (Oxford, Oxford University Press).
Tilley, J. R., Bold, T. & Garry, J. (2006) 'A gazdasági helyzet-értékelés meghatározó és a választói döntésre gyakorolt hatása', in Tóka, G. & Bátory Á. (eds) (2006).
Tilley, J. R., Bold, T. & Garry, J. (2008) 'Perceptions and Reality: Economic Voting and at the 2004 European Parliament Elections', *European Journal of Political Research*, 47, 5. [This is a translation into English of Tilley, J. R. *et al.* (2006).]
Tóka, G. (2006) 'Vezérek csodálói', in Karácsony, G. (ed.) (2006) *Parlamenti választás 2006* (Budapest, DKMKKA).
Tóka, G. & Bátory, Á. (eds) (2006) *A 2004. évi európai parlamenti választások* (Budapest, DKMKKA).
Van der Eijk, C. & Franklin, M. N. (eds) (1996) *Choosing Europe? The European Electorate and National Politics in the Face of the Union* (Ann Arbor, University of Michigan Press).
Zielonka, J. & Mair, P. (2002) 'Introduction: Diversity and Adaptation in the Enlarged European Union', in Mair, P. & Zielonka, J. (eds) (2002) *The Enlarged European Union: Diversity and Adaptation* (London, Frank Cass).

Index

Page numbers in *Italics* represent tables.
Page numbers in **Bold** represent figures.

acquis communautaire 54
Anderson, Benedict 10-11, 126
ANOVA analysis 82, 133
aristocratic nationalism 11
ascribed components 141
association phase 105
attachment: territorial *109*, 128; to Europe 130, **131**, 136
Austria: birth place 116; citizenship 14; EU or nation state 84; European identification 134; identity 116; primordalism 134; tax distribution 113, 129

Back, H. 6
balance of power 110
Baltic states 84
banks 2
Basque secessionist movement 76
Belgium 76; Christianity 116; European attachment 136; fear of Turkey 18; identity 116; multilingualism 12; tax redistribution 129, 140; threat from Russia 60; threat from Turkey 60; threat from USA 60
belongingness 8
Best, Heinrich 3, 5
birth place 114, 119, 120, 141; and nationality 40
border changes 14
Bosnia: Islam 18; language 12

Bosnia and Herzegovina 74, 76, 96
bourgeois nationalism 11
Brubaker, R. 128
Bruter, M. 126, 133
Bulgaria 5, 6, 30, 87; 2007 European Parliament elections 154; attachment to Europe 36; birth place 40; Christianity 18, 24, 41, 166; Christianity and citizenship 39; Communist Party 89; discontent in 151; economy 148; EU distrust of 94; EU policies support 154-5; EU strengthening 97, 102; EU trust in 91, 92, 100, *101*, 103; European attachment 136; European birth 44; European Commission 46, 98, 103; European identification 134; European parents 44-5; European Parliament 46, 48, 96; exclusion 24; good governance status 149; identity 34, 116; International Monetary Fund (IMF) 89-90; Intune survey 1, 89; language 41; legal citizenship 41; mastering European language 45; MPs' trust in EU institutions *98*; national identity 14, 15, 18; national parliament dissatisfaction 146; parents' nationality 40; political hostility 149; political system 89-90; pragmatic policies 157; primordalism 134; regional aid 155; tax distribution 113; territorial attachment 130; unification 99, 152, 157

INDEX

Bulgarian Socialist Party 89
bureaucratic nationalism 11
business associations 2
Byzantium 10

Carey, S. 127
Carrubba, C. 30
Catalan autonomist movement 76
Catholicism 9, 72
Central and Eastern European post-communist countries (CEEPC): elites 32; integration 31; and Southern Europe 30-2
Christianity 114, 116, 133; European identification 134; European identity 41; national citizenship 36; and national identity 12; and nationality 18, *19*
Citizens for European Development in Bulgaria (GERB) 154
citizenship 11, 33, 114, 116, 119, 120; democratic legitimation 126; elements of national *37-8*; legal 41; and nationality 14, *15*
City Belt 9-10
Coalition Attack (ATAKA) 149
cognitive mobilisation capacities 125
cognitive mobilisation theory 106
cohesion 4
Cold War 53
collective identity 10, 70, 133; classifications of 113, *see also* mass identity
collective memories 8
common destiny 8
common EU policies 112
common foreign policy 100, 103, 154
communism 18, 24, 28, 82; collapse of 31, 72-3; Greece 89
communities: attachment to *35*; imagined 10-11
Community Framework Programmes 94
competitiveness 6, 56, 112; USA 62
components of being a true national/European *132*
components of identification **135**
conditionality 32
conflict school 54
Constitutional Convention 33

Constitutional Treaty of the European Union (2005) 87
constructivism 54
Cooper, G. 128
corruption 90
Cotta, Maurizio 1
country performance: citizens' views 145-50
Cramer's rule 151
Croatia: language 12
cultural identity 11, 33
cultural traditions: political elites 39; sharing 39
culture: national identity 119
Cyprus 98
Czech Republic 83; atheism 114; attachment to Europe 36; benefits of EU membership 109; birth place 40; Christianity 41, 116; Christianity and citizenship 39; economic elites 108; European attachment 136; European cultural traditions 44; European identification 134; Euroscepticism 106, 109, 110, 112, 123-4, 153; identity 34, 116; Intune survey 1; national identity 113; parents' nationality 40; political elite 107; support for unification 111; tax distribution 112
Czechoslovakia 72

decisional component 133, 141
democracy 126; direct 144; transition to 31-2
democratic deficit 93, 144
democratic legitimation: citizenship 126
Democratic Party of Serbia 74, 90
democratisation 105
Denmark: European attachment 136; European identification 134; nation over EU 83; primordalism 134; tax distribution 113, 129; tax redistribution 140
diversity 7
Djindjic, Zoran 90

economic elites 2; cosmopolitanism 108, 123; nationality 12; positivity for Europe 123; social security 109

INDEX

economic freedom 56
economic performance: voting patterns 148
elite survey 1-3
elites 55-6; attitude to Russia 57; attitude to Turkey 58; differing attitudes towards nationality 113; exclusion 24; integration 30, 87, 155-8; nation building 11; nationality 25, 26; opinion on EU and nation-state *81, 83*; orientation towards EU or nation-state *84*; perception of threats **59**, *64-6*, **67**; political ideology 56; and religion 18; support for integration 156; unification 111; view on USA 58, 63; views compared with masses 158; views on Russia 63; views on Turkey 63; views on unification *165*
employers 2
enlargement 6, 54, 70, 105
entrepreneurs 2
equality 56, 58, 110
equality of opportunity *110*
establishers 82
Estonia 83; attachment to Europe 36; birth place 40; Christianity 41, 116; Christianity and citizenship 39; citizenship 14; economic growth 148; EU Commission 46; European attachment 136; European birth 44; European cultural traditions 44; European identification 134; European language mastering 45; European law 45; European parents 44-5; European Parliament 46; Euroscepticism 154; feeling European 45; good governance status 149; identity 33, 34, 36, 116; Intune survey 1; legal citizenship 41; low discontent in 151; nationality 40; parents' nationality 40; political landscape 149; pragmatic policies 157; Russia 55; Russians in 14; satisfaction in national parliament 146; statehood 152; tax distribution 113, 129; tax redistribution 140; unification 140; unification lack of support 152; unification views on 157
ethnic membership: social integration 126
ethnic minority parties 79, 93

ethnicity and religion 24
ethno-cultural components 133
ethnocentrism 14
Euro 148
Europe: attachment 36, 136; birth in 44; cultural traditions 41, 44; culture primordial components 133; fear of USA 55; identity and integration 106
European Atomic Energy Community (Euratom) 53
European citizenship *42-3*
European Commission 102; agreement to strengthen *97*, 98; support for 111; trust in 46, 48, 91, 96, 98
European Constitution: rejection of 105
European Economic Community (EEC): establishment 53
European Elections (2004) 6
European "feeling" 45, 122
European identity 33, 41, 49, 114, 120-3; affirmative replies *115*; building and threat framing 55-7; Christianity 41; components of *115*; constructivist approach 126; cultural 122; Germany 117; Hungary 117; meanings 126-7; national identity 41, 70, 115-16; pragmatic aspect 112; principal components analysis *121*; question of 105; Slovakia 117; threat perception 53
European institutions: trust in (by party) *92*; trust in *47-8*, 91-3, *92*
European language: knowledge of 114; mastering 45
European law 45
European Parliament 33, 154; agreement to strengthen *97*; political elites 46; strengthening 111; trust in 48, 91, 96
European state formation 9
European Union (EU): benefits of membership 72, 109, *109*; and change 29; common policies 112; distrust by left 94; fragmentation of 105; future of 98-102, 112; goals of 112; identification 133; main actors in *111*; opinions on strengthening *31*; participation of the people 3; polity and policy dimensions 150-5; primordial components of identification 134; reasons for or

against support 153; relative strength of institutions 96-8; Research and Technology Development policy 55; single defence policy 62; support for **137**; and USA 4, 5
Europeanisation 54; definition 56
Europessimist 56
Europhilia 157; national polity 145
Euroscepticism 4, 30, 87, 106, 122; Czech Republic 106, 109, 110, 112, 123-4, 153; Estonia 154; Great Britain 117; Greece 94; Hungary 154; national polity 145
exclusion 24

Fidesz 154
Flanders 9
Flemish section 116
foreign policy: common/single 100, 103, 112, 154-5, 157
France: Christianity 116; citizenship 14; EU constitution 87; EU support 159; European attachment 136; European identification 134; fear of Turkey 18; identity 116; primordalism 134; tax distribution 129; tax redistribution 140; territorial attachment 130
free market 112
Freud, S. 55
FRY *see* Yugoslavia
funds: policy agreement 112

GDP per capita *148*
Germany: citizenship 14; EU support 159; European attachment 136; European identification 134; European identity 117; identity 116; nationalism and militarism 116; primordalism 134; tax distribution 129; tax redistribution 140; threat from Russia 60; threat from Turkey 60; threat from USA 60
globalisation 56, 70, 108
Göncz, Borbála 3, 4, 112
good governance indicators *150*
governance: good 149; modes of 7
Grabowsky, J.K. 116
Great Britain 76; Christianity 116; European attachment 136; European culture 133; Euroscepticism 117; identity 116; low attachment to Europe 141; nation over EU 83, 84; national identity 14; tax redistribution 113, 129, 140; territorial attachment 130; unification 140
Greater Serbia 24
Greece 87; attachment to Europe 36; birth place 40; Christianity 18, 24, 41, 116; Christianity and citizenship 39; common foreign policy 100; cultural traditions 39; EC distrust by left 95; EEC advantages of joining 32; EU distrust reasons 96; EU strengthening 97; EU trust in 91, 92, 103; European attachment 136; European birth 44; European cultural traditions 44; European law 45; European parents 45; European Parliament 46; Euroscepticsim 94; exclusion 24; feeling European 45; identity 33, 34, 116; Intune survey 88; language 40; nationality 18; political system 88-9; strengthening EU 102; territorial attachment 130; and Turkey 18; unification 99
Greek Socialist Party 5
Greenfield, Liah 8-9
group identity 55, *see also* mass identity
growth rates 72
Gyurcsanyi, Prime Minister F. 149

Habermas, J. 126, 133
Haller, M. 126, 133
heterogeneity 49
history: and identity 9
Hooghe, L. 125
Horolets, A. 126
humanism 126
Hungary 76, 80; anti-EU party 154; attachment to Europe 36; birth place 40; Christianity 41; citizenship 14, 116; discontent in 151; dissatisfaction in national parliament 146; economy 148; elites view of EU 81; EU or nation-state 84; EU policies 154-5; European attachment 136; European birth 44; European cultural traditions 44; European identity 117; European

parents 44-5; European Parliament 46; Euroscepticism 154; feeling European 45; good governance status 149; identity 34, 36, 116; Intune survey 1; language 41; legal citizenship 41; parents nationality 40; pessimism in 148; political background 145; political hostility 149; pragmatic policies 157; regional aid 155; territorial attachment 130; unification support for 152; unification views on 157

identification: underlying structures of 131-4
identification process 128
identitarian approach 55
identity 3, 4; attachment to political communities *35*; collective 10; comparative perspective on 116-17; definition 32; European 4, 33, 41; factors of 117; and history 9; integration 32-3; Intune Survey 34-46; mass 8; multiple nature of 107-8; national 3, 8; political elites 34; territorial 108
immigration 24, 56
Index of orientation toward the EU or the nation-state (IOEU) 77-8
indigenous traditions 8
information deficit 125
Inglehart, R. 125
inherited components 141
integration 3, 29, 105; benefits of 125; comparison of mass and elite views 155-8; elite-driven 126; elites and masses 87; elites opinion 30; and European identity 106; future of 158; identity and representation 32-3; length of membership and positivity 123; mass attitudes to 29; national pride 127; policy dimension 154-5; political parties 153; political views 151-4; post-communist Serbia 73-5; pragmatic aspects 128-30; secessionist movements 73; and sovereignty 83; studies on 125; support for in poorly performing states 158-9; symbolic aspects 125, 130-1; views on 109-13
International Monetary Fund (IMF): Bulgaria 89-90

international relations: literature 54
Intune Project 1, 6, 91; elite working group 3
Intune survey 1-2, 11, 30, 77, 127, 145; Bulgaria 89; Czech Republic 106; elites 156; Greece 88; identity 34-46, 113; priming effect 120; sample size by country *2*
investment 72
Ireland: Reform Treaty 87
irredentist threat 76, 82
Isernia, Pierangelo 1
Islam 72
Italy: attachment to Europe 36; birth place 40; Christianity 18, 41, 116; Christianity and citizenship 39; cultural traditions 39; European attachment 136; European birth 44; European cultural traditions 44; European culture 133; European identification 134; European parents 44-5; European Parliament 46; exclusion 24; identity 116; language 40; tax redistribution 140

Jerez-Mir, Miguel 3, 4, 5

Kaczynszki twins 148
Kopeck y, P. 106, 110
Kosovo 12, 24, 74, 84, 96; and Serbia 74-5, 85, 90, 100
Kostunica, Vojislav 90-1

language: mastery of 40, 119, 120; and national identity 11-12, *13*
law: respect for 114, 120
law and order 114
laws: respect for 40, 119
Lazi , Mladen 5
League of Polish Families 154
League of Yugoslav Communists 90
left and right dividing lines 6, 102-3
left-right scale: self placement 93-6, *94*
Lengyel, György 3, 4, 112
liberals 79
Lisbon Treaty 105
Lithuania 76, 80; attachment to Europe 36; birth place 40; Christianity 18, 24, 41, 116; Christianity and citizenship

39; cultural traditions 39; elites view of EU 81; EU Commission 46; EU or nation state 84; European attachment 136; European cultural traditions 44; European culture 133; European identification 134; European parents 44-5; European Parliament 46; identity 34, 116; Intune survey 1; primordalism 134; risk of sovereignty 83; tax redistribution 113, 140; threat from Russia 60; threat from Turkey 60; threat from USA 60
local attachment 127
logistic regression analysis 136
logistic regression models *138-9*, 140

main actors EU *111*
Malta 98
Mansfeldová, Zdenka 3, 4
market economy 72
mass identity 8; constructivist approach 8
mass survey 1-3
masses: views compared with elites 158; views on integration 155-8; views on unification *151*, *165*
Matonytè, Irmina 4
Meciar, Vladimír 149
MEPs 33
military power 56
Milošević, S. 73, 78, 90, 96
minorities 24
modernisation 72
moral values 56
Morkevićius, Vaidas 4
Movement for Rights and Freedom 89
MPs 2; constituencies 108
Mudde, C. 106
multi-faith society 72
multiculturalism 58
multiple correspondence analysis (MCA) 134, 136, 140
Muslims 18

nation building 10, 105; elites 11
national citizenship: Christianity 36; elements of *37-8*
national identity 3, 8, 11, *12*, 106, 117-20; affirmative replies *115*; birth place of parents 14, *16*; Christianity 12, 24; civic component 119-20; components of *114*, 117, *118*, 123; culture 119; Czech Republic 113; and European identity 41, 70, 115-16; inherited 126; place of birth 14, *17*; voluntary 126
National Movement Simeon II 89, 149
national parliament dissatisfaction 146, *147*
national pride: threat of European integration 127
nationalism 56, 73; Serbia 74, 90
nationality: Christianity 18, *19*; criteria of 12; frequency of agreement to criteria *25*, *26*, *27*
nationhood: international acceptance 152
NATO: intervention in Serbia 74
Netherlands: EU constitution 87
New Democracy Party (Greece) 88, 91
new Europe 105, 146
New Serbia 74-5
newcomers 82
Nezi, Spyridoula 5

old Europe 105, 146, 156
origin 114, 120
Orthodox Christian Church 10, 18
Ottoman Empire 10

Panhellenic Socialist Movement 88
parents 44-5, 114
parents' nationality 40, 119, 120, 141
passive components 141
patriotism 33
peace 56
place of birth: national identity 14, *17*
Poland 30; attachment to Europe 36; birth place 40; Christianity 18, 24, 41, 116; Christianity and citizenship 39; citizenship 116; discontent in 151; economy 148; EU Commission 46; European attachment 136; European birth 44; European identification 134; European language mastering 45; European parents 44-5; European Parliament 46; exclusion 24; extremist parties 154; good governance status 149; identity 34, 116; Intune survey 1; language 40; legal citizenship 41;

national parliament dissatisfaction 146; parents nationality 40; political conflict 148; pragmatic policies 157; regional aid 155; support for EU 150; support for EU policies 154-5; tax distribution 113; territorial attachment 130; threat from Russia 60; threat from Turkey 60; threat from USA 60; unification support for 152; unification views on 157
policies: elite and mass views compared *158*; support for *155*
policy agreement: funds 112
political communities: attachment to *35*
political correctness 14
political elites 2; attachment to Europe 36; Christianity 41; cultural traditions 39; European law 45; European parents 44-5; European Parliament 46; identity 34; legal citizenship 41; local community attachment 108; mastery of language 40-1; national perspective 123; nationality 12; tax 140
political ideologies: threat perception *61*
political left 56; Russia 58-9, 60; USA 58, 60
political participation 126
political parties: allegiance and opinion 79; classification *104*; classification of 91; on EU issues 153; families 91, *104*; integration 153
political right 56; Russia 60; Turkey 58, 60, 67
political self categorisation 142
political self-placement 60, 142
politicians 2
politics of experience 55
Portugal 76, 80; advantages of joining EEC 32; attachment to Europe 36; Christianity 41; cultural traditions 39; elites view of EU 81; EU or nation-state 84; European cultural traditions 44; European language mastering 45; European Parliament 46; identity 34, 116; language 41; legal citizenship 41; parents nationality 40; tax redistribution 113, 140
pragmatism to EU 134-40, 157
predicted probabilities of elites perception: Russian threat **69**; Turkish threat **68**; USA threat **67**
prejudicial attitudes 55
priming effect: Intune survey 120
primordial components: European culture 133; European identification 134, 141
principal component analysis 131, 133
Protestantism 72
public opinion: Christianity 41; cultural traditions 39; European law 45; identity 33
Putnam, R. 29

racism 14
Radaelli, C. 56
Radical Party of Serbia 90
Real-Dato, José 3, 4, 5
Reform Treaty: Ireland 87
regression analysis 62
religion and ethnicity 24
religious confession: economic elites *21*; general population *22*; political elites *20*
religious identity 33
renaissance 126
representation 46-8, 144, 156; integration 32-3
representation of national interests *110*
right and left dividing lines 6
Risse, T. 56, 116
Rokkan, Stein 3, 9; conceptual map of Europe 9, 24
Roman law 126
Romania 90, 103; support for EU 150; trust in EU 100
Rome 9
Russia 4; Estonia 55; political left 58-9; political right and left 60; as a threat 57, 60; view of elites 63; and Warsaw Pact countries 57
Russian threat: predicted probabilities of elites perception **69**

sameness 8
Schengen zone 106
Scheuer, A. 151
Schmitt, H. 150
secessionist movements: EU integration 73
secessionist threat 76

Self Defence Party (Poland) 154
self-placement: on centre trust in EU 95;
  left-right scale 93-6, *94*
separatist threat 82
Serbia: attachment to Europe 36; birth
  place 40; blocked transformation
  5, 73-4; Christianity 18, 24, 41;
  citizenship 14; cultural traditions 39;
  EU Commission 46; EU distrust of 94;
  EU integration opinion 75; EU opinion
  on 85; EU strengthening 102; EU trust
  in 91, 92, 103; European attachment
  136; European birth 44; European
  identification 134; European language
  mastering 45; European parents 44-5;
  exclusion 24; feeling European 45;
  from communism to EU integration
  73-5; identity 34, 36; Intune survey 1,
  3; Islam 18; isolationist policy 74; and
  Kosovo 74-5, 85, 90; language 12, 40;
  legal citizenship 41; nationalism 74, 96;
  nationality 40; nativistic orientation 15;
  NATO intervention 74; negative view on
  EU 100; parents nationality 40; political
  party opinion 79; political system 90-1;
  Stabilisation and Association Agreement
  87, 91, 92; tax system 100; and Turkey
  18; UN sanctions 74; unification 99
Serbian Democratic Party 90
Serbian elites survey: EU and the nation
  state 78-80; EU and the nation
  state comparative perspective 80-5;
  hypothesis and methodology 75-8;
  opinion and education 80; opinion and
  life experience 80; opinion and
  networking 80; political party opinion 79
Serbian Radical Party 93
Siderov, Volen Nikolov 89
Siena: University of 1
Simeon II 89, 91
Slavic mission 10
Slovak National Party 149
Slovakia 83; attachment to Europe 36;
  Christianity 116; Christianity and
  citizenship 39; comparison of views on
  unification 157; Euro 148; European
  birth 44; European cultural traditions
  44; European identity 117; European
  parents 44-5; European Parliament 154;
  good governance status 149; identity 33,
  36, 116; Intune survey 1; low discontent
  in 151; parents nationality 40; political
  landscape 149; pragmatic policies 157;
  satisfaction in national parliament 146;
  statehood 152; tax redistribution 113;
  territorial attachment 130; unification
  support 152
Slovenia: birth place 40; economy 148;
  Euro 148; European Parliament 154;
  good governance status 149; lack
  of support for unification 152; low
  discontent in 151; political landscape
  149; satisfaction in national parliament
  146; statehood 152
Smith, Anthony 126
social constructivism 56, 69; European
  Studies 53-5
social democrats 79
social identity theory 55
social integration: ethnic membership 126
social security 4, 56, 100, 112, 154-5, 157;
  economic elites 109; USA 62
Socialist Party of Serbia 90
socialists 79
socio-economic differences 56
Sotiropoulos, Dimitri A. 5
Southern European support for Europe 32
sovereignty: endangered 76; and
  integration 83
Spain 76, 80; attachment to Europe 36;
  birth place 116; Christianity 18, 24,
  41, 116; Christianity and citizenship
  39; cultural traditions 39; elites
  view of EU 81; European birth 44;
  European cultural traditions 44;
  European identification 134; European
  language mastering 45; European law
  45; European parents 44-5; European
  Parliament 46; identity 33, 34, 36, 116;
  language 40; nationality 40; parents
  nationality 40; primordalism 134; pro-
  EU opinion 83; risk of sovereignty
  83; tax redistribution 140; territorial
  attachment 130; unification 140
Stabilisation and Association Agreement:
  Serbia 87

Stanichev, Sergei Dmitrievich 89
Stašková, Barbora Špicarová 3, 4
state sovereignty 76-7
state-building 73
statehood 152
Steenbergen, M. 30
supranational distribution: support for 128-9
supranational identity 127
surveys: warnings on 150
Synapismos 93

tax harmonisation 100, 102
tax redistribution 112, *112*, 127, 129, **129**, 136, 140, 141
tax system: common 100, 103; unified 112, 154-5, 157
territorial attachment *109*, 128, **131**
Thomassen, J. 6, 150
threat definition 54
threat perception: European identity 53; political ideologies *61*
threats 4; external 56; internal 56; perception of elites **59**
Toka, Panayiota 5
Treaty on the Functioning of the EU 54
Treaty of Rome (1957) 53
Turkey 4; elites views on 58; and political right 58; political right 67; as a threat 57, 59-60; threat to Europe 18, *23*; view of elites 63; views from political right and left 60
Turkish threat: European parents 62; predicted probabilities of elites perception **68**

UN sanctions: Serbia 74
unification 99, 106; agreement by country *99*; high support from left 140; mass views on *151*; perception of 140; strengthening of 127; support for *111*, 129, **130**, 136
Union of Democratic Forces (Bulgaria) 89
United States of America (USA): and EU 4, 5; European fear of 55; and political left 58; predicted probabilities of elites **67**; as a threat 57; as a treat 60; view of elites 63; views from political right and left 60, 62
University of Siena 1

van der Brug, W. 151
Vázquez-García, Rafael 3, 4, 5
voting: national and European 144
voting behaviour 153
voting patterns: economic performance 148
Vuleti : Vladimir 5

Walloon section 116
Warsaw Pact 57
welfare state: deficiencies in 56
Wessels, B. 30
Worldwide Governance Indicators: World Bank 149

Yugoslavia 72; disintegration 90, 96, 100

Zhivkov, Todor 89